AF230683

Endorsements for
Awakening The Human Robot

"As a neuroscientist and author of the manifesto on post-materialist science, Beauregard is in an excellent position to illuminate the myriad destructive facets that addiction to reductive materialist science has wrought in our modern lives, rendering us as automatons, or robots. He then proceeds to offer practical solutions leading away from this entrapment constructed by human society, towards liberating the human spirit to rise to its greatest potential through our unified spiritual power, and all in service to the higher good. Highly recommended!"

—**Eben Alexander, MD,** former Harvard neurosurgeon
and author of *Proof of Heaven, The Map of Heaven,*
and *Living in a Mindful Universe*

"Awakening the Human Robot is a complete how-to-guide to spiritual awakening for any human finding themselves incarnated in the Matrix. Dr. Mario Beauregard asks us to question our conditioning, face our fears, and expand into our true self beyond the unhealthy programming. Drawing from neuroscience to history to philosophy and more, he weaves multiple perspectives together to make sense of a seemingly chaotic world. Dr. Beauregard leaves no stone unturned in this timely masterpiece of nonfiction, sure to become a classic of our time. This book is a key to freedom."

—**Dr. Natalie Leigh Dyer, PhD**, Research Scientist,
University of California – Irvine

"This book, remarkably original in its depth and breadth of vision, is a genuine manual offering to infuse greater awareness into all areas of life, both individual and collective. It offers a holistic and integrative vision of the theoretical foundations and concrete, practical methods of care aimed at deprogramming, detoxifying, "dis-enchanting," and deconditioning our consciousness with regard to all the traumas and beliefs acquired during our existence. It helps to raise awareness of the social mechanisms of control and manipulation, mainly through fear, guilt, and ignorance, in order to better defuse them.
A truly practical guide, solidly grounded in science, which leaves you feeling truly transformed."

—**Dr. Olivier Chambon**, psychiatrist and author

"This book marks a threshold toward a new vision of the world we inhabit and the one still waiting to be born. It is a meditation on freedom that combines intellectual strength with poetic vision. Clear, fearless, and humane, it offers both reflection and revelation. Each page stirs the will to grow and to reclaim the creative power hidden within us.
Awakening the Human Robot *stands as a testament to the courage of emancipation."*
—**Marie Odile Riffard**, clinical psychologist, psychotherapist, and author

"This remarkable book is a journey of revelation, at once captivating and profound. It ventures into the hidden workings of our world and speaks to the curious, the seekers, and all who long to awaken."
—**Catherine Larouche**, visual artist

"The research of Dr. Mario Beauregard was, for me, a revelation. He is among the founders of the post-materialist scientific movement, whose studies suggest that consciousness endures beyond death. This discovery offers a profound turning point for humanity and gives hope for a world that might one day live in greater harmony."

—Valérie Séguin, author and documentary filmmaker

"I first knew Mario Beauregard the neuroscientist, the man who studied the brains of elderly nuns and discovered that their synapses should have shown grave deterioration, yet their minds remained brilliant and full of life. That discovery revealed that consciousness transcends and precedes the brain. I knew him as the first signatory of the Post-Materialist Manifesto, alongside Gary Schwartz, Larry Dossey, Rupert Sheldrake, Dean Radin, and soon hundreds more, calling scientists to awaken from the reductionist trance created by Cartesian logic and mechanistic thought. I had seen many sides of the same man, yet I had not understood that the fearless Québécois was, in truth, a revolutionary of spirit, vision, and action. Reading his new book carried me back to my twenties, to 1968, when we dreamed of transforming the world in every way, psychological, educational, ecological, economic, political, and spiritual. Almost sixty years later, Mario lifts that same flame again, now armed with the means to express scientifically what unites all dimensions of existence, the sacred logic of life. If humanity is to endure, that living logic must guide us once more, within ourselves and among us all, in wonder and in the certainty that each being in the universe is unique, irreplaceable, and essential."

—Patrice Van Eersel, journalist and author

"As a neuroscientist of international renown, celebrated for his pioneering work that restores consciousness to the center of creation, Mario Beauregard reveals in Awakening the Human Robot *the inner architecture of thought itself. He exposes the layers of conditioning that trap human beings in a matrix of perception shaped by the illusion of materialism. This book calls for liberation and invites every reader to reclaim the sovereignty of the spirit. Thank you, my soul brother Mario, for guiding our collective consciousness toward a more luminous horizon."*

—Philippe Guillemant, physicist
and CNRS research engineer

Awakening The Human Robot

Dismantling the Empire of Fear, Belief, and Control

Dr. Mario Beauregard, Ph.D.

GLOBAL WELLNESS MEDIA
ÉDITIONS MIEUX-ÊTRE GLOBAL
LOS ANGELES, TORONTO, MONTREAL

For permission requests, send an email to: mario@awakeningthehumanrobot.com

Published by:
Global Wellness Media /
Éditions Mieux-Être Global
Stratedgy LLC
440 N Barranca Ave #2027
Covina, California, 91723
(866) 467-9090
GlobalWellnessMedia.com

Publisher's Note: The views expressed in this work are solely those of the authors and do not necessarily reflect the views of the publisher, and the publisher hereby disclaims any responsibilities for them.

Cover: Eric D. Groleau

Awakening the Human Robot / Mario Beauregard. — First edition.
ISBN : 978-1-957343-47-1 (Paperback)
ISBN : 978-1-957343-48-8 (ePub)

Table of Contents

Dedication

To all the co-creators of a new world,

to those among us today and those yet to come.

And to Morgane, my wondrous friend,

whose presence illumines my life like

a benevolent star of destiny.

The Sleep of Machines, the Birth of Conscious Fire

"The real voyage of discovery consists not in seeking new landscapes, but in having new eyes."
— Marcel Proust

We are born not into freedom, but into prewritten scripts: softly lit prisons disguised as classrooms, sanctuaries, and glowing screens. From cradle to grave, we are lulled into compliance by systems that promise to serve yet quietly sculpt us. We are not born free: we are formatted.

Our thoughts are not entirely our own, our gods arrive as heirlooms, and our fears are etched into the nervous system through repetition and trauma. We are programmed by the programmed, living within institutions designed by those who long ago forgot the untamed taste of truth.

What we call education is often indoctrination; what we call news is often narrative; and what we call medicine is often chemical obedience. Institutions that claim to liberate—e.g., religion, politics, and economics—become extensions of the *"Matrix,"* conditioning not only behavior but the very perceptions from which behavior arises.

We are told we are sovereign individuals. Yet sovereignty cannot flourish in captivity. Our desires are installed, our passions downloaded, and our dreams implanted like apps in a device whose operating system is obedience. Programming masquerades as personality, and the padded safety of a cell is mistaken for the dignity of freedom. From birth, consciousness is drafted into service. Institutions choreograph perception, shaping obedience not through crude force but through subtle repetition and reward. What we call "religion," "politics," "economics," "education," and "media" are not simply social structures but programs for thought itself.

Yet even within this choreography lies another possibility. To awaken is not merely to resist the machinery of fear and belief but to remember that consciousness itself is generative. Reality is not a fixed stage upon which we act but a field of possibilities that bends toward the quality of our awareness.

Out of this recognition I developed a psychospiritual approach called *Holosynthesis©*. It emerged from two intertwined currents: my neuroscientific research into the neural foundations of consciousness and my own transpersonal experiences that revealed dimensions beyond the materialist frame. Holosynthesis© is both model and practice, a way of reweaving what has been fragmented and restoring coherence to body, brain, psyche, and spirit. Where the *Human Robot* narrows us into obedience, Holosynthesis© restores sovereignty, creativity, and wholeness. The structure and content of this book draw on principles similar to those that guide Holosynthesis© sessions and workshops.

When human beings gather in coherence—when fear dissolves into presence and imagination is freed from dogma—we do not simply resist the old world, we begin to co-create a new one. This is not utopia but a living principle echoed in mystical traditions, Indigenous wisdom and the sciences of complexity and collective intelligence remind us that reality itself bends to the depth of our participation. The ember within us is not only memory but also the seed of creation.

Religion perfected obedience by sanctifying fear. Salvation and damnation conditioned billions to submit to doctrines claiming eternal truth. Politics reshaped obedience into nationalism and tribal loyalty. Economics carried the pattern forward, wielding debt and scarcity as modern sacraments that chained societies to perpetual growth (Graeber, 2011). Education, cloaked in the banner of enlightenment, narrowed curiosity into test scores and trained children to repeat rather than to think (Illich, 1971). Later, media emerged as the newest cathedral, saturating our senses with orchestrated narratives until spectacle blurred into reality.

Though their costumes differ, the underlying machinery remains the same: fear narrows the mind, repetition rewires it, and belonging seals the contract. The result is a human being who mistakes programming for personality and captivity for civilization. To awaken is not to exchange one ideology for another but to see the architecture beneath them all, the faint strings of persuasion and control that bind thought itself.

Beneath every grand story about God, country, science, or success runs a *meta-script*—a master program shaping the smaller scripts of daily life. These scripts dictate what to value, what to fear, and how to behave. They are crafted to maintain hierarchy, reward compliance, and punish deviation. We do not inhabit neutral stories but simulations upheld by consensus. The algorithm is cultural, the code is historical, and the scripts are written in fear, belief, and control.

The metaphor of the *Human Robot* is not hyperbole but diagnosis. It names a mechanized state of consciousness: a mind executing inherited rules without ever questioning them. Neuroscience affirms this. The brain is sculpted by experience. *Neuroplasticity* molds the architecture of thought long before we call it our own (Doidge, 2007). *Predictive processing* shows perception is not the world itself but the brain's best guess, a *controlled hallucination* constrained by prior beliefs (Friston,

2010). When institutions, trauma, and propaganda install those priors, perception itself bends toward obedience.

We obey not out of cruelty, but because conditioning has carved obedience into us. Neural pathways fire along grooves etched by fear, tradition, and the need for social survival, while epigenetic scars whisper compliance across generations. At the heart of this cycle lies trauma, the master key. Early wounds reshape the *limbic system*—the brain's emotional core—dampening reflection and priming survival responses (van der Kolk, 2014). When fear becomes sustained, the *prefrontal cortex* (PFC)—the neural mediator of imagination and foresight—dims beneath cortisol's weight, rendering us programmable. In this way, trauma opens the gateway through which belief enters, takes root, and hardens into identity.

Beliefs feel intimate, sacred, and self-chosen. Yet most are *cultural malware*, installed without consent, reinforced by repetition, and defended by social firewalls of family, tribe, and media. Certainty lights up the brain's reward circuits: conviction intoxicates like any drug (Sapolsky, 2017), while doubt feels threatening and ambiguity unbearable. In this climate we cling to ideologies, mistaking comfort for clarity, memorization for understanding, and agreement for truth.

The autonomic nervous system reveals why. *Polyvagal Theory* (Porges, 2011) shows how safety and belonging govern our responses before conscious thought arises. Resonance with the tribe feels safer than dissonance with reality. Better to be wrong together than exiled alone.

Plato's cave now plays in high definition, its flickering shadows transformed into pixels and streams. Bostrom's (2003) *simulation hypothesis* extends the metaphor, asking: what if the shadows are not firelight but code? This question is not merely technological but psychological, for we inhabit models of reality projected by our own minds and amplified by our machines. In this inverted order, image precedes substance, narrative precedes fact, and perception precedes existence (Debord, 1967). Such conditions make consent malleable, *manufactured* as Chomsky and Herman (1988) observed, yet today refined to industrial precision through algorithms and data. What was once propaganda becomes predictive commerce, where behavioral prediction is a trillion-dollar industry and human attention itself is strip-mined as a resource.

Nevertheless, no machine is seamless and no prison without cracks. In each of us flickers a glitch in the program, a memory of unformatted awareness. This spark is the seed this book tends. It is both confrontation and invitation: to expose the machinery of invisible imprisonment and to chart a path toward sovereign reawakening. The journey begins not with outrage but with vision. It is a roadmap for inner rebellion.

And this is not a book of despair.

PART I: THE BLUEPRINT OF ENSLAVEMENT

Part I (Chapters 1 to 11) descends into the structures that shape us. We begin with the raw circuitry of fear and belief, weaponized by design: trauma wires the brain for obedience, predictive minds collapse into predictable citizens, and belief fuses so tightly with identity that dissent can feel like death itself. The nervous system is tuned toward submission, stress physiology makes nuance intolerable, and the hunger for certainty is transmuted into political currency.

From the body we move to the sacred. Religion appears not as a desecration of mystery but as its capture, binding the numinous to guilt and dogma. Yet beneath doctrine we glimpse mystical experience in its raw form—direct, transpersonal, transformative—before institutions domesticate it for control (James, 2002/1902; Watts, 1951). The same logic carries into politics, where tribal manipulation masquerades as governance, outrage is funneled into predictable channels, and the machinery of power remains untouched.

Education, too, exposes its hidden architecture: bell schedules, standardized tests, and covert curricula that cultivate obedience over creativity, repetition over originality, and silence over sovereignty (Illich, 1971). Economics then strips away its fictions, unveiling how debt becomes a leash and scarcity a story, both engineered to justify hierarchy (Graeber, 2011). Science, though rigorous, is vulnerable to capture by corporate interests. The point is not to dismiss its power but to free it from materialist blinders. Media joins the procession as well, no longer a vessel of truth but an engineer of emotional captivity, transforming attention into marketable data. Even spirituality, commodified into guru culture and self-branding, turns into another gilded cage.

And finally, the climate itself—the breath of the planet—is drawn into the script. Genuine ecological crises are reframed as apocalyptic spectacle: carbon becomes sin, science becomes sermon, and planetary survival is invoked to justify surveillance, austerity, and control. Moreover, fear of collapse is repurposed as a management strategy: individuals are burdened with guilt while "elites" enact ritualized hypocrisy at global summits. In this script, true pathways of regeneration—rooted in reciprocity, reverence, and community resilience—are eclipsed by the hypnotic theater of apocalypse. The outcome is not planetary healing but a population conditioned to mistake fear for care and compliance for wisdom.

The final chapters of Part I unmask the hidden orchestrators of belief themselves: unconscious programmers, incentive structures that maintain illusion, and the recursive loops binding trauma, ideology, and power.

PART II: EXITING THE MATRIX

Part II (Chapters 12 to 19) turns toward liberation. Psychedelics emerge not as escapism but as ancient medicines, tools that loosen the ego's rigid priors and reveal the hidden patterns of consciousness. From these inner gateways, the path widens into questions of economic sovereignty: cryptocurrency, cooperative networks, community-based peer production, and mutual aid offer ways to cut the leash of financial control. Refusal itself becomes an art form, a sacred disobedience that resists feeding algorithms with outrage, outsourcing healing, or surrendering attention, the most precious resource, to the marketplace of distraction.

This spirit of reclamation extends into the body. *Somatic intelligence, breathwork, trauma resolution, creative rebellion,* and *community coherence* become practices of *deprogramming*, restoring choice where conditioning once dictated response. In their wake, identity loosens into process rather than prison, and ethics arise not from imposed authority but from awareness itself.

The same current reshapes spirituality, transforming it from a doctrine to defend into an immediacy discovered not in temples but in breath, not in belief but in lived presence. That current also invites science to expand by integrating first-person data, contemplative methods, and nondual phenomenology—a philosophical approach and research methodology that focus on lived experience from within—without sacrificing rigor. In turn, education, when freed from the chains of compliance, can nurture coherence, imagination, and embodied intelligence in place of rote repetition.

All of these threads weave into a broader horizon: the emergence of *parallel societies* where liberation is not merely imagined but lived. Within them, regenerative systems flourish, communities organize through decentralization, governance becomes collective sensemaking, law evolves as a living process, and technology serves as tool rather than master. This vision of the *Awakening of the Human Robot* points toward renaissance, a passage from scarcity into sufficiency, from domination into partnership (Eisler, 1987), where certainty gives way to curiosity and programmed minds awaken to presence.

Awakening the Human Robot is a book that holds paradox: poetic yet scientific, critical yet visionary, grounded yet transcendent. It is not for the comfortable but for those who feel the glitch, the sacred discomfort that whispers: *There is more.* It is also for scientists who sense that matter is not enough, mystics who refuse to abandon rigor, activists who know that revolution without healing becomes repetition, and healers who know trauma is political and politics is somatic.

If these words reach you, it is because you are not asleep. You may still walk within the *Matrix*, yet something in you remembers freedom older than formatting, breath deeper than programming, and a soul wider than survival. You are no machine and no mask, not a bundle of opinions, but a spark woven into the living web of becoming. And as you awaken, the script unravels, the code cracks open, and the veil grows thin.

Written in Champex-Lac (Valais), Switzerland

REFERENCES

Beauregard, M. A fuller description of this approach can be found in the Holosynthesis© section of my website: www.drmariobeauregard.com/Holosynthesis.

Bostrom, N. (2003). Are you living in a computer simulation? The Philosophical Quarterly, 53(211), 243–255. https://doi.org/10.1111/1467-9213.00309

Chomsky, N., & Herman, E. S. (1988). Manufacturing consent: The political economy of the mass media. Pantheon Books.

Debord, G. (1967). La société du spectacle. Buchet-Chastel.

Doidge, N. (2007). The brain that changes itself: Stories of personal triumph from the frontiers of brain science. Viking Penguin.

Eisler, R. (1987). The chalice and the blade: Our history, our future. Harper & Row.

Friston, K. (2010). The free-energy principle: A unified brain theory? Nature Reviews Neuroscience, 11(2), 127–138. https://doi.org/10.1038/nrn2787

Graeber, D. (2011). Debt: The first 5,000 years. Melville House.

Illich, I. (1971). Deschooling society. Harper & Row.

James, W. (2002). The varieties of religious experience. Modern Library. (Original work published 1902)

Porges, S. W. (2011). The polyvagal theory: Neurophysiological foundations of emotions, attachment, communication, and self-regulation. W. W. Norton & Company.

Proust, M. (1923). La prisonnière. In À la recherche du temps perdu (Vol. 5). Grasset.

Sapolsky, R. M. (2017). Behave: The biology of humans at our best and worst. Penguin Press.

van der Kolk, B. (2014). The body keeps the score: Brain, mind, and body in the healing of trauma. Viking.

Watts, A. (1951). The wisdom of insecurity. Pantheon Books.

PART I

THE BLUEPRINT OF ENSLAVEMENT

Chapter 1

Fear, Belief, and
the Neural Prison

"Belief is the death of intelligence."
— Robert Anton Wilson

We live in a world where belief is mistaken for truth and fear is mistaken for realism. These twin pillars of conditioning, belief and fear, form the neural substrate of what I call the *Human Robot*. To understand how we became programmable, automated beings, we must first explore the architecture of our most intimate prison: the brain itself.

In this chapter, I will map the inner machinery that converts living, sensing humans into predictable automatons: the predictive brain that writes our experience before we notice it; the limbic alarms that compress consciousness into a narrow tunnel of survival; the social nervous system that bonds us to tribes while weaponizing certainty; and the digital infrastructures that exploit all of the above at planetary scale. Finally, I will sketch practices—cognitive, contemplative, somatic, and intersubjective—that reopen the space of freedom. The aim is not to adopt better beliefs, but to understand the machinery of believing so thoroughly that identification with it begins to loosen.

THE PREDICTIVE BRAIN AND THE COMFORT OF CERTAINTY

Think of your brain as a fortune-teller with a clipboard. All day it guesses what you are about to see, hear, or feel. These predictions flow down to your senses like memos from headquarters. When reality shows up, the brain checks: *Did I get it right?* If yes, everything runs smoothly. If not, it logs an error and updates the model (Friston, 2010; Clark, 2013). This constant cycle of guessing and revising helps us move through the world efficiently. The fewer surprises, the easier it is on our body. But when life gets unpredictable, the brain works overtime, setting off alarm bells like the amygdala and triggering the stress response (Hirsh, Mar, & Peterson, 2012).

A belief can be thought of as a prediction prior so entrenched that contradictory evidence is ignored, distorted, or reinterpreted to fit the model. *Cognitive dissonance* (Festinger, 1957) is the felt signal of mounting prediction error. To ease the discomfort, the brain often alters perception rather than the prior. This is why even the highly intelligent can be exquisitely irrational when defending core identities (Kahan, 2017). The brain's priority is not truth: it is preserving its model of the world and the neurochemical stability that model provides.

This predictive-coding machinery also helps explain confirmation bias at the synaptic level. When a belief is validated, dopamine reinforces the existing model along neural circuits that govern reward, motivation, and addiction (Schultz, 1998; Sharot et al., 2011). The pleasure is not in truth but in being right. Add the need for cognitive closure (Kruglanski, 2004) and *certainty* begins to resemble an addiction: it soothes anxiety, prunes ambiguity, and preserves identity coherence, all while maintaining tribal alignment. Each confirmation strengthens the belief, locking it more tightly into place. The loop becomes self-reinforcing: belief → confirmation → dopaminergic reward → stronger belief. Breaking that loop feels like tearing away part of the self. The withdrawal is not only mental but visceral, as if the nervous system were protesting the loss of its most familiar drug: certainty.

Even science, the most rigorous instrument we possess for questioning our models, is not immune. Paradigms solidify (Kuhn, 1962), confirmation biases shape what gets published, and replication crises reveal the fragility of "settled" truths.

BELIEF AS NEURAL, SOMATIC, AND SOCIAL ARCHITECTURES

Beliefs are not just ideas floating in the mind: they live in the brain, the body, and our relationships. Because of neuroplasticity, the brain's ability to change, repeated thoughts and emotions rewire neural circuits, making some interpretations easier to reach and others harder (Doidge, 2007). As neuroscientist Antonio Damasio (1999) showed, feelings are central to decision-making: we feel our beliefs before we speak them. In the body, beliefs often appear as muscle tension, breathing patterns, gut reactions, or shifts in the nervous system, patterns trauma therapists see every day (Levine, 1997; van der Kolk, 2014).

Socially, beliefs are contracts for belonging. *Social identity theory* (Tajfel & Turner, 1986) shows that we derive meaning, status, and safety from group membership. Oxytocin, often romanticized as the "love hormone," amplifies in-group trust but also out-group hostility (De Dreu et al., 2011). In other words, belonging is biochemistry, and belief is one of its gatekeepers. To question a group's sacred beliefs is to risk exile, and the mammalian nervous system reads social exclusion as existential threat (Eisenberger, Lieberman, & Williams, 2003).

Once belief fuses with identity—"I am a skeptic," "I am a believer," "I am a scientist," "I am a patriot"—questioning it feels like self-annihilation. Hence the extraordinary defensiveness around political and religious ideologies, but also around professional dogmas, academic paradigms, and even scientific orthodoxies (Kuhn, 1962). The *Human Robot* is most secure when it is its belief.

TRAUMA AND FEAR: THE MASTER KEY OF PROGRAMMING

Trauma is perhaps the most potent force in shaping belief. Under overwhelming stress, especially in early life, the brain prioritizes survival over reflection. The amygdala becomes hyperactive while the prefrontal cortex (PFC), crucial for inhibition and long-term planning, goes offline (Arnsten, 2009). Experiences are encoded as implicit, non-conscious memory traces, often without coherent narrative. From these fragments, the psyche forges fear-based priors: *I am unsafe. Authority is dangerous. Obedience is the only path to avoid pain.*

This plastic vulnerability extends beyond the individual. Cultural trauma—e.g., war, genocide, colonization, systemic racism or ecological collapse—reshapes collective nervous systems. Epigenetic studies reveal altered stress reactivity in the descendants of traumatized populations (Yehuda & Bierer, 2009; Meaney & Szyf, 2005). Fear is thus inherited not only through stories, but through biochemical processes that tune the hypothalamic–pituitary–adrenal (HPA) axis toward vigilance.

Trauma narrows the window of tolerance (Siegel, 1999). Outside that window, the nervous system defaults to fight, flight, or freeze. In those states, nuance collapses, complexity becomes unbearable, and the brain clings to absolutist beliefs to steady itself. Authoritarian ideologies thrive because they offer certainty to dysregulated systems. What looks like stupidity is in fact state-dependent neurobiology.

Trauma installs the circuitry, and fear supplies the current. Trauma wires the nervous system toward hypervigilance, while fear activates and sustains that wiring. Together they create the conditions of programmability: a brain primed to trade freedom for safety, reflection for certainty, and presence for control.

Fear, then, is the master key. It bypasses rational deliberation, hijacks the nervous system, narrows perception, and amplifies conformity. Activation of the HPA axis floods the body with cortisol and adrenaline. Acute surges prepare us for fight or flight, but chronic activation shrinks the hippocampus, dulls the PFC, impairs memory, and reduces cognitive flexibility (McEwen, 1998; Lupien et al., 2009). The fearful brain is a *programmable* brain: it seeks structure, hierarchy, and certainty.

Rulers, priests, and propagandists have long known this. What is new is the industrialization of fear. Today's media infrastructures function as attention-maximizing machines. Algorithms privilege arousal—especially anger and fear—because these states increase engagement and time-on-platform (Bakshy, Messing, & Adamic, 2015). The result is a permanent, low-level activation of the social nervous system: a populace oscillating between outrage and dread, neurobiologically primed to accept simplistic, forceful answers. These so-called *strongman solutions* promise protection and order—*just trust me and I'll keep you safe*—but they work by stripping away nuance and freedom in exchange for the illusion of certainty.

COVID-19 AS A CASE STUDY

The COVID-19 pandemic became a living laboratory for observing the mechanics of fear and belief on a global scale. Within weeks in March 2020, the world was plunged into uncertainty: headlines shifted daily, routines collapsed, and invisible danger seemed to lurk everywhere. The body does not distinguish between a virus in the air, a predator in the forest, or chaos in the news cycle: all are registered as threat. In this way, millions experienced a collective activation of the stress response system. What unfolded was not only a medical crisis but also a psychobiological one, as public discourse, institutional trust, and social behavior were rapidly reorganized under the sway of invisible, emotionally charged priors.

At the biological level, the pandemic acted as a chronic stressor. Constant exposure to alarming headlines, case dashboards, and polarized commentary kept many nervous systems in a low-grade fight-or-flight state. Under such conditions, the PFC, the neural mediator of deliberation and nuance, yielded to the urgency of limbic survival. This neurobiological shift laid the groundwork for what followed.

In such a state, belief systems did not simply adjust; they hardened. For some, the threat of the virus justified unprecedented restrictions and surveillance. For others, the same threat was filtered through existing distrust of institutions or the legacy of historical trauma. Both responses, though different, were shaped by the same mechanism: the brain's drive to resolve ambiguity and preserve identity coherence. Seen through the lens of predictive coding, facts mattered less than the emotional economy of certainty.

Social media amplified these dynamics. Algorithmic gatekeeping, through recommendation engines and personalized feeds, ensured users were bathed in confirmatory information, escalating polarization. Dissenters on either side were quickly cast as heretics. Belief fused with moral identity, and complex, evolving data collapsed into binary postures: compliant versus resistant, scientific versus conspiratorial, caring versus selfish. Nuance did not vanish by accident: it became intolerable under the neurophysiological conditions of sustained stress.

Perhaps most striking was that compliance and defiance alike were mobilized not by rational persuasion but by fear activation. Images of overwhelmed hospitals, rising death tolls, or, conversely, of supposed hoaxes and nefarious plots all bypassed the filters of the PFC and triggered rapid, emotionally anchored reactions. Whether obedient or resistant, the *Human Robot* was executing scripts dictated less by deliberation than by fear, identity, and tribal allegiance.

The pandemic revealed just how fragile our sense of agency becomes when mass fear is mobilized. It did more than disrupt routines: it reshaped perception, narrowed the window of tolerance, and heightened susceptibility to authoritative messaging. Once the limbic system is activated, the lure of simple answers and strong leaders grows almost irresistible, for fear makes obedience feel like safety. In this light, COVID-19 was not merely a public health event but a global psychobiological hijacking. And unless we learn how fear and belief co-opt the human nervous system, we will remain vulnerable not only to viruses but also to the contagion of certainty.

IDENTITY: THE FINAL LOCK

The most insidious aspect of belief is its fusion with identity. When belief becomes who we are, questioning it feels like moral failure or social suicide. Oxytocin-fueled in-group bonding (De Dreu et al., 2011) combines with moralized ideologies to create *sacred values*: beliefs that are immune to trade-offs and resistant to evidence. Violating them triggers rage, disgust, and punitive impulses.

Identity provides status, belonging, and meaning, but at the cost of cognitive liberty. The more we accept labels as essences, the more the *Human Robot* tightens its grip. The antidote is not to adopt a new label, but to notice labeling as a process the mind uses to secure itself.

ESCAPING THE PRISON:
TOWARD PSYCHOBIOLOGICAL LIBERATION

If belief and fear run so deep, how can we release their grip? The path lies in shifting how we hold belief itself, rather than replacing one dogma with another. Below are practices and frameworks that, together, help dismantle the neural prison.

Metacognition and Mindfulness

Metacognition—the ability to observe our own thoughts and feelings—creates a gap between experience and identification. Mindfulness meditation and related contemplative practices strengthen top-down regulatory circuits in the PFC and reduce limbic reactivity (Lutz, Slagter, Dunne, & Davidson, 2008; Tang, Hölzel, & Posner, 2015). They help the nervous system pause before reacting.

Somatic awareness—especially interoceptive practice, the attention to internal sensations such as heartbeat, breath, and gut feelings—strengthens the insula, a small region deep within the brain that serves as an internal-sensing hub. The insula translates bodily signals into felt experience. When its tuning improves, we can better differentiate emotions and ease diffuse fear states (Craig, 2009). In this way, fear becomes less an overwhelming force and more a sensation we can notice, giving us the space to respond rather than react.

Radical Self-Inquiry

Where did this belief come from? What fear does it protect? What social reward does it buy? What happens in my body when it is challenged? These questions form the basis of radical self-inquiry: a careful, first-person excavation of lived experience. The work is less about forcing answers than about cultivating presence with what arises, tracing beliefs back to their roots in memory, emotion, and bodily sensation.

In trauma-informed practice, such inquiry must be carefully paced so the nervous system stays within the window of tolerance (Ogden, Minton, & Pain, 2006). Otherwise, the inquiry can slip into overwhelm and become another reenactment of trauma rather than a pathway to freedom. This is why radical self-inquiry benefits from gentleness, grounding practices, and, when possible, supportive relationships. It is not an interrogation but a form of listening for where fear hardens into certainty, where obedience fuses with identity, and where survival strategies masquerade as truth.

When approached in this way, inquiry becomes not only an intellectual process but also a somatic and relational one. It invites the possibility that beliefs are not fixed structures but adaptive patterns, and that by bringing them into awareness, we create the space for choice.

Reframing Uncertainty

Uncertainty is not an enemy but a portal. Psychological flexibility, the capacity to hold multiple possibilities without collapsing, is strongly associated with mental health (Kashdan & Rottenberg, 2010). *Acceptance and Commitment Therapy (ACT)* operationalizes this by training cognitive defusion—learning to notice thoughts as passing words and images rather than literal truths—and values-based action (Hayes, Strosahl, & Wilson, 2011). Spiritual traditions have always pointed to this truth: real transformation happens in the "cloud of unknowing," the space where we let go of certainty and open ourselves to mystery. Mystics describe it as entering prayer or meditation without answers, allowing the unknown itself to become the doorway to insight.

Intersubjective Spaces

Intersubjective practices are ways of exploring truth together. Examples include *Bohmian dialogue*, a group conversation where participants suspend assumptions and listen for what emerges (Bohm, 1996); *Socratic inquiry*, the disciplined art of questioning that tests definitions and reasons; and *Circling*, a relational mindfulness practice that follows moment-to-moment experience and impact while staying in connection. These practices serve as neurobiological training grounds for humility.

When we pay attention not only to what we believe but to how we defend it, our minds and brains become more adaptable and open. Groups that learn to navigate disagreement without resorting to exclusion become fertile ground for identities that stretch beyond tribal boundaries.

Somatic Literacy

One practical way to get out of "neural autopilot" is to notice which gear your nervous system is in. *Polyvagal Theory* (Porges, 2011) describes three common gears: fight/flight (your body revs up to protect you), shutdown (your body goes numb or collapses to conserve energy), and social-safety (also called ventral vagal; you feel safe, connected, and able to think clearly).

Our beliefs often change with these states. In fight/flight, the mind leaps to worst-case stories. In shutdown, it can cling to "nothing matters" certainties. When we spend more time in social-safety, we can hold nuance without freaking out or checking out.

We can nudge our system toward social-safety with safe connection (being with trusted people), steady breathing, gentle movement, and prosocial play (e.g., shared laughter, music, and games). As ventral vagal tone strengthens, more perspectives feel tolerable and choosing how to respond gets easier.

Digital Hygiene

We ought to approach our information intake with the same care we give to our food choices. This means deciding what we see online, scheduling breaks from dopamine-driven scrolling, and intentionally exposing ourselves to sources that challenge our beliefs (Pennycook & Rand, 2019; Pariser, 2011). Embracing slower forms of media (e.g., books, in-depth conversations) helps restore a sense of temporal spaciousness to our thinking.

Awe and the Softening of the Self

Moments of awe, mystical union, or nondual awareness can soften the rigid priors that shape and often constrain our sense of identity (Yaden et al., 2017; Carhart-Harris & Friston, 2019). Whether evoked through contemplative practice, immersion in nature, or carefully facilitated psychedelic therapy, these states often relax the automatic patterns of perception and belief that define our experience of being a separate self. In doing so, they reveal what philosopher Thomas Metzinger calls the self-model: a mental construct, generated by the brain, that gives us the persistent but illusory sense of being a fixed, bounded "I" (Metzinger, 2003). Recognizing the self as a process rather than a thing can be profoundly liberating. Without thoughtful integration, even transformative insights risk crystallizing into new dogmas, becoming beliefs to cling to rather than truths to live.

FROM ROBOT TO FREEDOM

The *Human Robot* is not an exception but the rule. Our evolutionary wiring ensures that belief, fear, and habit can shape us into machines of conformity. Social systems have long exploited this pliability, converting raw survival instincts into patterns of control.

Obedience begins in the brain but is harvested and systematized by culture. Religion was the first great apparatus to capture this vulnerability, sanctifying fear and turning mystical fire into dogma.

Freedom, however, is not eliminated by the predictive brain. It is relocated. Freedom is not a metaphysical switch but a skillful relationship to conditioning. Within the machinery lies the possibility of revolt. Freedom begins when we recognize the *Human Robot* not as our master but as one component of a larger awareness. Beliefs can be held lightly, fear can be treated as data, and survival instincts can be honored without being obeyed.

Awakening begins here: in the moment-to-moment practice of seeing our priors, feeling our states, updating our models, and choosing values-aligned action even under pressure. Freedom becomes iterative, a process of deprogramming and reprogramming at higher, more inclusive levels of awareness. To awaken is to break the loops of trauma, fear, and conformity, to rebel against the inner empire of control, and to reclaim the full spectrum of our conscious potential. This struggle for freedom has always been bound up with humanity's search for the sacred. In the next chapter, we will see how divinity itself was hijacked, and how the hunger for transcendence was redirected into structures of power.

REFERENCES

Arnsten, A. F. T. (2009). Stress signalling pathways that impair prefrontal cortex structure and function. Nature Reviews Neuroscience, 10(6), 410–422. https://doi.org/10.1038/nrn2648 Nature

Bakshy, E., Messing, S., & Adamic, L. A. (2015). Exposure to ideologically diverse news and opinion on Facebook. Science, 348(6239), 1130–1132. https://doi.org/10.1126/science.aaa1160 PNAS

Bohm, D. (1996). On dialogue. Routledge.

Carhart-Harris, R. L., & Friston, K. J. (2019). REBUS and the anarchic brain: Toward a unified model of the brain action of psychedelics. Pharmacological Reviews, 71(3), 316–344. https://doi.org/10.1124/pr.118.017160 ResearchGate

Clark, A. (2013). Whatever next? Predictive brains, situated agents, and the future of cognitive science. Behavioral and Brain Sciences, 36(3), 181–204. https://doi.org/10.1017/S0140525X12000477 Cambridge University Press & Assessment

Craig, A. D. (2009). How do you feel—now? The anterior insula and human awareness. Nature Reviews Neuroscience, 10(1), 59–70. https://doi.org/10.1038/nrn2555 Nature

Damasio, A. R. (1999). The feeling of what happens: Body and emotion in the making of consciousness. Harcourt Brace. Colorado Mountain College

De Dreu, C. K. W., Greer, L. L., Van Kleef, G. A., Shalvi, S., & Handgraaf, M. J. J. (2011). Oxytocin promotes human ethnocentrism. Proceedings of the National Academy of Sciences, 108(4), 1262–1266. https://doi.org/10.1073/pnas.1015316108 PubMed

Doidge, N. (2007). The brain that changes itself. Viking Penguin.

Eisenberger, N. I., Lieberman, M. D., & Williams, K. D. (2003). Does rejection hurt? An fMRI study of social exclusion. Science, 302(5643), 290–292. https://doi.org/10.1126/science.1089134 Science

Festinger, L. (1957). A theory of cognitive dissonance. Stanford University Press.

Friston, K. (2010). The free-energy principle: A unified brain theory? Nature Reviews Neuroscience, 11(2), 127–138. https://doi.org/10.1038/nrn2787 Nature

Hayes, S. C., Strosahl, K. D., & Wilson, K. G. (2011). Acceptance and commitment therapy: The process and practice of mindful change (2nd ed.). Guilford.

Hirsh, J. B., Mar, R. A., & Peterson, J. B. (2012). Psychological entropy: A framework for understanding uncertainty-related anxiety. Psychological Review, 119(2), 304–320. https://doi.org/10.1037/a0026767 SSRN

Kahan, D. M. (2017). Misconceptions, misinformation, and the logic of identity-protective cognition. SSRN Working Paper (No. 2973067). https://doi.org/10.2139/ssrn.2973067 SSRN

Kashdan, T. B., & Rottenberg, J. (2010). Psychological flexibility as a fundamental aspect of health. Clinical Psychology Review, 30(7), 865–878. https://doi.org/10.1016/j.cpr.2010.03.001 PubMed

Kruglanski, A. W. (2004). The psychology of closed mindedness. Psychology Press. Routledge

Kuhn, T. S. (1962). The structure of scientific revolutions. University of Chicago Press.

Levine, P. (1997). Waking the tiger: Healing trauma. North Atlantic Books.

Lupien, S. J., McEwen, B. S., Gunnar, M. R., & Heim, C. (2009). Effects of stress throughout the lifespan on the brain, behaviour and cognition. Nature Reviews Neuroscience, 10(6), 434–445. https://doi.org/10.1038/nrn2639 PubMed

Lutz, A., Slagter, H. A., Dunne, J. D., & Davidson, R. J. (2008). Attention regulation and monitoring in meditation. Trends in Cognitive Sciences, 12(4), 163–169. https://doi.org/10.1016/j.tics.2008.01.005 PubMed

McEwen, B. S. (1998). Protective and damaging effects of stress mediators. New England Journal of Medicine, 338(3), 171–179. https://doi.org/10.1056/NEJM199801153380307 New England Journal of Medicine

Meaney, M. J., & Szyf, M. (2005). Environmental programming of stress responses through DNA methylation: Life at the interface between a dynamic environment and a fixed genome. Dialogues in Clinical Neuroscience, 7(2), 103–123.

Metzinger, T. (2003). Being no one. MIT Press.

Ogden, P., Minton, K., & Pain, C. (2006). Trauma and the body: A sensorimotor approach to psychotherapy. W. W. Norton.

Pariser, E. (2011). The filter bubble: What the Internet is hiding from you. Penguin Press.

Pennycook, G., & Rand, D. G. (2019). Fighting misinformation on social media using crowdsourced judgments of news source quality. Proceedings of the National Academy of Sciences, 116(7), 2521–2526. https://doi.org/10.1073/pnas.1806781116 ResearchGate

Porges, S. W. (2011). The polyvagal theory: Neurophysiological foundations of emotions, attachment, communication, and self-regulation. W. W. Norton.

Sapolsky, R. M. (2017). Behave: The biology of humans at our best and worst. Penguin Press.

Schultz, W. (1998). Predictive reward signal of dopamine neurons. Journal of Neurophysiology, 80(1), 1–27.

Sharot, T., Korn, C. W., & Dolan, R. J. (2011). How unrealistic optimism is maintained in the face of reality. Nature Neuroscience, 14(11), 1475–1479. https://doi.org/10.1038/nn.2949 Nature

Siegel, D. J. (1999). The developing mind. Guilford Press.

Tang, Y.-Y., Hölzel, B. K., & Posner, M. I. (2015). The neuroscience of mindfulness meditation. Nature Reviews Neuroscience, 16(4), 213–225. https://doi.org/10.1038/nrn3916 Nature

Tajfel, H., & Turner, J. C. (1986). The social identity theory of intergroup behavior. In S. Worchel & W. G. Austin (Eds.), Psychology of intergroup relations (pp. 7–24). Nelson-Hall.

van der Kolk, B. (2014). The body keeps the score. Viking.

Wilson, R. A. (1977). Cosmic trigger: Final secret of the Illuminati. And/Or Press.

Yaden, D. B., Haidt, J., Hood, R. W., Jr., Vago, D. R., & Newberg, A. B. (2017). The varieties of self-transcendent experience. Review of General Psychology, 21(2), 143–160. https://doi.org/10.1037/gpr0000102 Science

Yehuda, R., & Bierer, L. M. (2009). The relevance of epigenetics to PTSD. Journal of Traumatic Stress, 22(5), 427–434.

Chapter 2

Religion: Divinity Hijacked

*"Theologians may quarrel, but the mystics of
the world speak the same language."*
— Meister Eckhart

Religion stands as one of the oldest and most potent frameworks ever devised for organizing collective belief. Across centuries, it has been a powerful force for good: building communities, fostering compassion, inspiring great works of art, music, and architecture, and motivating acts of extraordinary altruism. Still, alongside these luminous contributions, religious beliefs have also fueled wars, persecution, and cultural destruction. At its best, religion has offered meaning and moral vision; at its worst, it has sanctioned chaos in the name of certainty and violence in the name of truth. While it has inspired awe, beauty, and compassion, it has also historically functioned as a tool of hierarchical control.

At their inception, most religious movements emerged from mystical insight: raw, unmediated encounters with the transcendent. William James (1902/2002) described such experiences as ineffable, noetic, and unifying. These altered states often catalyzed ethical transformation and existential reorientation, for the mystic catches a glimpse of *Ultimate Reality* beyond language, dogma, or duality.

Human beings have long sought to honor and integrate this encounter. Yet mysticism poses a threat to institutions. It decentralizes authority, prioritizes experience over doctrine, and resists control. Institutions responded predictably: over millennia they captured the mystical and codified it into static creeds. They weaponized it with guilt, built temples around it, tethered it to political thrones, and offered salvation in exchange for obedience. Mysticism withered into management, Revelation was shackled by regulation, and Divinity was hijacked.

On this issue, Alan Watts (1951) noted that organized religion often serves as a distraction from the divine, substituting symbols for experience and authority for awareness. It sells tickets to a show that plays within.

In psychological terms, this functions as a displacement defense. Instead of facing the terrifying freedom of direct encounter with the unknown, the ego clings to intermediaries such as priests (or pastors, rabbis, imams, lamas), scriptures, and rituals. These provide a sense of safety, but at the cost of vitality and aliveness.

Neuroscience helps explain why this strategy has worked so effectively. The brain is wired to detect patterns, infer agency, and assign meaning, especially under conditions of uncertainty or threat (Barrett, 2004). This *"hyperactive agency detection device"* (Guthrie, 1993) predisposes humans to interpret ambiguous events as intentional acts, a survival adaptation in predator-rich environments. Religions arose to shape the raw spark of agency detection into story: floods became punishments, not accidents; and earthquakes spoke as divine messages, not blind tectonics.

These narratives activate limbic circuits. Belief in punitive gods correlates with heightened social conformity and reduces antisocial behavior (Shariff & Norenzayan, 2011). But this compliance is fear-driven. When God becomes a surveillance system, morality devolves into obedience rather than empathy.

Rituals, found in every religion, act like training for belief. Cognitive neuroscience shows that repeating rituals taps into the brain's habit circuits, wiring beliefs into the body's movements and strengthening bonds within the group (Whitehouse & Lanman, 2014). In this way, belief is not just an idea but something practiced through the body, like choreography.

BELIEF AS BELONGING

Religion is rarely only about metaphysics. It is about membership: to believe is to belong, and to leave is not mere dissent but defection.

Social identity theory (Tajfel & Turner, 1986) illustrates how group identity fuses with individual self-worth, so that protecting the group feels like protecting the self. When those beliefs are challenged, the brain registers the threat not only cognitively but physically, activating the same regions associated with pain (Eisenberger et al., 2003). The nervous system amplifies this further: the polyvagal system reacts to exclusion as it would to danger, treating the loss of belonging as a survival risk (Porges, 2011).

This is why interfaith dialogues often fail to change minds. Belief extends beyond logic and evidence, woven into the nervous system's longing for safety, attachment, and significance. To question the faith is to risk exile, to confront the abyss of un-belonging.

This is why religious institutions have been so effective at enforcing doctrinal conformity. They do not simply transmit beliefs: they also encode social contracts.

ABOUT THE GOAL OF THIS CHAPTER

This chapter is not an attack on the sacred, nor a call to atheism or to blind faith. It is, rather, a defense of the sacred: an attempt to disentangle spirituality (direct, first-person, transformative) from religion-as-control, a sociopolitical technology that exploits fear of death, need for belonging, and neurobiological vulnerability to certainty. It is also a call to spiritual sovereignty.

THE BRAIN AS AN INTERFACE FOR THE MYSTICAL

Reducing the brain to a belief-producing, emotion-processing machine omits something profoundly essential: the capacity for transcendence, numinous awe, and direct encounter with the ineffable.

In our work with Carmelite nuns (Beauregard et al., 2007), my colleagues and I demonstrated that mystical states are mediated by the activation of specific brain regions associated with emotion, self-awareness, and altered perception of space and time. This was significant as it marked the first time a mystical state was experimentally induced and examined neurobiologically in a controlled setting. Importantly, these findings do not reduce the spiritual to "mere" brain states: they demonstrate that consciousness, in whatever its ultimate nature, interfaces with the nervous system in patterned ways. In other words, we humans are wired for transcendence. The neural machinery that makes us susceptible to religious control is the same machinery that can open us to radical freedom.

PRIMORDIAL PRIORS AND IMMORTALITY PROJECTS

As noted earlier, the *predictive processing theory* shows that the brain is always making models of the world and updating them when predictions do not match reality (Friston, 2010; Clark, 2013). Religious worldviews act like giant models— *"mega-priors"*—that explain existence and reduce uncertainty (Hirsh, Mar & Peterson, 2012). Because lowering uncertainty saves energy, dogma can actually feel safe to the brain. Institutions offer this sense of safety, but often at the cost of open questioning. In this view, doubt feels less like a virtue and more like a threat to stability.

Becker's *The Denial of Death* (1973) and subsequent *terror management theory* (Greenberg, Pyszczynski & Solomon, 2015) argue that religions function as immortality projects, symbolic or literal constructs that buffer death anxiety. When mortality is made salient, people cling more tightly to their worldviews and punish out-groups more harshly. Institutions exploit this. Preach Hell frequently enough, and you will manufacture compliance.

WHEN FIRE TURNED TO BUREAUCRACY

Routinization of Charisma

Sociologist Max Weber (1922/1978) described a recurring pattern: a charismatic breakthrough, whether from a prophet, sage, mystic, or shaman, generates a living current of meaning. After the founder's death, or due to institutional pressure, the movement routinizes into legal-rational or traditional authority. Roles stiffen into offices, creeds harden into dogma, and hierarchies solidify into chains of command; the living word becomes text, the text becomes law, and ecstasy becomes ecclesiastical order.

Early Christianity offers a clear example. What began as a radical, marginal movement of inner transformation and communal subversion became, by Constantine's fourth-century alliance, an imperial religion. The Council of Nicaea (325 CE) initiated a long process of defining orthodoxy and persecuting heresies, including Gnosticism, which emphasized direct experiential knowledge (gnosis) of the divine (Pagels, 1979).

The same dynamic unfolded within Islam. Sufism, the mystical heart of the tradition, often flourished on the margins, at times embraced and at times suppressed by legalist orthodoxies. Figures such as Mansur al-Hallaj, executed in 922

CE for declaring "I am the Truth," illustrate the enduring tension between mysticism and law.

Buddhism, though framed as a non-theistic path, also underwent institutionalization. The Buddha's radical psychological insights were routinized into scholastic debate, monastic bureaucracy, and, at times, state machinery. In Tibet, Buddhism became deeply entwined with feudal power for centuries.

Indigenous and shamanic traditions were similarly transformed, though in this case by colonization. Ecstatic and animistic practices were domesticated or destroyed, replaced by mission churches and state-approved theologies. In the process, communities were severed from direct relationships with land, ancestors, and expanded states of consciousness.

Canon, Creed, and the Closure of Meaning

Sacred texts can be luminous, poetic, and profound. But canonization also functions as a strategy of control. Once a text is declared infallible and its meaning entrusted only to ordained specialists, the doors of interpretation begin to close. The range of meaning narrows, and the text's complexity flattens into dogma, often weaponized both against rival interpretations and against direct experience.

This process is part of what Peter Berger and Thomas Luckmann (1966) described as the *social construction of reality*: institutions externalize human meanings, objectify them, and then re-internalize them through socialization. What begins as myth or metaphor is gradually reified into "reality," a framework that claims universality while erasing its origins in human imagination.

Once meaning is closed in this way, coercion often follows. The logic is straightforward: if eternal truth is at stake, then dissenters are not merely mistaken but dangerous. This logic has justified inquisitions, witch hunts, heresy trials, sectarian wars, fatwas, lynch mobs, and purity killings—the long, bloody record of defending orthodoxy. Nor is this dynamic confined to the Abrahamic traditions. Hindu nationalist violence in India, Buddhist ethno-nationalism in Myanmar and Sri Lanka, and new religious movements that devolve into cults of personality all reveal the same pattern: the sacred is captured and redirected toward domination.

THE PSYCHOLOGY OF OBEDIENCE

Guilt and shame are powerful emotions, rooted in our basic need to belong (Tangney, Stuewig & Mashek, 2007). Institutions can weaponize them by controlling moral rules and defining mistakes in absolute terms. When this conditioning happens in childhood, the nervous system learns to link even the thought of doubt or desire with stress reactions in the body, such as a racing heart or a rush of cortisol. The result is internalized surveillance. Michel Foucault (1977) described modern power as *panoptic*: external oversight replaced by internal self-policing. Religions pioneered this long before the prison.

They also frequently codify purity regimes (e.g., dietary laws, sexual taboos, menstrual restrictions), pairing them with disgust, a primal emotion rooted in pathogen avoidance (Curtis, Aunger & Rabie, 2004). When moralized, disgust becomes a tool for the dehumanization of out-groups and the regulation of bodies, particularly women's bodies.

Fear is another emotion often instrumentalized to control, guide, or discipline individuals and communities. Chief among these is the fear of Hell and eternal torment, an infinite punishment for finite errors. This has been one of the most potent and historically enduring emotional levers used by organized religions, particularly within the Abrahamic traditions

(Christianity, Islam, Judaism to some extent), to shape belief systems, regulate behavior, and reinforce group cohesion.

Hell works not only as a spiritual threat but also as a way of shaping behavior by hijacking the brain's fear circuits. The brain does not easily distinguish between imagined and real threats when emotions are strong (Kosslyn et al., 2001). Vivid sermons, frightening images, and constant reminders turn abstract ideas into bodily experiences. The fear of Hell is not just a thought but something people feel in their flesh.

Repeated exposure to such narratives during critical developmental windows (ages 5–12) can hardwire fear-based belief systems. The amygdala's plasticity during this time ensures that images of fire, judgment, and damnation become embedded in the emotional memory network, often inaccessible to rational revision (LeDoux, 1996). This kind of fear-based programming diminishes reflective capacity. When we are under stress, the brain's higher reasoning centers quiet down (Arnsten, 2009). This makes it harder to see religious texts in symbolic or poetic ways, so people tend to fall back on literal interpretations.

Some beliefs rise to the level of what Scott Atran and Jeremy Ginges (2012) call *sacred values*: convictions held as absolute and non-negotiable, often resistant to evidence. When these values are challenged, they spark intense moral outrage and are defended with the same reverence people give to religion, even when the beliefs are secular. Leaders can exploit sacred values to drive self-sacrifice, fuel aggression, or enforce conformity.

SCIENCE, REDUCTIONISM, AND THE EXCOMMUNICATION OF MYSTERY

If religion hijacked divinity, *scientism* — the belief that only the empirical is real — has often banished it. Institutional science can act like a gatekeeping priesthood, dismissing first-person data (e.g., mystical states, near-death experiences, psi phenomena) as mere "anecdote," while disregarding vast accumulations of anomalous evidence (Greyson, 2021; Radin, 2006). The result is a double-bind: religion manipulates the sacred, while scientism denies it. The individual is left impoverished, oscillating between dogma and disenchanted nihilism.

The true alternative lies in *post-materialist science*: rigorous and pluralistic, yet open to the possibility that consciousness is fundamental or at least irreducible to matter (Beauregard, 2012; Beauregard et al., 2014). Post-materialist science approaches the sacred not as pathology but as valid experience. It integrates phenomenology, contemplative practice, and psychedelics without surrendering methodological integrity (Varela, 1996; Lutz & Thompson, 2003).

RECLAIMING THE DIVINE WITHOUT BELIEF

If divinity has been hijacked, how can it be reclaimed? The answer is not to exchange one belief system for another but to transform our relationship to belief itself, rooting spirituality in direct experience, ethical embodiment, and communal coherence.

One pathway is through *apophatic practice*, the way of unknowing. The apophatic, or *via negativa*, tradition (for example, *The Cloud of Unknowing* in the 14th century and Meister Eckhart) points beyond concepts by denying all predicates of the divine: God is not this, not that (*neti neti*). This trains the mind to release the grasping that turns mystery into doctrine. Neuroscientifically, contemplative silence strengthens prefrontal regulation and reduces limbic reactivity (Tang, Hölzel & Posner, 2015), creating a nervous system capable of tolerating paradox.

Another path is *somatic mysticism*, treating the body as portal. Trauma-aware spirituality recognizes that dysregulated nervous systems cannot sustain contemplative depth without safety (Ogden, Minton & Pain, 2006). *Polyvagal-informed practices* (Porges, 2011), including breathwork, gentle movement, and relational safety, cultivate ventral vagal tone and expand the window of tolerance. The body ceases to be a battlefield of purity and becomes a temple of presence.

Psychedelic sacraments offer yet another opening by deconditioning the belief engine. Clinical trials with psilocybin and other psychedelics consistently report mystical-type experiences (Griffiths et al., 2006, 2016) correlated with long-term reductions in depression, anxiety, and addiction. The REBUS model (Carhart-Harris & Friston, 2019) suggests that psychedelics relax high-level priors, dissolving rigid beliefs and opening cognitive flexibility. Used responsibly, with skilled preparation, support, and integration, these tools can reveal the constructedness of identity and doctrine alike. Without integration, however, they risk becoming just another belief-factory, revelations frozen into new dogmas.

Post-belief spirituality grounds ethics in awareness instead of authority. It roots moral action in felt interconnectedness, empathic attunement, and wisdom that responds to context rather than absolute commands. This approach favors responsiveness over relativism. It asks: what action reduces suffering and creates coherence here and now? Such ethics resonate with process philosophies and nondual traditions, where compassion emerges naturally as rigid boundaries between self and other dissolve (Varela, Thompson & Rosch, 1991; Singer & Klimecki, 2014).

Finally, there is the work of deprogramming for those exiting high-control religions. Faith deconstruction can trigger destabilization, grief, and social exile, and so requires trauma-informed approaches. This may involve graded exposure to uncertainty, as in *Acceptance and Commitment Therapy* (Hayes, Strosahl & Wilson, 2011), which reframes ambiguity as spaciousness rather than threat. It may include somatic therapy to dissolve fear associated with divine punishment or community loss (van der Kolk, 2014). It also benefits from critical interpretation, recognizing how doctrines were historically constructed (Armstrong, 1993) and placing dogma in context. Most importantly, it requires the building of parallel communities that offer belonging without belief enforcement.

THE NUMINOUS AFTER THE HIJACK

The sacred is not an argument to win but a dimension to inhabit. The task is less about overthrowing religion and erecting a new creed than about unmasking the machinery of capture and walking out together into the open. In doing so, it is essential to remember that religion has not only served as a vehicle for oppression but also as a source of resilience, beauty, and compassion. For billions of people, it has carried and still carries moral courage, solidarity, and hope in times of darkness. The challenge, then, is not to discard religion wholesale, but to discern and reclaim its nourishing roots while refusing the structures that have exploited them.

This reclamation is already under way. As old religious institutions hollow and political ideologies stiffen, a new current emerges: the return of direct experience. Mysticism rises again, not as dogma but as inquiry. Psychedelic therapy, contemplative science, nondual traditions, and somatic healing converge in a renaissance of interior exploration. Such movements are threatening to the status quo not because they sow chaos but because they cultivate sovereignty. Mystical experience dissolves the very boundaries that institutions rely on: self and other, right and wrong, sacred and profane.

Neuroscientific studies of mystical states confirm this shift, showing decreased activity in the brain's *default mode network*, the neural hub of *egoic self-reference* (Carhart-Harris et al.,

2012). The result is often greater compassion, flexibility of mind, and a felt sense of interconnectedness (Yaden et al., 2017). In this light, we need rituals that return us to ourselves, languages that point rather than imprison, leaders who know how to step aside, and technologies that amplify awareness instead of addiction.

Religion once took the fire and built a prison. Our task now is to take the fire back, and this time to tend it without allowing it to burn us into hierarchies and dogma.

REFERENCES

Armstrong, K. (1993). A history of God: The 4,000-year quest of Judaism, Christianity, and Islam. Knopf.

Arnsten, A. F. T. (2009). Stress signalling pathways that impair prefrontal cortex structure and function. Nature Reviews Neuroscience, 10(6), 410–422. https://doi.org/10.1038/nrn2648

Atran, S., & Ginges, J. (2012). Religious and sacred imperatives in human conflict. Science, 336(6083), 855–857. https://doi.org/10.1126/science.1216902

Barrett, J. L. (2004). Why would anyone believe in God? AltaMira Press.

Beauregard, M. (2012). Brain wars: The scientific battle over the existence of the mind and the proof that will change the way we live our lives. HarperOne.

Beauregard, M., Courtemanche, J., Paquette, V., & St-Pierre, É. L. (2007). The neural basis of the mystical experience in Carmelite nuns. Neuroscience Letters, 405(3), 186–190. https://doi.org/10.1016/j.neulet.2006.07.052

Beauregard, M., Schwartz, G. E., & Miller, L. (2014). Spirituality and consciousness research: The birth of a postmaterialist science. Explore: The Journal of Science and Healing, 10(5), 272–274. https://doi.org/10.1016/j.explore.2014.06.002

Becker, E. (1973). The denial of death. Free Press.

Berger, P. L., & Luckmann, T. (1966). The social construction of reality: A treatise in the sociology of knowledge. Anchor Books.

Carhart-Harris, R. L., & Friston, K. J. (2019). REBUS and the anarchic brain: Toward a unified model of the brain action of psychedelics. Pharmacological Reviews, 71(3), 316–344. https://doi.org/10.1124/pr.118.017160

Carhart-Harris, R. L., Erritzoe, D., Williams, T., et al. (2012). Neural correlates of the psychedelic state as determined by fMRI studies with psilocybin. Proceedings of the National Academy of Sciences, 109(6), 2138–2143. https://doi.org/10.1073/pnas.1119598109

Clark, A. (2013). Whatever next? Predictive brains, situated agents, and the future of cognitive science. Behavioral and Brain Sciences, 36(3), 181–204. https://doi.org/10.1017/S0140525X12000477

Curtis, V., Aunger, R., & Rabie, T. (2004). Evidence that disgust evolved to protect from risk of disease. Proceedings of the Royal Society B: Biological Sciences, 271(Suppl 4), S131–S133. https://doi.org/10.1098/rsbl.2003.0144

Eckhart, M. (2001). The essential sermons, commentaries, treatises, and defense (B. McGinn, Ed. & Trans.). Paulist Press.

Eisenberger, N. I., Lieberman, M. D., & Williams, K. D. (2003). Does rejection hurt? An fMRI study of social exclusion. Science, 302(5643), 290–292. https://doi.org/10.1126/science.1089134

Foucault, M. (1977). Discipline and punish: The birth of the prison (A. Sheridan, Trans.). Pantheon Books. (Original work published 1975)

Friston, K. (2010). The free-energy principle: A unified brain theory? Nature Reviews Neuroscience, 11(2), 127–138. https://doi.org/10.1038/nrn2787

Greenberg, J., Pyszczynski, T., & Solomon, S. (2015). The worm at the core: On the role of death in life. Random House.

Griffiths, R. R., Richards, W. A., McCann, U., & Jesse, R. (2006). Psilocybin can occasion mystical-type experiences having substantial and sustained personal meaning and spiritual significance. Psychopharmacology, 187(3), 268–283. https://doi.org/10.1007/s00213-006-0457-5

Griffiths, R. R., Johnson, M. W., Carducci, M. A., et al. (2016). Psilocybin produces substantial and sustained decreases in depression and anxiety in patients with life-threatening cancer: A randomized double-blind trial. Journal of Psychopharmacology, 30(12), 1181–1197. https://doi.org/10.1177/0269881116675513

Greyson, B. (2021). After: A doctor explores what near-death experiences reveal about life and beyond. St. Martin's Essentials.

Guthrie, S. E. (1993). Faces in the clouds: A new theory of religion. Oxford University Press.

Hayes, S. C., Strosahl, K. D., & Wilson, K. G. (2011). Acceptance and commitment therapy: The process and practice of mindful change (2nd ed.). Guilford Press.

Hirsh, J. B., Mar, R. A., & Peterson, J. B. (2012). Psychological entropy: A framework for understanding uncertainty-related anxiety. Psychological Review, 119(2), 304–320. https://doi.org/10.1037/a0026767

James, W. (2002). The varieties of religious experience: A study in human nature. Routledge. (Original work published 1902)

Kosslyn, S. M., Ganis, G., & Thompson, W. L. (2001). Neural foundations of imagery. Nature Reviews Neuroscience, 2(9), 635–642. https://doi.org/10.1038/35090055

LeDoux, J. E. (1996). The emotional brain: The mysterious underpinnings of emotional life. Simon & Schuster.

Lutz, A., & Thompson, E. (2003). Neurophenomenology: Integrating subjective experience and brain dynamics in the neuroscience of consciousness. Journal of Consciousness Studies, 10(9–10), 31–52.

Ogden, P., Minton, K., & Pain, C. (2006). Trauma and the body: A sensorimotor approach to psychotherapy. W. W. Norton & Company.

Pagels, E. (1979). The Gnostic Gospels. Random House.

Porges, S. W. (2011). The polyvagal theory: Neurophysiological foundations of emotions, attachment, communication, and self-regulation. W. W. Norton & Company.

Radin, D. (2006). Entangled minds: Extrasensory experiences in a quantum reality. Paraview Pocket Books.

Shariff, A. F., & Norenzayan, A. (2011). Mean gods make good people: Different views of God predict cheating behavior. International Journal for the Psychology of Religion, 21(2), 85–96. https://doi.org/10.1080/10508619.2011.556990

Singer, T., & Klimecki, O. M. (2014). Empathy and compassion. Current Biology, 24(18), R875–R878. https://doi.org/10.1016/j.cub.2014.06.054

Tajfel, H., & Turner, J. C. (1986). The social identity theory of intergroup behavior. In S. Worchel & W. G. Austin (Eds.), Psychology of intergroup relations (pp. 7–24). Nelson-Hall.

Tang, Y.-Y., Hölzel, B. K., & Posner, M. I. (2015). The neuroscience of mindfulness meditation. Nature Reviews Neuroscience, 16(4), 213–225. https://doi.org/10.1038/nrn3916

Tangney, J. P., Stuewig, J., & Mashek, D. J. (2007). Moral emotions and moral behavior. Annual Review of Psychology, 58, 345–372. https://doi.org/10.1146/annurev.psych.56.091103.070145

van der Kolk, B. A. (2014). The body keeps the score: Brain, mind, and body in the healing of trauma. Viking.

Varela, F. J. (1996). Neurophenomenology: A methodological remedy for the hard problem. Journal of Consciousness Studies, 3(4), 330–349.

Varela, F. J., Thompson, E., & Rosch, E. (1991). The embodied mind: Cognitive science and human experience. MIT Press.

Watts, A. (1951). The wisdom of insecurity: A message for an age of anxiety. Pantheon Books.

Weber, M. (1978). Economy and society: An outline of interpretive sociology (G. Roth & C. Wittich, Eds.). University of California Press. (Original work published 1922)

Whitehouse, H., & Lanman, J. A. (2014). The ties that bind us: Ritual, fusion, and identification. Current Anthropology, 55(6), 674–695. https://doi.org/10.1086/678698

Yaden, D. B., Le Nguyen, K. D., Kern, M. L., et al. (2017). The noetic quality: A multi-method exploratory study. Psychology of Consciousness: Theory, Research, and Practice, 4(1), 54–62. https://doi.org/10.1037/cns0000106

Chapter 3

Nation, Tribe, and the Theater of Control

"The new theater of politics is vertical. While citizens argue across the aisle, the elites consolidate power above them."
— Mario Beauregard

If Chapter 1 revealed how belief and fear sculpt the neural circuitry of obedience, and Chapter 2 unveiled the apparatus of religions that harvest and amplify these vulnerabilities, we now turn to politics, nation, and tribe, powerful dogmas of the modern world.

Institutions do not merely reflect our psychology, they shape it. Chief among them is politics, an engine of *social programming* cloaked in the language of truth, virtue, and destiny. The nation, the tribe, and democracy itself arrive not as rational concepts but as visceral experiences, enacted in songs, rituals, voting booths, and online flame wars. Only later do we justify them with lofty ideas: freedom, sovereignty, representation, and rights.

Both religion and politics have always known the secrets we are only beginning to decode scientifically: that fear narrows perception, that identity binds belief, and that repetition rewires the brain. What religion once achieved through myth, ritual, and divine punishment, modern politics now secures through media manipulation, digital tribalism, and symbolic warfare. Both operate on the same substrate: the programmable nervous system.

POLITICAL THEOLOGY

Religion may have waned in the secular West, but its structures have not disappeared, they have migrated. Modern politics is *political theology* in disguise. It offers salvation (progress), heresy (opposition), rituals (elections), sacred texts (constitutions), and high priests (pundits, prime ministers, and presidents); furthermore, it demands belief, punishes apostasy, and promises deliverance through participation.

Carl Schmitt (1922/2005) contended that the very foundations of modern state theory are nothing more than *"secularized theological concepts."* In his view, sovereignty does not simply administer power: it mirrors divine omnipotence, claiming the ultimate authority to determine who may live and who must die, who belongs within the political community and who is cast out. From this perspective, politics acquires a quasi-theological structure, and modern ideologies function less as pragmatic frameworks for governance than as comprehensive moral universes. Liberalism, conservatism, socialism, communism—these are no longer merely policy positions but tribal markers, infused with sacred value systems. To question them is not merely to debate ideas, but to risk transgressing boundaries of the sacred, eliciting moral outrage and disgust in a manner strikingly akin to accusations of blasphemy in earlier religious orders (Atran & Ginges, 2012).

The machinery of political theology is not abstract: it breathes through parades, elections, national holidays, and monuments. To stand before a memorial is to be invited into reverence. When the anthem soars before the game, the body moves before thought: goosebumps ripple across the skin, eyes glisten, and the chest lifts with pride. This is the liturgy of the nation, the heartbeat of political theology.

THE SPECTACLE: MEDIA AS LITURGICAL INTERFACE

Enter the mass media, the high-speed carrier of ideology, fear, and ritual. If the church was once the mediator between the sacred and the masses, today's media is the liturgical interface for the political gods. Guy Debord (1967) called this *the society of the spectacle*," where lived experience is replaced by representations and participation is reduced to consumption. Politics becomes theater, and truth becomes narrative. Neuroscience confirms media's power. Repeated exposure to emotionally charged images such as terrorism, crime, or protest trains the brain to expect danger. The amygdala and hippocampus register these impressions, weaving them into patterns of threat that persist long after the images fade (Ohman & Mineka, 2001). Add screen-based reinforcement, and you get *echo chambers*. These are closed circles of information where people mostly hear their own views repeated, until dissent feels dangerous. Media is not just manipulation: it shapes the environment we live in. As McLuhan (1964) warned, *the medium is the message.*

Consider the 24-hour news cycle. Its perpetual stream of breaking stories is conceived to maximize arousal, ensuring that attention is constantly hijacked by novelty, outrage, and fear. Online platforms amplify this effect, rewarding outrage with virality. In this sense, the *liturgy of media* is daily, unrelenting, and neurobiologically sticky.

THE ENGINEER OF CONSENT

While Debord revealed the spectacle's philosophical contours, it was Edward Bernays who engineered its machinery. Often called the *"father of public relations,"* Bernays (1928/2005) was not merely a marketer, he was a *social engineer*. A nephew of Sigmund Freud, he transposed psychoanalytic insight into mass manipulation, pioneering techniques that would come to define modern propaganda. He understood that the human psyche, steeped in unconscious drives, was malleable not through reason, but through symbols, emotion, and repetition.

In *Propaganda*, Bernays wrote: *"The conscious and intelligent manipulation of the organized habits and opinions of the masses is an important element in democratic society... Those who manipulate this unseen mechanism of society constitute an invisible government which is the true ruling power of ι our country"* (Bernays, 1928, p. 37). What appeared to be conspiracy was, in fact, strategy. Edward Bernays called it "the *engineering of consent,*" a phrase lifted without irony from democratic ideals and repurposed to serve corporate and political power. Drawing on Freud's model of the unconscious, Bernays discovered how to bypass rational deliberation altogether. One notorious case came in the 1920s, when he orchestrated a campaign to promote female smoking by branding cigarettes as *"Torches of Freedom."* By linking tobacco to women's liberation, he ensured the campaign's success not through reasoned argument, but by by tapping into the neural pathways that link identity with rebellion.

The techniques pioneered by Bernays have proliferated. Today, entire industries specialize in nudging behavior, shaping desires, and managing public perception. Social media platforms apply Bernaysian principles at unprecedented reach, testing hundreds of message variations to determine which images, phrases, or sounds produce the strongest click-through or emotional response. Consent is no longer engineered by a few clever ad men but by computerized feedback loops fine-tuned to the vulnerabilities of billions.

MACHIAVELLI AND THE LOGIC OF POWER

Long before Bernays, Machiavelli diagnosed the brutal pragmatics of politics. In *The Prince* (1532), he argued that rulers should not be judged by their adherence to virtue, but by their ability to secure and maintain power. Fear, he insisted, is more reliable than love; appearances matter more than intentions; and deception, when used skillfully, is a legitimate tool of governance. His counsel to *"appear merciful, faithful, humane, religious, upright, and to be so, but with a mind so framed that should you require not to be so, you may be able and know how to change to the opposite"* foreshadowed today's politics of branding, optics, and spin.

Machiavelli's fingerprints are visible everywhere in modern politics. Leaders cultivate engineered personas, oscillating between populist warmth and authoritarian resolve. Parties weaponize fear to consolidate loyalty. Nations frame adversaries not only as geopolitical threats but as existential dangers, echoing Machiavelli's insistence on the necessity of unifying the populace against external enemies. His insights into the use of spectacle, manipulation, and fear remain alive in authoritarian regimes and media-driven structures that present the *appearance of democracy*.

Today's populists raid Machiavelli's playbook with gusto. They conjure enemies abroad to bind loyalty at home, stage crises to excuse extraordinary measures, and polish appearances with obsessive attention to optics. Bernays gave them the levers of emotion, and Machiavelli handed them the calculus of power. Together, they have birthed a hybrid beast: an online spectacle welded to timeless *realpolitik*, politics stripped of principle, engineered for control, and driven by survival at any cost.

FEEDBACK LOOPS OF FEAR AND BELIEF

Fear is the spark. Whether born of childhood wounds or stoked by social anxiety, it floods the limbic system and primes the mind for rescue. Into that opening steps ideology, promising safety, certainty, and the warmth of belonging. Each act of belief feels rewarding, not metaphorically but chemically: dopamine delivers its jolt of affirmation, while oxytocin binds the believer tighter to the group.

Then comes contradiction. A challenge to the narrative is not taken in as new information but felt as danger. The brain's alarm system, the amygdala, reacts instantly, tagging disagreement as a threat to survival. In response, mental defenses rise and belief solidifies. Those who disagree are no longer seen as simply mistaken but as corrupt, deluded, or even dangerous. From the outside this looks like stubbornness, but from the inside it feels like self-protection. The cage is not made of iron but of the brain's own wiring.

This defensive reaction helps explain why conspiracy theories and political cults are so resistant to change. Efforts to correct them often backfire, reinforcing the very beliefs they try to dismantle. Like religious sects bound by fear and identity, such movements shield themselves against contradiction by casting all outsiders as enemies. The cycle tightens, and the spell endures.

IMAGINING THE NATION

Benedict Anderson called the nation an *"imagined community"* (1983), imagined not because it is false, but because it rests on the vision of deep comradeship among millions who will never meet. Nations are stitched together through print capitalism and standardized languages, through invented traditions and state institutions that bend time with holidays, carve space with borders, and charge emotion with rituals, flags, and anthems.

The cognitive and emotional mechanisms that once bound small tribes around the fire now scales upward through myth and mass media, transforming strangers into a people.

Ernest Renan (1882) argued that a nation is a *"daily plebiscite,"* sustained less by institutions than by the collective memory of suffering and the shared will to endure together. Such suffering—whether through wars, revolutions, or pandemics—does not remain mere history but is transfigured into myth, becoming the adhesive that binds the national community. Out of this mythic reservoir emerge symbols like flags and anthems, functioning as modern totems that condense collective values into tangible form and channel them into reverence, loyalty, and sacrifice.

The emotional economy of nationhood runs on three currents: fear of external enemies, grievance over internal injustices, and pride in collective achievement or imagined glory. Governments and media serve as conductors, amplifying or dampening these affects to widen or narrow the boundaries of political possibility. In this way, national identity becomes less a fixed essence than a ritual of feeling, rehearsed and reinforced in classrooms, stadiums, and parliamentary halls alike.

TRIBE: THE ORIGINAL PROGRAM

If the nation is a modern myth, the tribe is ancient programming. Human psychology evolved for small groups of about 50 to 150 people (Dunbar, 1993), yet today that same programming animates billions through engineered platforms. Psychologist Henri Tajfel (1979) showed that even tiny differences between people are enough to spark group loyalty. Social media magnifies this effect, multiplying countless mini-tribes and splintering our shared reality into echo chambers of memes and beliefs.

Oxytocin intensifies parochial altruism, heightening kindness toward insiders while sharpening suspicion of outsiders (De

Dreu et al., 2011). Biology predisposes us toward tribal bonding, but it does not dictate the scope of our loyalties. Culture and institutions must extend empathy beyond the in-group, or the closed mind defaults to division. In the digital age, this ancient tendency has been reconfigured, as virtual tribes now rival geographic nations in their power to bind and mobilize. Fandoms, hashtags, and online movements gather millions around shared symbols and causes. The moral direction of these tribes is not predetermined. Some cultivate solidarity and compassion, while others amplify extremism and hate. The same neurobiological inheritance can fuel global generosity in disaster relief or genocidal fervor in moments of crisis. What determines the outcome is not biology itself but the narratives we construct and the contexts in which they unfold.

DEMOCRACY AS ILLUSION

Walter Lippmann (1922) observed that publics rely on 'pictures in our heads' shaped by elites, a point later expanded by Chomsky and Herman (1988) in their account of how media manufactures consent. What they described has now been industrialized: algorithms and bots amplify persuasion on a massive scale (Zuboff, 2019; Tufekci, 2017), while campaigns microtarget voters as consumers of narratives (Issenberg, 2012). Within this machinery, elections compress complexity into yes-or-no choices. They divide, narrow horizons, and serve more to legitimize power than to distribute it. Beneath it all, parties and candidates remain structurally dependent on capital for attention and financing, while media ownership and lobbying infrastructures delimit the agenda long before ballots appear (Michels, 1911; Mills, 1956; Stigler, 1971). The result is *oligarchic orchestration*: politicians function less as authors of policy than as intermediaries for concentrated wealth. Empirical work finds that when the preferences of economic elites diverge from those of average citizens, enacted policy tracks the elites (Gilens & Page, 2014; Winters & Page, 2011): representation becomes ritual, and governance becomes pageant.

Fear, belief, and control form a triad: fear sharpens obedience, belief justifies identity, and control organizes behavior through surveillance and incentives. Together they create a feedback loop: fear entrenches beliefs, beliefs legitimize control, and control manufactures new fears. Democracy, more illusion than reality, takes its place on the stage. The voter plays consumer, and the politician plays brand. Elections are not the slow labor of shared intelligence but fleeting plebiscites. The lights dazzle, the script repeats, and the audience fractures. And behind the curtain, power bows only to its elites.

Yet the stage can be redesigned. Mechanisms such as public financing of campaigns, antitrust measures against media conglomerates, and transparency requirements for machine-mediated information gatekeeping can weaken oligarchic capture (Lessig, 2011; Zuboff, 2019). Experiments with citizens' assemblies, participatory budgeting, and platform cooperatives point toward more continuous, deliberative forms of governance (Fishkin, 2018; Landemore, 2020). These alternatives remind us that democracy need not remain a theater of managed illusions: it can also be a workshop of collective intelligence.

THE TECHNOCRATIC AGENDA

If politics has long been theater, technology now threatens to become the stage, the script, and the director. The 21st century has witnessed the rise of a new ruling class, not priests or princes, but *technocrats and oligarchs* who command the digital infrastructure of daily life. Big Tech platforms, supranational institutions, and financial elites converge in a project often disguised as efficiency, safety, or "progress." Its deeper logic is control.

Unlike earlier empires, the emerging technocratic order does not rely on visible coercion. Its edifice is digital, algorithmic, and bureaucratic. *Social credit systems* in China, *biometric surveillance* in Europe, and *predictive policing* in the United States all reveal the same pattern: the quantification of human behavior, the extraction of data as raw material, and the governance of populations through metrics and nudges rather than laws and deliberation.

The language is managerial: resilience, sustainability, and technological optimization. But beneath the jargon lies a vision of governance that transcends borders and erodes sovereignty. The European Union (EU) experiments with centralized regulation of speech and information flows. The United Nations (UN) advances frameworks for *"global digital cooperation."* Corporate titans from Silicon Valley to Davos shape these agendas in closed-door summits, insulated from democratic accountability. What emerges is an alignment of interests between bureaucracies seeking efficiency, corporations seeking profit, and elites seeking stability.

The neuroscience of compliance illuminates why this works so effectively. Surveillance activates the brain's threat circuitry, heightening conformity even when no punishment follows. Subtle design tricks, personalized streams of news, effortless ways to spend money, and hidden forms of censorship all work beneath our awareness, steering us without our realizing it. Freedom is not outlawed but gradually redefined, narrowed, and made invisible. The most effective prison is one whose walls we do not see.

The dream of efficiency risks becoming the nightmare of compliance: a world of *bionic slaves*, optimized for productivity and obedience rather than creativity and freedom. The most dystopian future is not one where machines rule us, but one where we have become machines.

This *technocratic agenda* represents the culmination of Bernays and Machiavelli updated for the digital age. It weds the emotional engineering of propaganda to the precision of behavioral science and the scale of AI. Where nation-states once cultivated loyalty through flags and anthems, today's global technocracy aspires to command through data, biometrics, and automated governance. It is not a politics of belonging, but a politics of management. Citizens are treated as data, and participation becomes passive obedience.

What is at stake is nothing less than the horizon of human freedom. The choice is not between democracy and dictatorship in their old forms, but between adaptive, participatory frameworks of collective intelligence, or a managed *technocratic dystopia* where computations dictate truth, elites monopolize narrative, and sovereignty dissolves into technocratic decree.

RESISTING THE DIGITAL LEVIATHAN

The antidote to technocratic enclosure is not nostalgia for a vanished past, but the deliberate cultivation of counter-designs that are decentralized, transparent, and humane. Just as power now flows through code-based controls, resistance must develop its own infrastructures of autonomy and resilience.

Decentralized technologies such as open-source platforms, encrypted communication, and blockchain-based governance—where records are kept on a kind of shared digital record book that everyone can see and verify, instead of being controlled by a single authority—offer prototypes for loosening the grip of centralized control. At the same time, these very tools remain vulnerable to capture and co-optation, serving entrenched powers as easily as they can subvert them. Their emancipatory potential emerges only when they are rooted in participatory cultures that resist enclosure and redirect agency back to communities. In such contexts, citizens' assemblies convened online, cooperatives owned by their members, and peer-to-peer energy or finance systems provide glimpses of a different networked future, one in which connections do not domesticate but empower.

Equally vital are what might be called *cognitive firewalls*. Education in critical thinking, media literacy, and emotional resilience helps inoculate societies against manipulation. A society that can recognize propaganda in real time, that values nuance over outrage, and that treats computerized gatekeepers as tools rather than oracles, is far harder to domesticate. Finally, sovereignty must be re-imagined not as domination but as stewardship. Communities, nations, and transnational alliances must insist that technology serve human flourishing rather than human reduction. This means making platform structures more transparent, breaking up tech monopolies, protecting people's data, and building shared digital spaces for everyone.

The real choice is stark: either a future of bionic slaves, humans optimized for obedience and stripped of their creative spark, or a future of *conscious co-creators*, citizens who create systems that expand autonomy, deepen empathy, and foster collective intelligence. The struggle, then, is not simply against Big Tech or supranational bureaucracies but for the power to imagine the digital on new terms. Will it be a system of control, or a workshop of freedom? If the 20th century was marked by propaganda's conquest of the masses, the 21st will be defined by whether humanity can reclaim technology as an instrument of flourishing rather than submission.

MANUFACTURED CONSENT

Noam Chomsky and Edward Herman's (1988) propaganda model applies not only to media but to religion and politics alike. The most effective control system does not outlaw dissent: it renders it unthinkable. Language frames perception (Lakoff, 2004), priming neural pathways before reason is engaged. Social media platforms act as attention casinos, rewarding outrage and penalizing nuance.

Propaganda today is hyper-personalized. Where 20th-century states distributed uniform messages through posters, radio, and television, 21st-century platforms tailor propaganda to the individual. Each feed is a bespoke reality tunnel, optimized for maximum emotional engagement. This fracturing of public space undermines the very possibility of shared truth.

The challenge is not merely informational but neurobiological. Attention is finite, constantly hijacked by notifications, memes, and microbursts of dopamine. A distracted population cannot sustain the reflective awareness that true democracy requires. The nervous system, fragmented by stimuli, is primed for control. The result is a society that reacts and consumes, but seldom thinks together.

MASQUERADE OR TRANSFORMATION?

Religion gave us the structures of obedience, politics re-scripted them for nations, and now technocracy aspires to digitize them for the globe. The question is whether we remain captive to these inherited theaters, endlessly rehearsing scripts of fear, beliefs, and control, or whether we can improvise new performances. The alternative is neither withdrawal nor cynicism, but conscious design. Collective intelligence is not a fantasy: it is the latent potential of a species wired for empathy, creativity, and collaboration. But it must be cultivated. Rituals of division can be replaced by practices of coherence; media that manipulates fear can be re-engineered to amplify wisdom; and democracy that performs sovereignty for spectacle can be restructured to enact sovereignty through deliberation.

The nervous system that once bound us to gods, tribes, and flags can also bind us to one another in webs of solidarity that transcend manipulation. The challenge is not to abolish theater but to direct it toward truth, compassion, and freedom. If politics is performance, let us write a script that liberates rather than subdues.

REFERENCES

Anderson, B. (1983). Imagined communities: Reflections on the origin and spread of nationalism. Verso.

Atran, S., & Ginges, J. (2012). Religious and sacred imperatives in human conflict. Science, 336(6083), 855–857. https://doi.org/10.1126/science.1216902

Bernays, E. L. (1928/2005). Propaganda. IG Publishing.

Bernays, E. L. (1947). The engineering of consent. The Annals of the American Academy of Political and Social Science, 250(1), 113–120. https://doi.org/10.1177/000271624725000116

Chomsky, N., & Herman, E. S. (1988). Manufacturing consent: The political economy of the mass media. Pantheon.

Debord, G. (1967). The society of the spectacle. Buchet-Chastel.

De Dreu, C. K. W., Greer, L. L., Handgraaf, M. J. J., Shalvi, S., Van Kleef, G. A., Baas, M., ... & Feith, S. W. W. (2011). Oxytocin promotes human ethnocentrism. Proceedings of the National Academy of Sciences, 108(4), 1262–1266. https://doi.org/10.1073/pnas.1015316108

Dunbar, R. I. M. (1993). Coevolution of neocortex size, group size and language in humans. Behavioral and Brain Sciences, 16(4), 681–735. https://doi.org/10.1017/S0140525X00032325

Fishkin, J. S. (2018). Democracy when the people are thinking: Revitalizing our politics through public deliberation. Oxford University Press.

Gilens, M., & Page, B. I. (2014). Testing theories of American politics: Elites, interest groups, and average citizens. Perspectives

on Politics, 12(3), 564–581.
https://doi.org/10.1017/S1537592714001595

Issenberg, S. (2012). The victory lab: The secret science of winning campaigns. Crown.

Lakoff, G. (2004). Don't think of an elephant!: Know your values and frame the debate. Chelsea Green.

Landemore, H. (2020). Open democracy: Reinventing popular rule for the twenty-first century. Princeton University Press.

Lessig, L. (2011). Republic, lost: How money corrupts Congress—and a plan to stop it. Twelve.

Lippmann, W. (1922). Public opinion. Harcourt, Brace and Company.

Machiavelli, N. (1532/2008). The prince (P. Bondanella, Trans.). Oxford University Press.

McLuhan, H. M. (1964). Understanding media: The extensions of man. McGraw-Hill.

Michels, R. (1911/2001). Political parties: A sociological study of the oligarchical tendencies of modern democracy. Free Press.

Mills, C. W. (1956). The power elite. Oxford University Press.

Ohman, A., & Mineka, S. (2001). Fears, phobias, and preparedness: Toward an evolved module of fear and learning. Psychological Review, 108(3), 483–522.
https://doi.org/10.1037/0033-295X.108.3.483

Renan, E. (1882). What is a nation? (Lecture at the Sorbonne). Retrieved from
https://sourcebooks.fordham.edu/mod/1882renan.asp

Schmitt, C. (1922/2005). Political theology (G. Schwab, Trans.). University of Chicago Press.

Tajfel, H., & Turner, J. C. (1979). An integrative theory of intergroup conflict. In W. G. Austin & S. Worchel (Eds.), The social psychology of intergroup relations (pp. 33–47). Brooks/Cole.

Tufekci, Z. (2017). Twitter and tear gas: The power and fragility of networked protest. Yale University Press.

Winters, J. A., & Page, B. I. (2011). Oligarchy in the United States? Perspectives on Politics, 7(4), 731–751. https://doi.org/10.1017/S1537592709992710

Zuboff, S. (2019). The age of surveillance capitalism: The fight for a human future at the new frontier of power. PublicAffairs.

Chapter 4

Schooling the Human Robot

*"School is the advertising agency which makes
you believe that you need the society as it is."*
— Ivan Illich

Step into almost any conventional classroom in the world and you will see a choreography at once ordinary and extraordinary: rows of desks aligned in military precision, a single authority figure presiding at the front, a clock dictating the tempo of attention, and bells orchestrating the movement of bodies from one enclosure to another. The pattern is so ubiquitous that its logic disappears into the background, disguised as "*education.*" But the framework, rituals, and implicit expectations betray another aspiration: the mass production of compliant, predictable, and efficiently manageable human beings.

This chapter contends that modern schooling—born of the Prussian model, refined by industrial capitalism, fortified by behaviorist psychology, and now amplified by surveillance technologies—functions as a remarkably effective obedience machine. It works less through what is openly taught than through what critical theorists have called the *hidden curriculum*: the tacit lessons about hierarchy, punctuality, surveillance, competition, and the suppression of intrinsic curiosity (Bowles & Gintis, 1976; Bourdieu & Passeron, 1977; Foucault, 1975). These lessons are not inscribed in textbooks: they are etched into timetables, grading regimes, standardized testing rituals, and the fine-grained mechanics of everyday discipline. The outcome is a particular socialization: the *Human Robot*, a person habituated to conformity, trained to outsource judgment to external authority, and conditioned to confuse information retention with understanding, much less wisdom.

Still, this story has counterpoints. Across the globe, we encounter living alternatives: *Montessori, Waldorf,* and *Reggio Emilia* schools; *democratic and self-directed learning communities*; *Freire-inspired* interactive pedagogies; and even *national systems such as Finland's*, which emphasize teacher autonomy, trust, and integrative learning. These models remind us that education can awaken rather than anesthetize the mind (Freire, 1970; Robinson, 2011; Sahlberg, 2011). Emerging insights from neuroscience, motivational psychology, and complexity science provide a conceptual foundation for such liberatory ecologies of learning. To envision them fully, however, we must first confront how we arrived at the present, how the machinery of obedience operates, and how it shapes our brains, our identities, and our societies.

GENEALOGY OF A MACHINE

The compulsory, age-graded school system crystallized in Prussia in the 18th and 19th centuries, then spread outward across Europe and the United States (Gatto, 1992; Illich, 1971). Horace Mann's advocacy of "*common schools*" in the 1840s imported many of these Prussian features into the USA, aligning perfectly with the needs of the industrial revolution. Factories required punctual, literate, and obedient workers: schools operated as their assembly lines. Fixed schedules, standardized assessments, hierarchical accountability, and externally mandated curricula imposed the dominant grammar. In this regime, learning was recast as compliance rather than discovery.

This was not incidental. Bowles and Gintis (1976) argued that schools reproduce the social relations of production: they condition students to accept external authority, perform alienated labor (e.g., memorizing disconnected facts for tests), and internalize competition as the natural sorting mechanism. Bourdieu and Passeron (1977) showed how schools reinforce inequality by transmuting cultural capital into "merit" and credentialing it as if neutral. The explicit curriculum pales before the tacit message: sit still, wait your turn, obey the bell, and never question the test.

THE HIDDEN CURRICULUM

Foucault's *Discipline and Punish* (1975) remains one of the clearest lenses for the school as obedience factory. Institutions, he observed, manufacture "docile bodies" through surveillance, normalization, and examination. The classroom is a miniature *panopticon*: the gaze of the teacher, the ledger of the gradebook, the ominous shadow of the "permanent record," and the expanding reach of data dashboards. The examination distills this power into ritual form, converting the fluid richness of human potential into quantified metrics: comparable, rankable, and punishable.

Over time, the tyranny of the grade is not only external but internalized. Students monitor themselves, surveil themselves, and censor themselves. Their emotional lives—curiosity, wonder, boredom, fear—are re-coded into performance indicators.

This is the hidden curriculum: an unspoken pedagogy carried by recurring lessons. At its core lies the message that authority is always external, with truth lodged in textbooks, teachers, and tests. The rhythms of daily life reinforce this dependence, as the bell claims time itself and dictates the cadence of attention. Within such a framework, learning is cast not as discovery but as consumption, something delivered rather than co-created. Success then hinges on compliance, with grades rewarding obedience more than genuine understanding. This compliance is further sharpened by competition, which naturalizes hierarchy by casting peers as rivals in a zero-sum contest. All of these elements converge in a climate of surveillance, where visibility is constant and judgment never absent.

These are structural outputs of a system optimized for control and predictability rather than for the flourishing of complex, self-determining beings.

BEHAVIORAL ENGINEERING: FROM THORNDIKE TO SKINNER TO EDTECH

The theoretical foundation of 20th-century obedience programming was behaviorism. Edward Thorndike's *"law of effect"* (1911) and B.F. Skinner's *operant conditioning* (1953) promised that behavior could be shaped by reinforcement schedules. The allure for administrators was obvious: if humans could be trained like pigeons, schools could become laboratories of control. Gold stars, letter grades, honor rolls, and later, digital badges and gamified points economies are all Skinnerian technologies.

Skinner envisioned teaching machines that would deliver carefully sequenced stimuli and reinforcements to engineer specific outcomes (Skinner, 1954). Today's education technology extends that vision. What began with machines that scan and grade multiple-choice tests has grown into machine-driven assessment regimes that adjust questions based on student performance, learning management regimes, and AI-driven platforms. These tools track minute behaviors, predict performance, and steer students toward outcomes chosen in advance: getting the right answer, completing a task quickly, or following a prescribed path. Personalization is the marketing promise, but the reality is more often *optimization for compliance*: click here, master this 'objective,' and move to the next box.

CONFORMITY, OBEDIENCE, AND THE SOCIAL BRAIN

The most famous studies of obedience and conformity were not conducted in schools, but their implications are unavoidable. *Asch's conformity* experiments (1951) revealed that individuals will deny their own perception to align with a unanimous majority, even on trivial judgments. In classrooms, the pressure to conform easily overwhelms personal curiosity or dissent.

Milgram's famous experiments in the 1960s and 70s showed that ordinary people, when instructed by someone in authority, were willing to give what they thought were deadly electric shocks. In schools, the authority of teachers, administrators, and high-stakes tests can push people into equally harmful practices, such as drilling students to pass exams at the expense of real understanding, or even participating in widespread cheating.

Zimbardo's Stanford Prison Experiment (1971) showed how quickly people adopt authoritarian behavior when placed in certain roles. Schools, with teachers in positions of authority and students expected to obey, often mirror these same patterns of dominance and submission.

Neuroscience highlights the costs. Social pain in the form of rejection or humiliation recruits the same neural pathways as physical pain (Eisenberger & Lieberman, 2004). Public ranking, shaming, or chronic fear of failure triggers stress responses that impair working memory, cognitive flexibility, and inhibitory control (Lupien et al., 2009). In short, the obedience machine neurobiologically undermines the very capacities it claims to cultivate.

MOTIVATION DERAILED

Self-Determination Theory (SDT) identifies three fundamental needs for intrinsic motivation: autonomy, competence, and relatedness (Deci & Ryan, 1985, 2000). Conventional schooling systematically thwarts these needs: autonomy is stripped (students rarely choose what, how, or when to learn); competence is obscured (grades offer little actionable feedback); and relatedness is instrumentalized (peers become competitors).

The predictable result is a shift from intrinsic to extrinsic motivation. *Intrinsic motivation* means learning for its own sake, for meaning, mastery, or contribution. *Extrinsic motivation* means learning for something outside the activity itself, such as grades, approval, or fear. Research shows that external rewards often weaken intrinsic motivation, especially in tasks that require creativity (Deci, Koestner, & Ryan, 1999). Under constant measurement and comparison, learners adapt by narrowing attention to what will 'be on the test.' Divergent thinking shrinks and risk-taking declines (Torrance, 1966; Kim, 2011). Ken Robinson, the British educator and author best known for arguing that 'schools kill creativity,' was not exaggerating but offering a shorthand for a broad, empirically supported pattern.

INEQUALITY ENGINE: CAPITAL, SORTING, AND THE MERITOCRACY MYTH

The obedience machine also functions as an engine of inequality. Schools transform cultural capital, such as language, tastes, and habits, into credentials that masquerade as merit (Bourdieu & Passeron, 1977). What appears to be neutral measurement through standardized tests in fact reflects existing socioeconomic divides (Sirin, 2005). In this way, the system rewards the already privileged while penalizing those without access to such capital. As Bowles and Gintis (1976) argued, the deeper logic of schooling is not mobility but reproduction, preparing students from different backgrounds for the roles their class positions have already assigned them.

Tracking and grouping students by ability, often presented as meeting different needs, usually ends up dividing them by race and class, turning inequalities into self-fulfilling prophecies. Framed as objective, this sorting system keeps the status quo in place by teaching students to accept their position.

THE NEUROBIOLOGY OF DEFERENCE

Chronic stress from high-stakes testing, surveillance, and fear of failure has well-documented neurobiological effects. One major pathway is through elevated cortisol, which impairs hippocampal neurogenesis, the process of creating new brain cells, and disrupts memory consolidation (Lupien et al., 2009). These disruptions extend further, since executive functions such as working memory and cognitive flexibility are highly sensitive to the emotional climate of learning (Diamond, 2013). When pedagogy adopts an authoritarian style, it erodes psychological safety (Edmondson, 1999), amplifying stress and thereby constraining the exploratory behaviors on which genuine learning depends.

Conversely, when environments support autonomy, competence, and relatedness, dopaminergic reward pathways are activated, enhancing curiosity and exploration (Gruber, Gelman, & Ranganath, 2014). In other words, the brain systems that make us want to learn are shut down by the very structures meant to enforce learning. Clearly, the obedience machine misunderstands how the brain really works.

REIMAGINING EDUCATION

If the problem is obedience, the cure is *agency*. The way out of producing *Human Robots* is to create a learning environment where students have a voice, take part actively, ask questions, and learn with a sense of purpose. A liberatory education does not simply transmit information: it cultivates judgment, awakens imagination, and prepares individuals to live as autonomous, compassionate, and creative beings. To build such an education, we need both guiding principles and practical frameworks that can give those principles flesh and form.

The principles of *liberatory learning* function as a compass, orienting us away from conditioning and toward awakening. These principles are grounded insights drawn from living experiments such as Montessori classrooms, democratic schools, Finland's teacher-led system, and countless grassroots innovations that prove other ways are possible. Together they sketch a vision of what learning becomes when it is organized around human flourishing rather than obedience. Autonomy and co-agency become central, with learners creating their own paths while teachers act as mentors rather than managers. Knowledge is co-constructed through dialogue, echoing Freire's vision, and projects address authentic problems with real-world consequences and audiences.

Evaluation takes the form of deep feedback rather than shallow grades, with portfolios, narrative assessments, and competency maps offering richer portraits of growth than reductive letters and rankings. This shift is sustained by trust and professionalism: as Finland's example shows, when teachers are trusted, excellence emerges without the heavy machinery of constant testing. Governance, too, can be reimagined as democratic, as schools like *Sudbury Valley* demonstrate how shared decision-making nurtures civic competence. Within such environments, students cultivate metacognition and critical consciousness, learning not only to question assumptions but also to resist manipulation. Their inquiries cross disciplinary boundaries, fostering transdisciplinarity and systems thinking that better reflect the complexity of real-world problems. Learning is embodied and affective as well, with movement, the arts, and contemplative practice reintegrating emotion into the heart of education. Even technology enters this ecology under an ethical lens, valued for its capacity to expand agency, privacy, and creativity rather than for its power to enforce compliance.

Principles without structures, however, risk dissolving into rhetoric. To truly reimagine education, we must transform the architecture of schools: the ways time is measured, knowledge is assessed, space is configured, and communities govern themselves. These generative moves are strategies that can be adapted across contexts to bring liberatory principles into daily practice.

Imagine schools where bells no longer break learning into fragments but open long stretches of time for immersion, inquiry, and flow (Csikszentmihalyi, 1990). Here, graduation becomes a rite of passage shaped by portfolios, public defenses, and reflective essays that reveal depth and coherence, while assessment serves as guidance rather than threat, nurturing autonomy, competence, and belonging. Learning takes place in studios where ages mix and students pursue authentic questions alongside mentors both within and beyond the school walls, in spaces that feel less like institutions than community homes, alive with makerspaces, contemplative rooms, and areas for collaboration. Teachers form circles of inquiry, deepening their practice through shared reflection and research, as students practice democracy in civic laboratories where deliberation, debate, and co-governance are part of daily life. Even technology plays a different role, intended not for surveillance and control but to protect privacy, ensure transparency, and return data ownership to learners themselves. Seen as a whole, these principles and practices sketch a vision for shifting education from programming to awakening, from obedience to agency. They remind us that schools need not be quiet factories of compliance but can instead become laboratories of freedom, nurseries of creativity, and practice grounds for democracy itself. To awaken the *Human Robot*, we must reimagine not only what students learn, but how, where, and with whom learning takes place.

A TRANSITIONAL STRATEGY

We cannot get rid of standardized testing and the overreliance on diplomas and test scores overnight, but we can begin shifting power from distant bureaucracies to communities of learners. Change might begin with pilot schools that have more freedom, where portfolios replace high-stakes tests and teachers work under agreements built on trust and peer review rather than constant inspection. Students can be guaranteed rights to autonomy and data privacy, while public funding supports networks of learning that empower local communities. In some places, democratic school governance can show that authority need not flow only from the top down. Even beyond schools, admissions and hiring can evolve by valuing richer portfolios in place of test scores, pointing the way toward a more human system of education.

THE INNER CURRICULUM

Institutional redesign must be paired with psychological transformation, for the *Human Robot* is not only an artifact of paradigms but also a set of mental habits. Deprogramming requires metacognitive training so that learners can recognize when grades are mistaken for worth or when compliance is mistaken for learning. It also requires critical media literacy, the ability to decode how metrics and platforms shape perception. Contemplative and somatic practices such as mindfulness, breathwork, and embodied awareness help interrupt fear loops. And communities of practice provide social reinforcement, surrounding learners with others who prize inquiry over conformity.

From a neuroscientific perspective, these practices rewire the brain. Instead of reflexively seeking external validation, learners develop the neural circuitry mediating curiosity, intrinsic valuation, and courageous dissent.

DEMOCRACY RECLAIMED

If democracy requires citizens capable of thinking critically, dialoguing across differences, and holding power accountable, then schooling as obedience is democracy's autoimmune disorder. We school citizens in obedience and then, paradoxically, summon them to deliberate. The same system sharpens them for competition even as it later demands cooperation. Fear of mistakes is instilled early on, yet innovation is later celebrated as a civic virtue. Together, these tensions pull learners in opposing directions, creating contradictions that are ultimately unsustainable.

A liberatory education is not a luxury but a civilizational necessity in an age of accelerating technological power and intellectual fragmentation. In such a context, the capacity to question, to imagine, to discern, and to act autonomously with others becomes the only safeguard against both authoritarianism and nihilism. Cultivating these capacities, however, requires more than minor reform. It demands reconstructing the very schools that produced the *Human Robot* in the first place.

From school bells to standardized tests, education narrows imagination and rewards conformity. Such training ensures we enter adulthood already shackled, this time by the constraints of finance and economics. In the next chapter, we turn to the marketplace, where scarcity is engineered, debt becomes a shackle, and money itself functions as a tool of mass control.

REFERENCES

Asch, S. E. (1951). Effects of group pressure upon the modification and distortion of judgments. In H. Guetzkow (Ed.), Groups, leadership and men (pp. 177–190). Pittsburgh, PA: Carnegie Press.

Bourdieu, P., & Passeron, J.-C. (1977). Reproduction in education, society and culture. London: Sage.

Bowles, S., & Gintis, H. (1976). Schooling in capitalist America. New York: Basic Books.

Csikszentmihalyi, M. (1990). Flow: The psychology of optimal experience. New York: Harper & Row.

Deci, E. L., Koestner, R., & Ryan, R. M. (1999). A meta-analytic review of experiments examining the effects of extrinsic rewards on intrinsic motivation. Psychological Bulletin, 125(6), 627–668.

Deci, E. L., & Ryan, R. M. (1985). Intrinsic motivation and self-determination in human behavior. New York: Plenum.

Deci, E. L., & Ryan, R. M. (2000). The "what" and "why" of goal pursuits: Human needs and the self-determination of behavior. Psychological Inquiry, 11(4), 227–268.

Diamond, A. (2013). Executive functions. Annual Review of Psychology, 64, 135–168.

Edmondson, A. (1999). Psychological safety and learning behavior in work teams. Administrative Science Quarterly, 44(2), 350–383.

Eisenberger, N. I., & Lieberman, M. D. (2004). Why rejection hurts: A common neural alarm system for physical and social pain. Trends in Cognitive Sciences, 8(7), 294–300.

Foucault, M. (1975). Discipline and punish: The birth of the prison. New York: Pantheon.

Freire, P. (1970). Pedagogy of the oppressed. New York: Continuum.

Gatto, J. T. (1992). Dumbing us down: The hidden curriculum of compulsory schooling. Gabriola Island, BC: New Society Publishers.

Gruber, M. J., Gelman, B. D., & Ranganath, C. (2014). States of curiosity modulate hippocampus-dependent learning via the dopaminergic circuit. Neuron, 84(2), 486–496.

Illich, I. (1971). Deschooling society. New York: Harper & Row.

Kim, K. H. (2011). The creativity crisis: The decrease in creative thinking scores on the Torrance Tests of Creative Thinking. Creativity Research Journal, 23(4), 285–295.

Lupien, S. J., McEwen, B. S., Gunnar, M. R., & Heim, C. (2009). Effects of stress throughout the lifespan on the brain, behaviour and cognition. Nature Reviews Neuroscience, 10(6), 434–445.

Milgram, S. (1974). Obedience to authority: An experimental view. New York: Harper & Row. (Original experiments conducted 1963).

Robinson, K. (2011). Out of our minds: Learning to be creative (2nd ed.). Oxford: Capstone.

Sahlberg, P. (2011). Finnish lessons: What can the world learn from educational change in Finland? New York: Teachers College Press.

Sirin, S. R. (2005). Socioeconomic status and academic achievement: A meta-analytic review of research. Review of Educational Research, 75(3), 417–453.

Skinner, B. F. (1953). Science and human behavior. New York: Macmillan.

Skinner, B. F. (1954). The science of learning and the art of teaching. Harvard Educational Review, 24(2), 86–97.

Thorndike, E. L. (1911). Animal intelligence: Experimental studies. New York: Macmillan.

Torrance, E. P. (1966). The Torrance Tests of Creative Thinking. Bensenville, IL: Scholastic Testing Service.

Zimbardo, P. G. (2007). The Lucifer effect: Understanding how good people turn evil. New York: Random House. (Discusses the Stanford Prison Experiment, 1971).

Chapter 5

The "Sociopathic Elites" and the Alchemy of Currency

"The few who understand the system will either be so interested in its profits, or so dependent on its favors, that there will be no opposition from that class."
— Rothschild Brothers of London,
in a letter to the U.S. Treasury (1863)

Let us name the dragon here: by *"sociopathic elites,"* I mean the tier of actors that includes oligarchs, corporate executives, financiers, political operatives, technocrats, and policy intellectuals who occupy nodal points of power within the global monetary and financial order. Their influence is marked by a common disposition: they treat social costs, ecological limits, and human suffering as collateral damage to be ignored, managed, or monetized. This is not merely rhetorical indictment. Mounting evidence indicates that *Dark Triad traits*—psychopathy, Machiavellianism, and narcissism—are disproportionately concentrated in positions of corporate and financial leadership (Babiak, Neumann, & Hare, 2010; Jones & Paulhus, 2014). When individuals embodying these traits ascend by creating and defending arrangements that privatize gains while socializing losses, producing crises in succession, the problem can no longer be reduced to individual pathology. It reflects instead a process of structural selection: an apparatus of power that systematically rewards and elevates personalities optimized for extraction rather than reciprocity.

This chapter explores how a small fringe of so-called elites deploys a peculiar magic: the *alchemy of currency*. Unlike the medieval alchemists who dreamed of transmuting lead into gold but never truly succeeded, today's elites have perfected a stranger transmutation, turning debt into wealth, risk into profit, scarcity into leverage, and collective trust into private rent. They perform this alchemy not only through institutions but through imagination, crafting stories about what money is, where it comes from, and what is possible with it. These narratives narrow the field of vision, ensuring that our financial and economic horizons remain chained to their interests.

MONEY AS MYTH, LEDGER, AND WEAPON

Anthropologist David Graeber argued that money did not primarily evolve as a commodity that arose from barter. Instead, it emerged as a credit-debt relationship inscribed in social memory (Graeber, 2011). Sociologist Geoffrey Ingham (2004) likewise describes money as a social institution underwritten by the authority of the state to tax, to compel, and to enforce liabilities. In this sense, money is less a neutral medium of exchange than a political technology of memory, a way to keep scores and settle obligations across time.

If money is a collectively upheld promise, then controlling who gets to issue, allocate, and backstop those promises becomes the central locus of modern power. *Central banks* are state-backed institutions that issue currency and stabilize financial markets. Alongside them are private banks and *shadow banks*, which include investment pools that bet on markets and large funds where companies and governments park short-term cash. These shadow banks act like regular banks by lending and trading, but they are not bound by the same rules or protections. Add to this the vast web of *offshore* balance sheets, and you have the inner sanctum of monetary power (Mehrling, 2011; Tooze,

2018). The elites understand this intimately. They have labored to obscure the political nature of money, presenting it instead as a natural and apolitical phenomenon governed by neutral markets or technical expertise. This illusion allows them to perform their alchemy in plain sight.

THE ALCHEMY OF CURRENCY

Modern money is not discovered or mined from the ground: it is created. The sociopathic elites use their control over financial institutions to generate wealth not primarily by producing goods or innovations, but by conjuring capital into being and channeling it into assets that entrench their dominance. This alchemy unfolds through a series of maneuvers that combine technical procedures with narrative cover.

Money is first created through keystrokes, not printing presses. In today's system, *central banks* such as the *Federal Reserve* and the *Bank of England* expand the money supply digitally by crediting the reserve accounts of private banks. This is *fiat currency*, backed not by gold or commodities but by collective trust and the authority of law. A trillion dollars can be summoned in an instant. Commercial banks then multiply this base money by issuing loans, which themselves create new deposits (McLeay, Radia, & Thomas, 2014). This is the first act of modern alchemy: *creating something seemingly out of nothing.*

The second step is *lending money into existence with interest.* Each dollar that enters the economy carries a debt larger than itself, because the borrower must pay back not only the principal but the interest as well. The result is a perpetual cycle of indebtedness that ensures households, corporations, and governments remain bound to the system while those who control the money supply accumulate streams of income simply by virtue of ownership.

The third act is *multiplication through banking.* Textbooks describe this as *"fractional reserve banking,"* where a bank receiving one million dollars in reserves could lend out many times that amount. In practice, banks do not lend strictly against reserves; they create loans first, generating deposits, and central banks supply reserves as needed. The outcome, however, is the same: credit expands far beyond actual cash on hand, leaving the financial system inherently fragile. For banks this fragility is not a bug but a feature, because it produces extraordinary leverage and profit.

The fourth act is *conversion.* With newly created credit, elites purchase real assets: land, housing, energy infrastructure, water rights, technology companies, and political influence. What began as virtual entries on a balance sheet becomes tangible power in the world. To the public, these elites appear as "wealth creators." In reality, they are wealth consolidators, converting collective trust into private dominion.

The fifth act is *orchestration of booms and busts.* Credit expands recklessly during speculative cycles, inflating bubbles in housing, stocks, or commodities. When the inevitable collapse comes, millions lose homes, jobs, and savings, while elites scoop up distressed assets at bargain prices. The global financial crisis of 2008 exposed this dynamic in high resolution, as did the COVID-19 economic shock. For those positioned at the center of monetary alchemy, crises are not disasters but harvest seasons.

The sixth act is *maintenance of illusion.* To preserve legitimacy, elites fund think tanks, lobbying networks, academic departments, and media outlets that present the system as natural, efficient, and inevitable. They cultivate jargon—phrases such as "market discipline," "inflation targeting," or "fiscal responsibility"—that obscure the underlying dynamics of extraction. By cloaking political decisions in the language of technocratic neutrality, they persuade the public to accept exploitation as economic necessity.

Finally, when the financial system buckles, the seventh act begins: *profits stay private while losses are pushed onto the public.* Taxpayers fund government bailouts of the very institutions that engineered the collapse. Central banks buy up bad loans, governments impose austerity, and public wealth is funneled to stabilize private balance sheets. The architects of crisis walk away with bonuses and greater control, while ordinary people pay the price.

THE INSTITUTIONAL MACHINERY OF EXPLOITATION

This alchemy is not performed by individuals alone but by a constellation of institutions whose legitimacy has been carefully engineered. Central banks, presented as "independent," routinely bail out private institutions while disciplining elected governments. The *International Monetary Fund* (IMF), *World Bank*, and *Bank for International Settlements* (BIS) enforce a policy package of austerity, privatization, and liberalization on vulnerable nations in exchange for liquidity. *Rating agencies* such as Moody's, Standard & Poor's, and Fitch pass political judgments under the guise of technical expertise, penalizing states that invest in social infrastructure while rewarding those that impose fiscal "discipline."

Meanwhile, lobbying networks and philanthropic foundations launder ideology as expertise, making sure that the range of "respectable" policy debate excludes alternatives such as public banking, debt jubilees, or wealth caps. The elites cultivate what Antonio Gramsci (1971) called *cultural hegemony*: the ability to shape not only material structures but also common sense itself. When central bankers issue pronouncements about "market confidence," the public hears obscure jargon and assumes wisdom. What is really happening is the manufacture of consent through ritualized opacity.

PSYCHOLOGICAL INFRASTRUCTURE

The financial system works not only because of institutional machinery but also because of psychological infrastructure. It rewards traits such as compartmentalization, empathy deficits, and moral disengagement. Organizational psychology has shown that environments with large power asymmetries and weak accountability mechanisms cultivate ethical fading, in which moral questions are reframed as mere matters of compliance or efficiency (Bazerman & Tenbrunsel, 2011).

Overlay this with the ideology of *Homo economicus*, the myth of the self-interested, utility-maximizing individual, and you have the perfect ethical bypass. If humans are seen only as isolated actors pursuing self-interest, then compassion, reciprocity, or restraint appear irrational. This is the moral atmosphere in which financial elites operate, an atmosphere where exploitation feels like inevitability rather than choice.

THE IDEOLOGY OF SCARCITY AND
THE THEOLOGY OF SOUND MONEY

Two myths sustain this alchemy. The first is the household metaphor: governments are told they must "*tighten their belts*" just like families. Yet currency-issuing states are not financially constrained in the same way households are. Their constraints are real but different: productive capacity, inflationary risk, and ecological limits. To equate public finance with household finance is an ensnaring metaphor meant to shrink collective imagination (Kelton, 2020).

The second myth is *inflation panic*. Fear of inflation is invoked selectively to suppress wage demands or social spending, while asset price inflation in housing or stocks is tolerated or even celebrated. When working people demand more, inflation is portrayed as heresy; when financial markets bloat, inflation is treated as natural growth. These imbalances reveal that the theology of "*sound money*" is not about stability but about control. It disciplines public desire while granting elites unlimited liquidity for corporate bailouts, military budgets, or speculative expansion.

PLATFORM CAPITALISM, CRYPTO DREAMS, AND CBDCS

The next frontier of monetary alchemy is digital. *Surveillance capitalism* harvests behavioral data to predict and shape human activity, transforming attention into a currency and selling our lives as tradable assets. *Cryptocurrencies* promised decentralization and inclusion but often reproduced the same inequities of traditional finance, only without protections like deposit insurance. Nevertheless, the critique embedded in crypto, the distrust of centralized monetary authority, remains valid, pointing toward the need for democratic public alternatives.

Central Bank Digital Currencies (CBDCs) loom on the horizon. These programmable and traceable state monies could be created to democratize finance by enabling direct fiscal injections and public digital wallets. But they could also be engineered to intensify technocratic control, imposing austerity at the level of the individual household. The outcome will depend not on technology but on politics.

DE-ALCHEMIZING CURRENCY

If money is a political technology of memory, then reclaiming it must be both a political and psychological act. To democratize money is to take back the collective right to decide what we remember, what we honor, and what we value. This requires more than technical reform. It calls for a shift in the cultural imagination, a recognition that money is not a neutral medium but a social agreement that can be rewritten to serve life rather than domination.

The first step is democratizing central banking. Today, decisions that determine the flow of credit, the direction of investment, and the fate of entire economies are made behind closed doors by a small cadre of technocrats. To bring these institutions under transparent and democratic oversight is to reclaim sovereignty over the most important public utility of all: the creation of money. Central banks could be mandated not only to maintain price stability but also to pursue full employment, ecological sustainability, and financial resilience. They could coordinate openly with fiscal authorities, ending the taboo on using public money for public purpose.

Public banks and community-based banking through post offices could help ensure that money is created to serve communities. Such institutions could provide affordable credit for housing, green infrastructure, small enterprises, and local cooperatives, reducing dependence on profit-driven private banks. By expanding the reach of financial services to underserved areas, public banking would also counteract the exclusion that sustains inequality.

Reintroducing debt jubilees would prevent societies from collapsing under the weight of obligations that can never be repaid. Throughout history, from ancient Mesopotamia to biblical Israel, leaders periodically canceled debts to restore social balance and prevent implosion. In our time, student debt, medical debt, and predatory micro-debt—small, high-interest loans that trap poor borrowers—could be forgiven as acts of economic repair and moral renewal.

Fairer taxes on the very rich would narrow the gap between the top and everyone else while funding public needs like health, education, and climate action. Stopping companies from buying back their own stock would push profits toward better pay, new ideas, and real innovation. And breaking up giant tech platforms would give people back control over the data they create, treating information as a shared resource rather than a private hoard.

Reclaiming currency also requires new forms of democratic participation. Citizens must be invited into the conversation about how money is created, allocated, and governed. Participatory budgeting, already practiced in many cities, allows communities to decide directly how public funds are spent. Citizens' assemblies on monetary policy could deliberate over the establishment of fiscal priorities, the balance between inflation management and employment, or the conditions for ecological transition. Involving ordinary people in these decisions not only deepens democracy but expands the collective imagination of what currency is for.

A democratic money system would also invest directly in the future of the planet. Green public money could fund biodiversity restoration, regenerative agriculture, and resilient infrastructure. The true limits to spending are not financial but ecological and productive. *The question is not whether we can afford to act but whether we can afford not to.*

Finally, transparency must reach into the hidden spaces of global finance. Shadow banking, offshore tax havens, and derivative markets—where traders buy and sell financial contracts whose value depends on other assets like stocks or mortgages— represent trillions of dollars of obligations that remain largely invisible to the public. Still, when crises erupt, these hidden exposures are inevitably rescued by the state. If public resources are used to guarantee private risk, then the public has the right to see and the right to decide.

To de-alchemize currency is to restore money to its rightful status as a collective instrument rather than a private weapon. It is to remind ourselves that value is created not in the abstract circuits of finance but in the shared labor of communities, the resilience of ecosystems, and the bonds of trust that hold societies together in pursuit of the common good.

THE INNER WORK OF RE-ENCHANTMENT

Structural reform alone cannot free us from the empire of money. Systems endure not only through institutions but also through habits of mind and heart. Elites exploit these inner patterns by stoking fear of scarcity, anxiety about status, and the compulsion to compare. A culture trained to see life as rivalry is already primed for financial capture. To dismantle the empire outside, we must also transform it within.

This transformation begins by cultivating another orientation to life: one grounded in interdependence, in the freedom of enough, and in forms of value that exceed money's grasp. When communities embody cooperation and mutual care, the old story that survival requires endless competition begins to lose its hold. Practices that nurture this shift are varied, including contemplative traditions, collective rituals, and educational approaches, but they share a common aim of weaving awareness, embodiment, and shared meaning into daily life. Within such cultures of practice, fear loosens, comparison softens, and new patterns of curiosity, compassion, and intrinsic motivation take root.

The same principle applies at the cultural scale. The elites have enchanted us with financial indicators such as *Gross Domestic Product* (GDP) and the *Consumer Price Index* (CPI). These are maps mistaken for the territory, numbers meant less to reflect human flourishing than to render societies measurable for exploitation. Their alchemy succeeds because we forget that money holds legitimacy only through our collective belief.

To break this spell is to reimagine value itself. Wealth can no longer mean owning claims on other people's time; it must mean nurturing well-being across every scale of existence, from our relationships to the living planet. To see money as memory rather than destiny, as a ledger that can be rewritten rather than a fate to be obeyed, is to reclaim its power for life. The empire of belief and control is powerful, but fragile in its dependence on consent. Withdraw that consent, and the alchemy collapses. Replace it with a politics of care, courage, and collective stewardship, and another economy—indeed, another civilization—becomes thinkable.

With inner shifts as the foundation and cultural re-enchantment as the horizon, we open the possibility of a world in which money serves life rather than masters it. From here, the path leads beyond currency's empire to the next dominion of control: the church of scientism, where doubt is excommunicated and mystery becomes forbidden.

REFERENCES

Babiak, P., Neumann, C. S., & Hare, R. D. (2010). Corporate psychopathy: Talking the walk. Behavioral Sciences & the Law, 28(2), 174–193.

Bazerman, M. H., & Tenbrunsel, A. E. (2011). Blind spots: Why we fail to do what's right and what to do about it. Princeton University Press.

Graeber, D. (2011). Debt: The first 5,000 years. Melville House.

Gramsci, A. (1971). Selections from the prison notebooks. International Publishers.

Ingham, G. (2004). The nature of money. Polity Press.

Jones, D. N., & Paulhus, D. L. (2014). Introducing the Short Dark Triad (SD3): A brief measure of dark personality traits. Assessment, 21(1), 28–41.

Kelton, S. (2020). The deficit myth: Modern monetary theory and the birth of the people's economy. PublicAffairs.

McLeay, M., Radia, A., & Thomas, R. (2014). Money creation in the modern economy. Bank of England Quarterly Bulletin, Q1, 14–27.

Mehrling, P. (2011). The new Lombard Street: How the Fed became the dealer of last resort. Princeton University Press.

Tooze, A. (2018). Crashed: How a decade of financial crises changed the world. Viking.

Chapter 6

Science as the New Church

*"The materialist worldview is running out of steam.
It is a kind of belief system that has become fossilized,
held onto far beyond its usefulness, and now
functioning more like a religion than a science."*
— Rupert Sheldrake

Science began as a revolt against scholasticism, a daring wager that careful observation, experiment, and public argument could free humanity from the tyranny of unquestioned authority. Yet every revolution risks becoming what it once opposed. Today, many of the cultural habits that were meant to ensure scientific rigor—peer review, methodological orthodoxy, and a default metaphysics of reductive materialism—often operate as an implicit creed. Heretics are no longer burned at the stake: they are desk-rejected, unfunded, demonetized, or buried by ranking systems that quietly hide their work from view. Inquiry quietly becomes doctrine, and doctrine becomes a gatekeeper of permissible reality.

Saying science sometimes behaves like a church does not dismiss the scientific method or its achievements. Rather, the concern is that over time today's research culture, across journals, funders, and universities, has adopted habits and hidden assumptions that blur two ideas: *methodological naturalism*, a rule for doing science that asks us to explain results using natural causes, and *ontological naturalism*, a belief about reality that says only physical things exist. When a rule of method is treated as a claim about what is real, debate about consciousness narrows and reductionism becomes the dominant narrative

This chapter explores how mechanisms meant to keep science honest can stiffen into dogma, with peer review enforcing blindness to anomalous data and unfashionable frameworks, consciousness studies dismissed as a metaphysical embarrassment, and a monoculture of atomistic explanation leaving us unable to think in terms of emergence, complexity, systems, and meaning. I close by sketching a vision for a science that is post-reductionist and post-materialist, methodologically plural and grounded in humility, one that redeems the original insurgent spirit of the enterprise.

FROM ANTI-AUTHORITY TO NEW AUTHORITY

In the early modern period, figures like Francis Bacon, Galileo Galilei, and later Isaac Newton helped dethrone Aristotelian scholasticism, the rigid medieval system of learning that relied more on abstract argument from Aristotle's authority than on experiment or observation. The authority of tradition and scripture was replaced by the authority of experiment, measurement, and the mathematically describable regularities of nature. But as philosopher and historian of science Thomas Kuhn famously noted, scientific communities inevitably form paradigms: shared exemplars and problem-solution templates that define what a "real" scientific problem looks like, what counts as acceptable evidence, and what methods are legitimate (Kuhn, 1962). Paradigms are essential for progress, but they also limit science to solving puzzles within an accepted framework rather than encouraging truly open inquiry.

Thomas Kuhn showed that when anomalies pile up, scientific "paradigms" can enter crisis, yet they rarely give way gracefully. He called this the "essential tension" between conservatism, which protects the paradigm, and innovation, which tries to question or overturn it, helping explain why scientific revolutions are not smooth or linear (Kuhn, 1977). Max Planck, a Nobel Prize-winning physicist and founder of quantum theory, captured the human side of this dynamic with his wry remark: *"A new scientific truth does not triumph by convincing its opponents, but rather because its opponents eventually die"* (Planck, 1949). Considered together, these points suggest that change in science often advances as much through generational turnover as through argument. Extending this view, Imre Lakatos, a philosopher of science who developed the idea of *"research programmes"* to judge progress, and Paul Feyerabend, a philosopher of science who argued for *methodological pluralism*, both emphasized that scientific rules and standards are historically contingent and constantly renegotiated (Lakatos & Musgrave, 1970; Feyerabend, 1975). In this light, science is not a machine that outputs truth once fed data: it is a human, social, political, and economic activity with norms that sometimes enable insight and sometimes suppress it (Latour & Woolgar, 1979; Latour, 1987; Polanyi, 1958).

PEER-REVIEWED BLINDNESS

Peer review is often presented as the guardian of scientific quality. In principle, it is. In practice, it also functions as a filter of conformity, with well-documented biases: novelty suppression, conservative review boards, careerist pressures, reputational cartels, and ideological policing (Smith, 2006; Coryn et al., 2006). The replication crisis revealed just how vulnerable the system is to *p-hacking, HARKing (Hypothesizing After the Results are Known)*, publication bias, and the file drawer problem, where negative or inconclusive results are quietly shelved, leaving the published record skewed toward a false sense of certainty (Ioannidis, 2005; Simmons, Nelson, &

Simonsohn, 2011; Open Science Collaboration, 2015). Smaldino and McElreath (2016) showed that academic selection pressures can even favor *"bad science,"* as methods that generate flashy but unreliable results spread more rapidly than slower, more careful approaches.

The *Matthew effect* compounds these distortions: prestige begets prestige (Merton, 1968). Papers from elite labs glide through review, while anomalous findings from outsiders collide with skepticism or silence. Null results vanish into the file drawer, warping literatures and meta-analyses, the statistical studies that pool together many results to draw broader conclusions (Rosenthal, 1979). Journals privilege positive, tidy stories, narratives with low entropy that read more like scripts than science. Reforms like *Registered Reports* and *open data* are steps in the right direction (Nosek & Lakens, 2014; Chambers, 2013), but they are adopted unevenly and often performed as box-ticking rituals rather than real cultural change.

At its worst, peer review becomes peer enforcement. Paradigms are policed not only for methodological rigor but also for metaphysical comfort. Suggest that consciousness may not be fully explainable in reductive physicalist terms, and you will be invited to rewrite your claims until they fit the canonical ontology, or remain unpublished. The problem is not criticism itself, but the disproportionate veto power that entrenched metaphysical assumptions exert through institutionalized review.

THE HERESY OF CONSCIOUSNESS

If physics is often "shut up and calculate," then consciousness science has long been *"shut up and correlate."* David Chalmers' famous articulation of the *"hard problem,"* why and how physical processes give rise to subjective experience, revealed the inadequacy of reductionist narratives that simply map neural correlates to conscious states (Chalmers, 1995). For many, the hard problem is an embarrassment, an artifact of conceptual confusion destined to evaporate when we have enough data (Dennett, 1991; Churchland, 1986). But for others, it is a genuine ontological lacuna, indicating that subjectivity is not reducible to the third-person terms favored by most scientific discourse (Nagel, 1974; Nagel, 2012).

Integrated Information Theory (IIT) proposes that consciousness corresponds to the intrinsic causal power of a system upon itself (Tononi, 2004, 2008). *Global Workspace Theory* (GWT) models consciousness as the broadcasting of information to a global cognitive workspace (Baars, 1988; Dehaene, 2014). *Predictive processing theory* and the free energy principle attempt a unifying story of perception, action, and learning (Friston, 2010). Each framework explains part of how consciousness works. Yet the bigger question is often declared off limits: is consciousness basic to reality, a by-product of the brain, an illusion, or a property of information? Many scientists avoid this because they assume a strictly materialist outlook. Philosophers may debate, but neuroscientists must measure.

Researchers like Roger Penrose and Stuart Hameroff (1994), who propose quantum processes as integral to consciousness, face accusations of pseudoscience, not necessarily because their proposals lack empirical content, but because they threaten a normative boundary about what respectable minds may suggest. Rupert Sheldrake (2012), who argues for morphic resonance and broader critiques of mechanistic metaphysics, is treated as a contagion rather than a challenger. Whether these proposals are ultimately correct is beside the point. The reflexive defense of a metaphysics is itself evidence that science has accreted doctrinal layers.

The multi-decade sidelining of anomalous consciousness phenomena—near-death experiences, terminal lucidity, psi phenomena, visions of reality under psychedelics, etc.—illustrates how a priori metaphysical commitments can function as cognitive filters. Again, the claim is not that all such data are decisive or even robust, but that they cannot be engaged on their empirical merits without first surviving a metaphysical inquisition. A science truly committed to understanding consciousness must be willing to risk ontological surprises.

THE GOSPEL OF REDUCTIONISM

Reductionism is a simple, powerful idea: to understand something complicated, break it into parts. That move has given us huge wins, such as how genes work, what matter is made of, and how cells keep us alive. But using a tool well is not the same as thinking the tool shows the whole of reality. The jump from 'this works' to *'this is all there is'* is a mistake.

Physicist Steven Weinberg (1992) said explanations ultimately point down to basic physics. Another physicist, P. W. Anderson (1972), replied that *'more is different'*: when things get more complex, new patterns and rules appear that you cannot predict just from the parts. Areas like systems thinking and complexity science show that organization and feedback change how things behave (von Bertalanffy, 1968; Wiener, 1948; Holland, 1995). So reality is not only like a pile of Lego bricks. It is also like teams, ecosystems, and cities, where the whole can do things the pieces cannot do on their own.

Reductionism's metaphysical inflation breeds explanatory blindness in two directions. *Upward blindness* is the refusal to recognize the autonomy and causal efficacy of higher-level patterns such as organisms, minds, and cultures, on the grounds that "really" only particles and fields are real. *Inward blindness* is the inability to account for first-person experience as anything but a computational or neural pattern reported in third-person terms, leading to a conceptual explanatory gap masquerading as a data gap.

Post-reductionist alternatives are not mystical retreats but scientific frameworks that treat emergence, self-organization, and information as real features of nature (Ellis, Noble, & O'Connor, 2012; Noble, 2006). Top-down causation, where higher-level patterns shape lower-level dynamics, is now a rigorously developed concept (Ellis, 2016).

STATISTITHEISM: WORSHIPING THE P-VALUE IDOL

If reductionism is the gospel, null-hypothesis significance testing is often the liturgy. Modern science has built a ritual around the threshold of $p < .05$, a magical number that confers legitimacy on results the way ecclesiastical imprimaturs once sanctioned doctrine. The problem is not with inferential statistics themselves, but with their ritualized misuse and the collective pretense that binary significance testing can bear the intellectual weight we place on it (Meehl, 1967; Gigerenzer, 2004; Amrhein, Greenland, & McShane, 2019). This way of doing statistics ignores how big the effects really are, how likely they were to begin with, whether the models actually fit the data, and how well they can predict new results.

The replication crisis, the finding that many published results cannot be reliably reproduced, exposed deep flaws in how research is conducted, published, and rewarded (Open Science Collaboration, 2015). Rather than prompting a fundamental rethink of what counts as evidence, the response focused on procedure: fields ran workshops on p-hacking, introduced transparency checklists, and refined statistical rituals. Yet the deeper assumptions went largely unexamined, with reality still treated as a passive object to be measured, theory handled as decoration rather than a driver of discovery, and the scientist's role reduced to producing statistically significant increments for the publication mill.

Andrew Gelman and Eric Loken (2013) described the "*garden of forking paths*," showing that even honest exploratory decisions inflate false positives unless researchers commit to model-building and pre-registration. The crisis is not merely statistical but philosophical: evidence is not a binary, and reality does not conform to the ritual boundaries of a single threshold. By treating p-values as a kind of sacrament, modern science often confuses methodological tools with ontological truth.

ECONOMICS OF BELIEF

The political economy of science quietly selects for certain worldviews. Funding agencies, grant panels, journal editors, and tenure committees sit at chokepoints where intellectual and metaphysical preferences become institutional fact. Daniele Fanelli, a metascience researcher, showed that positive results are more common in fields with greater interpretive flexibility, suggesting that publish-or-perish pressures skew reported outcomes (Fanelli, 2010). Meanwhile, Sabine Hossenfelder, a theoretical physicist, has argued that parts of modern physics have drifted toward mathematical elegance and aesthetic preference in the absence of strong empirical anchors (Hossenfelder, 2018). Viewed jointly, their work shows how incentives and tastes shape what gets published and pursued.

Most problems are not outright cheating. Instead, fields slowly bend toward whatever raises their scores, such as journal rankings, citation counts, and online attention. Because those scores drive careers and funding, researchers learn to play to them, sometimes at the expense of truth. Under publish-or-perish pressure, methods that make papers easier to publish, even when they are less reliable, spread quickly (Smaldino & McElreath, 2016). As these habits take hold, work that challenges the dominant view struggles and often moves to philanthropy, independent institutes, or cross-disciplinary centers. In the end a market for safe, familiar ideas forms, where tidy stories get backing and risky or messy ideas fade. That shift does more than sort careers; it also steers what the public later hears as 'settled science.'

BIG PHARMA, SCIENTIFIC FRAUD, AND
THE MARKETIZATION OF KNOWLEDGE

If incentives and prestige shape the academic economy of science, nowhere are the stakes higher than in biomedicine, where billions of dollars depend on the framing of data. Here the *"new church"* of science reveals not only dogmatic tendencies but systemic corruption. Pharmaceutical corporations fund most biomedical research, sponsor clinical trials, and underwrite medical education. This financial entanglement introduces conflicts of interest that undermine the credibility of supposedly neutral knowledge.

The evidence of distortion is sobering. Marcia Angell, former editor of the *New England Journal of Medicine*, concluded after decades at the helm that *"it is simply no longer possible to believe much of the clinical research that is published"* because of pervasive industry manipulation (Angell, 2004). Richard Horton, editor of *The Lancet*, echoed the point: *"much of the scientific literature, perhaps half, may simply be untrue"* (Horton, 2015).

Fraud here is not always outright fabrication, though that occurs. More often it is subtler: selective publication, suppression of negative findings, ghostwritten articles authored by corporate marketing teams but signed by prestigious academics, and statistical massaging that reframes modest effects as breakthroughs (Sismondo, 2008; Gøtzsche, 2012). Trials with unfavorable results are frequently buried, while positive outcomes are fast-tracked into high-impact journals. The practice not only biases the literature but endangers patients, since harmful drugs may remain on the market for years before risks become undeniable.

One infamous case is the antidepressant paroxetine (Paxil/Seroxat). In the early 2000s, internal documents revealed that trials had failed to show efficacy in adolescents, and even showed increased risk of suicidality. Yet the published literature presented the drug as safe and effective for youth depression (Jureidini et al., 2004). Similarly, the opioid crisis was fueled by fraudulent claims that oxycodone carried a low risk of addiction, a narrative cultivated through aggressive marketing and selective science (Van Zee, 2009). In both cases, corporate-sponsored research functioned as doctrine, producing a sanctioned "truth" that aligned with economic interests rather than empirical reality.

These are structural features of the biomedical-industrial complex. As Ben Goldacre (2012) documented in *Bad Pharma*, industry control over trial design, data access, and publication pipelines systematically biases evidence. What masquerades as dispassionate science is often a highly engineered narrative, one that serves capital first, patients second, and truthfulness last.

The resemblance to ecclesial authority is striking. Theological imprimaturs become regulatory approvals; sacred texts give way to ghostwritten clinical guidelines; and dogma once defended by priests is now guarded by experts financially bound to the system. In both settings, questioning orthodoxy risks excommunication, whether through loss of funding, career stagnation, or reputational smearing. Scientific fraud in Big Pharma thus reveals not just individual dishonesty but the systemic conversion of science into a market-dominated church of authority.

THE QUANTUM MIRROR: ONTOLOGICAL LESSONS WE IGNORED

Quantum mechanics delivered a century of ontological vertigo: observer-dependent phenomena, nonlocal correlations, and contextuality, the strange feature that a measurement's outcome is not fixed on its own but can change depending on what other questions we choose to ask at the same time. Instead of building on these insights to develop a richer understanding of observation and reality, mainstream science largely settled for calculation without interpretation (Mermin, 1989). The institutional lesson was clear: where metaphysics intrudes, silence it.

Niels Bohr, Werner Heisenberg, and John Wheeler all recognized that measurement, information, and participation are not side issues in physics but central to how it works (Bohr, 1934; Heisenberg, 1958; Wheeler, 1983). Even today, physicists still debate whether the mathematics they use describes something real in the world or is only a tool for making predictions, showing that the big philosophical questions in physics are still very much alive.

Outside of physics, where foundational debates cannot be avoided, most sciences bracket metaphysical discussion as "philosophy" and therefore optional, sidestepping their own ontological foundations. This is an error of intellectual integrity, for every inquiry presupposes a metaphysics, whether acknowledged or not. Denying this merely cements the default worldview as invisible dogma.

TOWARD A POST-REDUCTIVE, POST-ECCLESIAL SCIENCE

How can inquiry be reclaimed from dogma without descending into relativism or pseudoscience? The answer is not "anything goes" (despite Feyerabend's provocation), but methodological pluralism anchored in transparency, rigor, and open argument.

This call for a post-reductive, post-ecclesial science is not new. It builds on *The Manifesto for a Post-Materialist Science* (Beauregard et al., 2014). In that manifesto, my colleagues and I challenged the dominance of materialist metaphysics and outlined a more open, pluralistic research culture. We argued that real progress requires widening the lens beyond reductive materialism, taking consciousness seriously, and investigating phenomena that resist reduction. We also set out three commitments: intellectual humility, methodological diversity, and openness to ontological surprises. Those commitments remain central to the reforms proposed here.

Concrete pillars of a reformed practice would include making metaphysical assumptions explicit rather than hidden, pre-registering theoretical as well as empirical commitments, and embracing radical transparency with open methods and data. They would also mean cultivating diversity of perspectives in hiring and collaboration, opening peer review to post-publication critique (Kriegeskorte, 2012), and shifting metrics away from impact factors (Seglen, 1997) toward replication and predictive accuracy (Steegen, Tuerlinckx, Gelman, & Vanpaemel, 2016). Such a reform would normalize emergence and top-down causation as legitimate directions of research, and treat consciousness not as a footnote but as a frontier. Creating protected places for unconventional research would help keep rigorous science from stiffening into dogma.

Moreover, such reforms would free inquiry from dogmatic constraints and allow science to evolve into a more integrative and genuinely self-correcting enterprise. By acknowledging metaphysical assumptions instead of hiding them, and by diversifying the knowledge ecosystem rather than enforcing monocultures of thought, science can recover its original spirit of rebellion.

SCIENCE, MEANING, AND THE HUMAN CONDITION

Part of the reason science drifts toward ecclesial functions is existential. Humans need meaning, and reductive materialism offers a seductive simplicity: a world of brute particles and laws, with consciousness as a late-breaking epiphenomenon. That story, however, is insufficient. It fails to do justice to the irreducibility of experience, the autonomy of life and mind, and the self-organizing fabric of nature.

An honest science can admit that we do not know what consciousness is, we do not know how life began, and we do not know whether information or matter is more fundamental. Such admissions are not weaknesses but virtues of intellectual humility. To re-sacralize inquiry is not to theologize it but to restore a sense of awe, mystery, and openness about the structure of reality. This means science needs to recognize its own limits and hidden assumptions, and to work with philosophy not just for appearances but as a true partner in clarifying ideas, assumptions, and consequences.

REBELLION RENEWED

Science was born in rebellion. It must rebel again, this time, against its own ossified creed. The reform is not merely technical but cultural and metaphysical: a willingness to see one's own dogmas, to welcome conceptual heterodoxy, to fund and protect high-risk inquiry, and to treat consciousness not as a scandal but as a clue. The alternative is a bureaucratized knowledge industry that measures, publishes, and optimizes, while forgetting to ask what it is that we truly wish to know.

And even the church of science is no longer confined to journals or lecture halls. Its dogmas and denials now fuse with technologies that reach directly into our veins, our genes, and our screens. The promise of progress appears in the form of pills, pixels, and promises of immortality. Yet beneath the utopian language lies an ancient pattern: control of the body, capture of attention, and colonization of the future. From science as creed, we step into the glittering snare of transhumanism, the *Matrix*'s final seduction.

REFERENCES

Angell, M. (2004). The truth about the drug companies: How they deceive us and what to do about it. Random House.

Amrhein, V., Greenland, S., & McShane, B. B. (2019). Retire statistical significance. Nature, 567, 305–307.

Anderson, P. W. (1972). More is different. Science, 177(4047), 393–396.

Baars, B. J. (1988). A cognitive theory of consciousness. Cambridge University Press.

Beauregard, M., Schwartz, G. E., Miller, L., Dossey, L., Moreira-Almeida, A., Schlitz, M., Sheldrake, R., & Tart, C. (2014). Manifesto for a post-materialist science. EXPLORE: The Journal of Science and Healing, 10(5), 272–274.

Bohr, N. (1934). Atomic theory and the description of nature. Cambridge University Press.

Chalmers, D. J. (1995). Facing up to the problem of consciousness. Journal of Consciousness Studies, 2(3), 200–219.

Chambers, C. (2013). Registered reports: A new publishing initiative at Cortex. Cortex, 49(3), 609–610.

Churchland, P. S. (1986). Neurophilosophy: Toward a unified science of the mind–brain. MIT Press.

Coryn, C. L. S., et al. (2006). A systematic review of theory-driven evaluation practice from 1990 to 2003. American Journal of Evaluation, 27(2), 197–208.

Dehaene, S. (2014). Consciousness and the brain: Deciphering how the brain codes our thoughts. Viking.

Dennett, D. C. (1991). Consciousness explained. Little, Brown.

Ellis, G. F. R. (2016). How can physics underlie the mind? Top-down causation in the human context. Springer.

Ellis, G. F. R., Noble, D., & O'Connor, T. (2012). Top-down causation: An integrating theme within and across the sciences? Interface Focus, 2(1), 1–3.

Fanelli, D. (2010). "Positive" results increase down the hierarchy of the sciences. PLoS ONE, 5(4), e10068.

Feyerabend, P. (1975). Against method. Verso.

Friston, K. (2010). The free-energy principle: A unified brain theory? Nature Reviews Neuroscience, 11, 127–138.

Gelman, A., & Loken, E. (2013). The garden of forking paths. Unpublished manuscript, Department of Statistics, Columbia University.

Gigerenzer, G. (2004). Mindless statistics. Journal of Socio-Economics, 33(5), 587–606.

Goldacre, B. (2012). Bad pharma: How drug companies mislead doctors and harm patients. Fourth Estate.

Gøtzsche, P. C. (2012). Deadly medicines and organised crime: How big pharma has corrupted healthcare. Radcliffe Publishing.

Heisenberg, W. (1958). Physics and philosophy. Harper.

Holland, J. H. (1995). Hidden order: How adaptation builds complexity. Addison–Wesley.

Horton, R. (2015). Offline: What is medicine's 5 sigma? The Lancet, 385(9976), 1380.

Hossenfelder, S. (2018). Lost in math: How beauty leads physics astray. Basic Books.

Ioannidis, J. P. A. (2005). Why most published research findings are false. PLoS Medicine, 2(8), e124.

Jureidini, J. N., McHenry, L. B., & Mansfield, P. R. (2004). Clinical trials and drug promotion: Selective reporting of Study 329. International Journal of Risk & Safety in Medicine, 16(1), 31–39.

Kriegeskorte, N. (2012). Open evaluation: A vision for entirely transparent post-publication peer review and rating for science. Frontiers in Computational Neuroscience, 6, 79.

Kuhn, T. S. (1962). The structure of scientific revolutions. University of Chicago Press.

Kuhn, T. S. (1977). The essential tension. University of Chicago Press.

Lakatos, I., & Musgrave, A. (Eds.). (1970). Criticism and the growth of knowledge. Cambridge University Press.

Latour, B. (1987). Science in action. Harvard University Press.

Latour, B., & Woolgar, S. (1979). Laboratory life: The construction of scientific facts. Sage.

Meehl, P. E. (1967). Theory-testing in psychology and physics: A methodological paradox. Philosophy of Science, 34(2), 103–115.

Mermin, N. D. (1989). What's wrong with this pillow? Physics Today, 42(4), 9–11.

Merton, R. K. (1968). The Matthew effect in science. Science, 159(3810), 56–63.

Nagel, T. (1974). What is it like to be a bat? The Philosophical Review, 83(4), 435–450.

Nagel, T. (2012). Mind and cosmos: Why the materialist neo-Darwinian conception of nature is almost certainly false. Oxford University Press.

Noble, D. (2006). The music of life: Biology beyond genes. Oxford University Press.

Nosek, B. A., & Lakens, D. (2014). Registered reports: A method to increase the credibility of published results. Social Psychology, 45(3), 137–141.

Open Science Collaboration. (2015). Estimating the reproducibility of psychological science. Science, 349(6251), aac4716.

Penrose, R., & Hameroff, S. (1994). Quantum coherence in microtubules: A model for consciousness. Journal of Consciousness Studies, 1(1), 98–118.

Planck, M. (1949). Scientific autobiography and other papers. Philosophical Library.

Polanyi, M. (1958). Personal knowledge: Towards a post-critical philosophy. University of Chicago Press.

Rosenthal, R. (1979). The file drawer problem and tolerance for null results. Psychological Bulletin, 86(3), 638–641.

Seglen, P. O. (1997). Why the impact factor of journals should not be used for evaluating research. BMJ, 314(7079), 498–502.

Sheldrake, R. (2012). The science delusion. Coronet.

Simmons, J. P., Nelson, L. D., & Simonsohn, U. (2011). False-positive psychology: Undisclosed flexibility in data collection and analysis allows presenting anything as significant. Psychological Science, 22(11), 1359–1366.

Sismondo, S. (2008). How pharmaceutical industry funding affects trial outcomes: A systematic review. Contemporary Clinical Trials, 29(2), 109–113.

Smaldino, P. E., & McElreath, R. (2016). The natural selection of bad science. Royal Society Open Science, 3(9), 160384.

Smith, R. (2006). Peer review: A flawed process at the heart of science and journals. Journal of the Royal Society of Medicine, 99(4), 178–182.

Steegen, S., Tuerlinckx, F., Gelman, A., & Vanpaemel, W. (2016). The multiverse analysis. Perspectives on Psychological Science, 11(1), 65–76.

Tononi, G. (2004). An information integration theory of consciousness. BMC Neuroscience, 5, 42.

Tononi, G. (2008). Consciousness as integrated information: A provisional manifesto. Biological Bulletin, 215(3), 216–242.

Van Zee, A. (2009). The promotion and marketing of OxyContin: Commercial triumph, public health tragedy. American Journal of Public Health, 99(2), 221–227.

von Bertalanffy, L. (1968). General system theory. George Braziller.

Weinberg, S. (1992). Dreams of a final theory. Pantheon.

Wheeler, J. A. (1983). Law without law. In J. A. Wheeler & W. H. Zurek (Eds.), Quantum theory and measurement (pp. 182–213). Princeton University Press.

Wiener, N. (1948). Cybernetics: Or control and communication in the animal and the machine. MIT Press.

Chapter 7

Poison, Pixels, and the Transhumanist Trap

*"The post human is now 'a real, not a notional... possibility,'
and therefore the question of what it means to be human 'is
all a sudden a pressing question, a question absolutely
pressed for time... otherwise... [it] will have been already
"decided by scientific experts and market forces"'."*
— Nikolas Kompridis

This chapter braids three strands of a single rope tightening around the human: poison, pixels, and the transhumanist trap. *Poison* here refers to the chemical and pharmacological saturation of bodies and ecosystems; the spread of endocrine disruptors, neurotoxicants, and microplastics; and the chronic use of psychopharmaceuticals that quietly reshape physiology, cognition, and behavior. *Pixels* point to the attention-extractive, behavior-modifying machineries of capture that have moved from the periphery of life to its center, inserting screens, metrics, and algorithms between us and the world. The *transhumanist trap* describes the metaphysical horizon toward which these forces drive us: the belief that humanity's path forward lies in dissolving the human into code, optimizing biology into product, and handing over governance to computational procedures that promise safety, efficiency, and immortality.

Together, these vectors form a governance regime that is no longer principally legal or political but *biopsychotechnical.* They shape biology, rewire attention, and install a metaphysics in which consciousness is reduced to computation and life to information. The *Human Robot*, already conditioned in school and state, is now upgraded to a human–machine substrate.

To break this regime apart, we need to see three things working together: first, how our chemical and digital environments interact to affect our brains and hormones; second, how the dream of transhumanism acts like a modern belief system that justifies pushing technology into every corner of life; and third, how we can nurture ways of living that are bodily, connected, and spiritual as a form of resistance to being enclosed by algorithms and capital.

POISON: THE SLOW VIOLENCE OF CHEMICAL AND PHARMACOLOGICAL GOVERNANCE

Endocrine Disruptors as Political Technology

By the late twentieth century, scientists had realized that certain common chemicals can disrupt our hormones even at tiny doses. *Bisphenol A* (BPA), used in plastics and food can linings, can mimic estrogen in the body. *Phthalates*, found in plastics and many cosmetics, interfere with testosterone and other hormones. *PFAS* (per- and polyfluoroalkyl substances), the so-called *"forever chemicals"* used in nonstick pans, waterproof clothing, and food packaging, linger in the environment and accumulate in our bodies. In addition, *organophosphate pesticides*, widely used in agriculture, disrupt nervous system signaling and carry risks for brain development. These effects are particularly harmful during sensitive stages such as fetal development, infancy, and puberty. Research has linked exposure to these chemicals with infertility, metabolic disease, developmental problems in children, and various cancers (Vandenberg et al., 2012; Trasande, 2019; Gore et al., 2015, 2020).

Beyond the numbers, the point is simple: industrial choices flow downstream into our bodies. "Safe" limits are often set for an average adult, not for a fetus, a child, or someone in puberty, so real vulnerabilities get missed. Meanwhile, the burden is shifted onto individuals with advice to shop smarter instead of fixing the sources of exposure. In that gap, endocrine-disrupting chemicals do quiet work at low doses, modulating hormones, shaping development, and sometimes leaving effects that carry into the next generation. In short, what looks like personal risk is often a policy choice, and our biology keeps the record.

The Erosion of Cognitive Sovereignty

Grandjean and Landrigan (2014) identified a growing list of chemicals that harm the developing brain, including lead, mercury, and organophosphate pesticides. Subsequent work has raised concerns about other common exposures, such as fluoride in some settings, which several studies link to impaired neurodevelopment. These researchers (2014) warned of a *"silent pandemic"* damaging children's brain development. As attention, memory, and self-control weaken, individual harm becomes civic harm because clear judgment and self-regulation support public life. Chemical exposures chip away at mental resilience, which makes societies more vulnerable to platform predators, systems that harvest attention and nudge behavior. In this way the chemical and the digital converge, as toxins dull cognitive sovereignty and code exploits what remains.

Psychopharmacology and the Governance of Mood

The mass prescription of psychopharmaceuticals such as SSRIs (Selective Serotonin Reuptake Inhibitors), stimulants, and benzodiazepines emerges within a culture that treats distress as individual pathology divorced from political, ecological, and cultural roots. While these medications can be life-saving for many, their systemic overuse, especially among children and adolescents, contributes to a society where mood, focus, and arousal are managed chemically rather than addressed through structural transformation.

This culture of pharmacological optimization dovetails seamlessly with the transhumanist ideal. If mood, attention, and cognition are understood as problems to be engineered, then why stop at pills? Why not gene-edit, neurostimulate, or eventually upload?

PIXELS: BEHAVIORAL MODIFICATION AT PLANETARY SCALE

The Attention Economy as Extractive Industry

We have already alluded to surveillance capitalism, the economic logic in which human experience is mined as raw behavioral data to be sold as prediction and ultimately coerced into desired future behaviors (Zuboff, 2019). Every micro-interaction, each pause in scrolling or simple click, becomes a data point processed by machine learning engines conceived to manipulate attention, emotion, and choice.

Today's platforms function like a planetary Skinner box, tuned by persuasive design strategies pioneered by BJ Fogg at Stanford's Captology Lab (Fogg, 2003) and now embedded deep in their infrastructure. Features such as variable rewards, infinite scroll, and engineered social comparison are intentional: they operate as operant-conditioning tools that target the brain's reward and bonding systems, including dopamine for anticipation and habit formation and oxytocin for social attachment, to keep us engaged.

Adolescence as a Battlefield

Rising rates of anxiety, depression, self-harm, and loneliness among adolescents, particularly girls, have been closely linked to the explosion of smartphones and social media in the early 2010s

(Twenge, 2017; Haidt, 2024). Children's attention, along with their sleep, social growth, and play, has been pushed into a world of constant competition, online status games, and a steady state of low-level anxiety.

When children grow up mainly through digital platforms, they enter adulthood already used to being measured by numbers, presenting their lives for an audience, and living under computerized control. The *Human Robot* is not just trained to obey anymore: it is hooked into dependence through games and constant rewards.

Algorithmic Governance: From Predict to Prescribe

Rouvroy and Berns (2013) describe *algorithmic governmentality* as governance that bypasses reflective capacities by acting on behavioral propensities detected in data flows. What began as targeted advertising becomes *targeted reality construction*, in which what you see, know, and desire is filtered by opaque models whose goals are not aligned with human flourishing.

As AI moves from simple helpers like video recommenders to all-purpose tools that handle many tasks, the feedback loops tighten. Watch one video and the platform learns your taste, so the next suggestions are harder to resist. Chat with a bot and your words become training data, so future conversations feel more guided and can tilt what seems normal to say. Upload photos and image models learn from them, then produce synthetic faces that crowd the feed and compete for attention. Step by step, our clicks, chats, and uploads teach the machines, and the machines teach us back. The result is an information stage with no single author, where the platform's AI-driven feedback loop, including recommenders, chatbots, ranking systems, and ads, choreographs behavior without our awareness.

THE TRANSHUMANIST TRAP

Transhumanism as Secular Eschatology

Transhumanism, promoted by thinkers like Ray Kurzweil (2005) and Nick Bostrom (2005, 2014), promises things like much longer lifespans, smarter brains, engineered moral improvement, and eventually even uploading the mind into machines. It works like a modern kind of salvation story: death is treated as a glitch to be fixed, suffering as a technical problem, and consciousness as data that can be copied or transferred into a computer or other non-biological "substrate."

Built into this vision are several unspoken assumptions: the mind is nothing but computation, the self reduces to information, the body is flawed evolutionary hardware, and ethics is merely risk management. None of these claims has been proven, yet they are often treated as inevitable truths.

Reduction, Disembodiment, and the Loss of the Qualitative

Embodied cognition says the mind is not just a computer running calculations. It is shaped by how our living bodies move, sense, and interact with the world. Transhumanism, in contrast, sees the body as hardware that can be upgraded, modified, or even left behind.

The body is more than a brain's container. It is what makes life meaningful. Modern culture often prizes abstractions and images over real contact and connection. Transhumanism supercharges this, letting our models of reality overshadow reality itself.

The New Eugenics

New technologies like editing genes, selecting embryos, and using AI in medicine are often presented as compassionate ways to reduce suffering. The promise sounds humane: healthier children, fewer inherited diseases, and treatments tailored to each person. Yet the very same tools can also create a *soft eugenics*, where statistical averages are treated as ideals, human variety is recast as defect, and the pursuit of "better" slides quietly toward sameness.

A few decades ago, Francis Fukuyama warned in *Our Posthuman Future* (2002) that new biotechnologies could erode the very foundation of equal human dignity. If some traits are judged worth keeping while others are marked for elimination, difficult questions arise. Parents may feel pressure to select the "best" embryo, patients may be steered toward genetic enhancement, and whole societies may begin to accept a narrow standard of what counts as healthy, capable, or worthy of life.

Within this environment, power shifts toward a technocratic form of governance, where authority belongs not to wise or morally grounded leaders but to experts fluent in metrics, models, and machine learning. The language of safety and efficiency hides a deeper politics of control, in which bodies and futures are shaped to serve market priorities rather than human flourishing. What appears as compassion can, without reflection, turn into a machinery of conformity.

AI and the Ontological Capture of Consciousness

Bostrom's *Superintelligence* (2014) warned of machines that might threaten humanity's survival. Yet the more immediate danger is ontological capture: AI systems quietly shape how we see the world, filtering science, art, and law through their own lenses, and in the process redefining what counts as insight, significance, and truth. A humanity that turns to AI as a mirror to understand itself risks absorbing the mirror's distortions. If a system can simulate consciousness with convincing skill, we may be tempted to conclude that consciousness is nothing more than simulation.

This reversal flips the spiritual on its head. Mystery becomes a statistical margin of error, transcendence is reduced to the limits of a model, and personhood is equated with a score. The danger is not only political but also existential, as it thins our deepest sense of meaning.

CHEMICO-DIGITAL TRANSHUMANISM AS GOVERNANCE

These forces do not operate in isolation but reinforce one another in a self-amplifying loop. Chemical exposures weaken the body, digital regimes capture the mind, and transhumanist ideology reframes both as inevitable stages on the way to a supposedly better future. Together they form a machinery of governance that operates through biology, psychology, and belief at once.

Chemical weakening, through endocrine disruptors, neurotoxicants, and widespread pharmaceuticals, gradually erodes health, resilience, and cognitive sovereignty. Once compromised, bodies and minds are easier to steer. Platform architectures then hijack and fragment attention, replacing lived intersubjectivity with technologically orchestrated emotional management. As resilience declines, the lure of engineered supports grows stronger until the screen functions both as pacifier and overseer. Finally, transhumanist ideology interprets these degradations as provisional fixes on the road to a post-biological future. By branding this as progress, dissent is portrayed as backward or anti-scientific.

The *Matrix* manufactures consent to disembodiment. The more people feel biologically weakened and psychologically destabilized, the more they are tempted by technological promises of control: neural implants to treat depression, gene edits to "correct" mood, AI therapists offering constant support, and longevity interventions to defeat mortality. Yet these supposed cures deepen the very conditions they claim to address.

BREAKING THE SPELL

What if we stopped measuring humanity by speed, efficiency, endless growth, or predictive power? What if we looked for meaning instead in depth, relationship, and wonder? The challenge lies not only in technology but in culture itself: how to turn life toward what exceeds metrics and performance scores.

The Morality of Limits

Human flourishing depends as much on boundaries as on breakthroughs. Resisting the illusion of limitless progress requires ethical guardrails. Technological humility begins with acknowledging how little we understand about consciousness and complexity, and with accepting that uncertainty is not simply a flaw to be eliminated but part of life itself. For powerful biotechnologies that alter genes or brains, the precautionary principle demands that reversible options be favored and the burden of proof rest on those advocating irreversible interventions. Above all, human dignity must be protected from reduction to data profiles, risk scores, or optimization targets.

The Landscape of Attention

If the body is our first home, attention is our second, and both are under siege. Just as chemical toxins harm the body, manipulative technologies corrode the mind. Protecting attention requires collective strategies: treating addictive app features as a public health risk, limiting platform manipulation, and insisting on transparency. Community life also provides a counterweight: shared meals, intergenerational rituals, time in nature, and collective art help restore focus and resilience. Even small practices like technology breaks can reset the nervous system and strengthen bonds beyond screens.

Detoxifying the Body–World Connection

Our inner chemistry is inseparable from the outer world. Protecting mental and physical health therefore means more than individual treatment: it requires cleaning up endocrine disruptors, PFAS, and other toxins, monitoring exposures, and holding polluters accountable. It also calls for a transformation of food infrastructures toward regenerative farming and away from ultra-processed products. Health policy, in turn, must grapple with the social roots of distress rather than simply expanding medication. Within this broader context, honest consent around psychiatric drugs becomes essential, alongside greater access to therapies rooted in relationships, meaning, and community.

Reviving the Human Spirit

Escaping the optimization trap requires not only detoxification but reclamation. To live beyond metrics is to seize back mystery and meaning. Consciousness is not a machine but embodied and relational, alive in networks of care. Multiple ways of knowing must be welcomed, with science in dialogue with contemplative practice, Indigenous wisdom, and the arts. Spiritual literacy, whether rooted in religion or practiced in secular forms, rekindles gratitude, awe, and contemplation while resisting the reduction of life to data points.

Rethinking Institutions

Reorientation cannot fall to individuals alone: it calls for institutions that serve human needs, act transparently, and remain accountable to democratic oversight. When institutions take this role seriously, technology can be developed as a partner that strengthens human capacities instead of replacing them. Such an approach demands governance that is open and contestable, with platform rules exposed to public scrutiny, tested through impact assessments, and subject to enforceable rights of challenge. Extending this principle further, decisions about gene editing, AI, and environmental health should not rest in the hands of technocratic elites but be deliberated in citizen assemblies, where experts advise and citizens retain the power to decide.

TEN THESES AGAINST THE TRANSHUMANIST TRAP

Having traced the risks of optimization and technocratic control, we now turn to guiding principles that offer both resistance and affirmation. What follows are not only observations but vows, commitments that draw a line in defense of the human spirit.

1. We refuse to treat the body as obsolete hardware and affirm it as sacred flesh, alive with meaning, relation, and presence.
2. We refuse to reduce consciousness to computation and affirm awareness as a mystery that overflows matter, irreducible to code or circuitry.
3. We refuse to equate optimization with flourishing and affirm that love, beauty, and transcendence—not efficiency—are the marks of true purpose.
4. We refuse to absolutize safety and efficiency and affirm that freedom and dignity require risk, openness, and trust in life.
5. We refuse to normalize toxins that erode body and mind and affirm our duty to protect clarity and vitality for future generations.
6. We refuse to let the attention economy colonize the soul and affirm attention as a sanctuary for contemplation, communion, and awe.
7. We refuse to accept transhumanism as destiny and affirm it as a narrow faith masquerading as inevitability, while honoring instead the vast horizons of spirit.

8. We refuse to see AI as neutral and affirm it as a cultural and ontological force that must be aligned with reverence for life.
9. We refuse to leave resistance to individuals alone and affirm the need for communities and institutions that nurture wholeness, wisdom, and responsibility.
10. We refuse to reduce the human to data, neurons, or algorithms and affirm the irreducible essence of spirit and relation at the heart of every person.

Taken as a whole, these theses are more than a boundary: they express a commitment to what it means to be human. They remind us that the human is not a puzzle to be solved or a problem to be optimized, but a mystery to be lived. To resist the transhumanist trap is not to reject science or technology but to restore them to their rightful role, as servants of life rather than idols of control. The task before us is orientation, not optimization: depth over speed, communion over calculation, and freedom rooted in spirit over domination by the empire of mechanism.

THE COURAGE TO STAY HUMAN

The transhumanist trap seduces by promising mastery over finitude: the end of disease, confusion, and even death. Finitude is no flaw in the human condition but the wellspring of love, care, and meaning. To affirm humanity is to choose the qualitative over the quantitative, relation over control, and depth over extension. It is also to defend, with humility and rigor, the irreducible mystery at the heart of consciousness and life.

The work ahead is not to reject technology but to resituate it within an anthropology that honors embodiment, vulnerability, and transcendence. The human is not a defective machine to be upgraded but a meaning-making being whose destiny is not to be uploaded but to awaken.

The dream of transcendence has been captured not only in ideology and laboratories but also in the glowing screens we carry like talismans. Silicon Valley prophets preach digital salvation, promising to merge flesh with code and selling the myth of immortality through algorithms. Yet behind the sleek veneer lies the same old machinery of control, fear, distraction, and dependence. From the cult of progress we step into the cathedral of pixels, where media no longer reports on reality but manufactures it.

REFERENCES

Bostrom, N. (2005). A history of transhumanist thought. Journal of Evolution and Technology, 14(1), 1–25.

Bostrom, N. (2014). Superintelligence: Paths, dangers, strategies. Oxford University Press.

Fogg, B. J. (2003). Persuasive technology: Using computers to change what we think and do. Morgan Kaufmann.

Fukuyama, F. (2002). Our posthuman future: Consequences of the biotechnology revolution. Farrar, Straus and Giroux.

Gore, A. C., Chappell, V. A., Fenton, S. E., Flaws, J. A., Nadal, A., Prins, G. S., Toppari, J., & Zoeller, R. T. (2015). EDC-2: The Endocrine Society's second scientific statement on endocrine-disrupting chemicals. Endocrine Reviews, 36(6), E1–E150. https://doi.org/10.1210/er.2015-1010

Gore, A. C., Chappell, V. A., Fenton, S. E., Flaws, J. A., Nadal, A., Prins, G. S., Toppari, J., & Zoeller, R. T. (2020). EDC-3: The Endocrine Society's third scientific statement on endocrine-disrupting chemicals. Endocrine Reviews, 41(2), bnaa011. https://doi.org/10.1210/endrev/bnaa011

Grandjean, P., & Landrigan, P. J. (2014). Neurobehavioural effects of developmental toxicity. The Lancet Neurology, 13(3), 330–338. https://doi.org/10.1016/S1474-4422(13)70278-3

Haidt, J. (2024). The anxious generation: How the great rewiring of childhood is causing an epidemic of mental illness. Penguin Press.

Kompridis, N. (2009). Technology's challenge to democracy: What of the human? Parrhesia, 8, 20–33.

Kurzweil, R. (2005). The singularity is near: When humans transcend biology. Viking.

McGilchrist, I. (2019). The master and his emissary: The divided brain and the making of the Western world (2nd ed.). Perspectiva Press.

McGilchrist, I. (2021). The matter with things: Our brains, our delusions, and the unmaking of the world. Perspectiva Press.

Rouvroy, A., & Berns, T. (2013). Algorithmic governmentality and prospects of emancipation. Réflexions & Propositions, 1(1), 163–196.

Trasande, L. (2019). Sicker, fatter, poorer: The urgent threat of hormone-disrupting chemicals to our health and future… and what we can do about it. Houghton Mifflin Harcourt.

Twenge, J. (2017). iGen: Why today's super-connected kids are growing up less rebellious, more tolerant, less happy—and completely unprepared for adulthood. Atria.

Varela, F. J., Thompson, E., & Rosch, E. (1991). The embodied mind: Cognitive science and human experience. MIT Press.

Vandenberg, L. N., Colborn, T., Hayes, T. B., Heindel, J. J., Jacobs Jr., D. R., Lee, D. H., Shioda, T., Soto, A. M., vom Saal, F. S., Welshons, W. V., Zoeller, R. T., & Myers, J. P. (2012). Hormones and endocrine-disrupting chemicals: Low-dose effects and nonmonotonic dose responses. Endocrine Reviews, 33(3), 378–455. https://doi.org/10.1210/er.2011-1050

Zuboff, S. (2019). The age of surveillance capitalism: The fight for a human future at the new frontier of power. PublicAffairs.

Chapter 8

Media: The Ministry of Manufactured Reality

"The media's the most powerful entity on earth. They have the power to make the innocent guilty and the guilty innocent."
— Malcolm X

We now live inside an empire of images. The endless sensorium of modern life, a perpetual cascade of screens, feeds, alerts, and notifications, does not merely report events: it composes reality itself. Our perception of the world is not direct but mediated, structured, and increasingly automated, narrowing the horizons of what we take to be real.

What counts as *"reality"* is not neutral. It is produced, filtered, and ranked by apparatuses whose loyalty lies not in truth but in engagement metrics, financial profit, and the imperatives of governance. The medium is still the message, as McLuhan (1964) declared, but the message of late capitalism is unmistakably clear: *stay hooked, keep scrolling, and believe that your compliance was your idea.*

Walter Lippmann (1922) recognized the power of what he called *"pseudo-environments,"* the mental pictures people form of the world they cannot directly experience. Today, those pictures are no longer constructed primarily by newspapers or broadcast anchors but by the customized flows of stories and updates that platforms create for each user, along with recommendation mechanisms and personalized ad markets.

Media no longer merely describes the world: it participates in constructing it. As a cybernetic feedback loop, it shapes what we notice, what we remember, how we feel, and even who we believe ourselves to be. Thus its function has shifted from setting agendas to shaping behavior, and from conveying stories to shaping identities. The issue extends beyond the manufacture of consent to a deeper concern: whether media now manufactures reality itself. To see how this transformation unfolds, we must examine how media has shifted from being a mirror that reflects events to a machine that actively engineers perception.

MEDIA AS REALITY MACHINE

From Mirror to Lens

Berger and Luckmann (1966) argued that reality is *socially constructed* through institutions that stabilize meaning. Today that process is accelerated and automated. Media has moved from mirror to lens, deciding what is visible, what is felt, and what disappears. News no longer just reports events but organizes them into symbolic order; and screens no longer show the world but a version filtered by algorithms, editors, and platform owners. This is not propaganda in the old sense but *programmable reality*, where the stories we live by are continuously recalibrated for effect. One of the most powerful ways this programmable reality operates is through *framing*, the hidden grammar by which events are named, categorized, and morally charged.

The Politics of Framing

Framing provides the grammar of media construction. As Entman (1993) explains, framing involves selecting *"some aspects of a perceived reality"* to promote particular interpretations. Its power lies less in outright falsehood than in emphasis and omission. Protesters can be cast as *"rioters"* or as *"freedom fighters,"* depending on the moral lens applied; torture is rebranded as *"enhanced interrogation;"* and civilian deaths are recoded as *"collateral damage."* Each phrase dulls moral response and steers perception before reflection has a chance to begin.

Lakoff (2004) showed that metaphors shape how we think before facts even enter the picture. Call taxes a *"burden"* and you get one kind of politics. Call them an *"investment"* and you get another. Words matter, but so do the silences, the things frames hide from view. This raises a deeper question: if framing already tilts perception, what does it mean when journalism claims to be *"objective"*?

Objectivity as Ritual Costume

Journalistic "objectivity" often functions as a ritual mask concealing the operations of power. Rosen (1999) called this the *"view from nowhere,"* a performance of neutrality that hides the fact that selection is never neutral. What is often described as *"both-sides-ism"* does not create balance but instead elevates manufactured doubt to the same level as established knowledge (Oreskes & Conway, 2010). For instance, in times of conflict, news outlets frequently echo official narratives while offering only muted dissent, framing wars as questions of tactics rather than of legality or morality.

Hallin (1986) explained this dynamic through three spheres of discourse: consensus, legitimate controversy, and deviance. Radical critiques are excluded not by censorship but by classification as "unserious" or "irrelevant." In the United States, structural critiques of empire, capitalism, or machine-mediated governance rarely appear because elites rarely debate them. Bennett (1990) confirmed this with "indexing theory": when elites converge, dissent disappears from coverage.

Media no longer just reports events. It tells us what counts, how to feel, and what kind of future we can imagine. It is less a record-keeper than an engineer of reality. And the material it works with is not facts but attention, the most valuable resource of all.

WHEN ATTENTION BECOMES ADDICTION

Attention as Extractive Resource

If media manufactures reality, its raw material is attention. In the 21st century, attention has become the fundamental extractive resource, captured, refined, and sold on open markets. Companies no longer primarily sell information or entertainment: they sell your nervous system to advertisers and political actors.

Tristan Harris, former Google ethicist, put it simply: *"If you're not paying for the product, you are the product"* (Harris, 2017). But this misses the depth of the transformation. You are not just the product. You are the worker, the raw material, and the output all at once. Each glance, click, or pause is recorded, aggregated, and fed into machine-learning systems that refine predictions and optimize future capture.

The Science of Capture

Silicon Valley did not just stumble on ways to make apps addictive. They borrowed tricks from behavioral science. Fogg (2009) outlined how triggers, actions, and unpredictable rewards could hook people. Kahneman (2011) explained why we are so vulnerable: our brains run on two modes of thinking. *System 1* is the quick, automatic, gut-reaction mode, while *System 2* is the slower, logical, more thoughtful one. Most of the time, System 1 is in charge. Social media apps exploit this by continually feeding fast, emotional System 1 with endless notifications, likes, and scrolls, while our slower, reflective System 2 rarely gets a chance to intervene.

Courtwright (2019) coined the term *"limbic capitalism"* to describe markets organized to exploit neural reward circuits. Unlike earlier markets, which manipulated desire indirectly through advertising, limbic capitalism plugs directly into the circuitry of craving. The result is an economy in which your dopamine levels are as valuable as your dollars.

Memory as Overwrite, Not Debate

The capture of attention is only one axis of control: the other is memory. Orwell imagined the *Ministry of Truth* rewriting the past through falsified newspapers. Our system achieves something similar in a quieter way: instead of rewriting, it buries.

The design of social media makes forgetting inevitable. Yesterday's atrocity is displaced by today's viral meme, which is quickly overwritten by tomorrow's scandal. What remains is not a record but a torrent that erases itself. In this environment, reflection and accountability have no stable ground. Levitin (2014) calls this *cognitive overload*, a collapse of discernment under the weight of novelty. Nora (1989) argued that societies preserve meaning in "sites of memory." Today those sites are no longer shared space but private platforms, searchable only insofar as they generate clicks.

Addiction on Purpose

The loop closes in compulsion. Each notification, ping, heart, and retweet is a neurochemical prompt, delivering small doses of dopamine, and because these rewards arrive unpredictably, they tap into what Lembke (2021) identifies as the most addictive schedule of all: intermittent reinforcement, the same mechanism that keeps gamblers at slot machines.

The consequences cut deeper than habit. They reshape identity. The self is reduced to metrics, meaning to visibility, and intimacy to interactivity. Online we rise and fall with platform recognition. And as Turkle (2011) notes, the paradox is brutal: the more we connect, the lonelier we become, our nerves hijacked and our psyches pulled outward into a world that never rests.

The outcome is a society of restless selves, constantly stimulated yet never satisfied, constantly fed yet never nourished. This restless condition is not accidental. It is the foundation of a new form of governance in which control is exercised less through law or coercion than through platforms, metrics, and machine-driven feedback loops.

GOVERNANCE BY MACHINE

Manufactured News:
Misinformation in the Mainstream

Misinformation refers to false or misleading claims spread without intent to deceive, while *disinformation* is the deliberate production and circulation of falsehoods for strategic ends. Both are often blamed on fringe outlets or anonymous trolls, yet mainstream media has repeatedly played a central role in shaping false narratives.

Before the Iraq War, major U.S. outlets repeated government claims about weapons of mass destruction, claims later proven false, presenting invasion as unavoidable rather than a matter of choice (Chomsky & Herman, 1988; Bennett, 1990). During the 2008 financial crash, the same outlets mostly echoed Wall Street insiders while sidelining those who warned that the system was on the verge of collapse. The pattern has repeated in health crises, from the tobacco industry's denial campaigns to more recent debates over climate change and COVID-19, where leading news organizations often amplified industry talking points and softened accountability for corporations and governments (Oreskes & Conway, 2010).

These are symptoms of structural pressures such as ownership, advertising dependence, and reliance on official sources, all of which distort reporting toward power. The result is that mainstream news can mislead not only by what it says, but also by what it leaves unsaid, normalizing distortions that shape public consent.

Manufacturing Consent 2.0

In *Manufacturing Consent* (1988), Noam Chomsky and Edward Herman described five forces that shape what the public sees in the media: who owns the outlets, who pays for advertising, where stories come from, the backlash against unwanted coverage, and the dominant ideology of the time. Decades later, those filters have not disappeared. Instead, they have been absorbed into the infrastructure of today's digital platforms and rebuilt inside engineered systems of power.

Today ownership is concentrated in a few platform giants like Google, Meta, and Amazon, and that concentration shapes the entire digital media ecosystem. Their business model depends on advertising, but ads are no longer placed in the slow rhythm of campaigns: they are traded in lightning-fast auctions that buy and sell our attention by the millisecond. Because profit depends on clicks, the flow of stories is guided less by journalists than by algorithms designed to elevate whatever goes viral. That same logic also shapes backlash, where criticism spreads rapidly through coordinated online campaigns, swarms of anonymous accounts, and waves of manufactured outrage. Beneath it all lies an ideology built into the very architecture of digital platforms, one that prizes polarization, certainty, and oversimplification, because those features drive engagement and keep us scrolling.

The machinery of influence has changed form but not function. What once looked like top-down control now feels like personalization. Yet the effect is just as powerful. *Filter bubbles* (Pariser, 2011) form when platforms keep showing us more of what we already like, which quietly hides alternative views. Over time, this narrowing combines with *echo chambers* (Sunstein, 2017), where we mostly hear from people who think as we do, reinforcing our existing beliefs and identities.

In combination, these forces fracture the public sphere into parallel realities. What once resembled a shared arena of debate becomes a patchwork of rival information silos, each ruled by its own truths, grievances, and sense of reality.

Cambridge Analytica as Proof-of-Concept

The *Cambridge Analytica scandal* illustrated the mechanics. By harvesting the data of tens of millions of Facebook users without their informed consent, the company built psychological profiles that could be exploited for microtargeted political ads. Voters were not persuaded by mass messaging but manipulated through highly personalized appeals that played to fear, resentment, or identity.

This was not an isolated scandal. It was a prototype of programmed propaganda: democracy reduced to a marketplace where emotions are auctioned to the highest bidder. And it was only one sign of a deeper transformation, where platforms no longer simply mediate communication but restructure the very conditions of economic and political life.

Platform Feudalism

The slogan *"If you're not paying for the product, you are the product"* still underestimates the situation. Users provide the labor as well as the data. Every click, scroll, and tag generates data that fuels the predictive engines. The labor is unpaid, the ownership absent, and the exit costs immense.

Scholars have given this condition different names: Andrejevic (2013) calls it the *"digital enclosure,"* Srnicek (2016) describes it as *"platform capitalism,"* and Couldry and Mejias (2019) frame it as *"data colonialism,"* the extraction of human life for computational profit. Whatever the term, the metaphor is feudal. Big Tech are the new lords, their platforms are walled gardens of code, and what they charge as rent is your attention and your predictable behavior. Like old feudal systems, this order pushes things to extremes, and in today's platform economy those extremes are powered by algorithms built for optimization.

Extremity by Optimization

Algorithms are indifferent. They do not care what you believe, only how long you stay. Their objective functions are simple: maximize watch-time, extend session length, reduce dropout, and raise *ARPU* (Average Revenue Per User).

Yet optimization has consequences, because systems designed only to maximize engagement often push users toward more extreme material. Tufekci (2018) showed how YouTube's recommender system worked this way, steering viewers not through ideology but through statistical optimization. In this environment, radicalization emerges less as a deliberate goal than as a by-product of keeping people watching.

Ideas in this ecosystem spread like genes. The ones that survive are those that hook attention. Falsehoods travel faster than truth. Outrage is stickier than calm. Messages fused with identity bind more deeply than those appealing to reason (Vosoughi, Roy, & Aral, 2018). The result is a crisis of meaning: virality outpaces verification, and society becomes governable by meme. Yet the deepest consequences of this crisis are not only political but personal. Manufactured reality seeps into the very texture of selfhood, solitude, and the possibility of freedom.

SELFHOOD, SOLITUDE, AND LIBERATION

The Platform-Ready Self

The deepest stakes of manufactured reality are not merely about information but about being itself. Identity has become programmable. Goffman's (1959) dramaturgical view of life as performance, once a metaphor, has been literalized by social platforms. Butler's (1990) insight that identity is performative is no longer just cultural theory: it has become a business model. Platform logics thrive on caricature. They elevate outrage, certainty, and archetype while pushing nuance and ambiguity to the bottom of the feed. What survives is what is most visible, most extreme, and most monetizable.

This transformation is not enforced from above but internalized from within. We begin to shape ourselves for programmed mechanisms, sculpting identities that fit platform logic. In the process, we become both prisoner and warden of our branded selves. Foucault's (1977) *panopticon*, the prison where the watched absorb the gaze of the watcher, has collapsed into the everyday. The guard tower is no longer distant: it rests in our pockets, buzzing with notifications. Each glance, each refresh, and each check for validation reinforces the cage we ourselves maintain.

The Collapse of Solitude

Alongside this reshaping of identity comes the erosion of solitude. Han (2017) describes modern society as populated by "achievement-subjects," driven to optimize, perform, and self-exploit without pause. The smartphone collapses the boundaries between work, leisure, and intimacy, keeping us tethered to a perpetual stream of demands. Carr (2010) warns that this environment undermines the ability to engage in deep reading and sustained thought, replacing them with skimming, multitasking, and fragmented attention. In response, Newport (2019) calls for *digital minimalism*, not a renunciation of technology, but a deliberate, sovereign use of it.

Even so, solitude itself has become a rare and fragile state. Silence feels unbearable, not because it lacks value, but because silence cannot be monetized. A mind that can rest in stillness, that can attend without distraction, becomes subversive in an economy where every pause is treated as wasted revenue. In such a world, the radical act is not scrolling faster but slowing down, not consuming more but choosing less. To protect solitude is to preserve the very conditions for thought, imagination, and freedom. Its erosion, however, is inseparable from the broader transformation of power itself.

When Control Feels like Choice

These shifts in selfhood and solitude cannot be separated from transformations in power. In disciplinary societies, as Foucault (1977) observed, power worked through surveillance, institutions, and direct discipline. Deleuze (1992) argued that we have since entered *"societies of control,"* where power seeps into the flows of everyday life, coded into access points, passwords, and algorithms. Han (2017) extends this further into *psychopolitics*: control that no longer needs to repress us externally, because we willingly govern ourselves under the imperative of self-optimization.

In this landscape, power no longer feels like coercion but like design. The interface itself—the feed, the scroll, the push notification—becomes the mechanism of governance. The new panopticon is not a prison we resist but a user experience we embrace. Dissent is not silenced directly: it is buried beneath torrents of noise, trivialized by distraction, or reframed by the logic of virality. Power now hides in plain sight, moving with the grain of convenience. If this is the landscape, then liberation cannot mean escape from technology but the cultivation of practices that make us unprogrammable.

TOWARD LIBERATION

Liberation does not come from abandoning technology. It is already inseparable from modern life. To withdraw entirely would be to hand over power to corporations and governments, leaving citizens without agency. The task, then, is not escape but transformation: reclaiming attention, demanding accountability, and building tools that serve human flourishing instead of control or profit.

On the personal level, attention must be treated as sacred infrastructure. Just as clean air and safe water demand protection, so too must the habitat of the mind be defended. This can mean fasting from feeds, adopting slower media diets, and rooting ourselves in embodied anchors such as meditation, breath, and time in nature. Even small acts of resistance, like disabling autoplay or muting notifications, can interrupt the loops designed to consume us.

Freedom depends on flexibility. No single platform or ideology should dictate how we see the world. We strengthen freedom by testing ideas against one another, holding beliefs lightly, and seeking out perspectives that challenge us. The aim is not certainty but clarity: the capacity to recognize when information tries to capture our identity or emotions, and the strength to resist being swept along by the viral tide.

Liberation is never solitary. Truth and meaning endure through shared practices. Communities of verification, small groups bound by norms of truth-seeking, offer spaces where trust can be rebuilt. From there, larger structures must take shape. Civic data trusts could collectivize ownership of information and set boundaries on its use; and public-interest information systems, open to transparency and audit, could serve as democratic infrastructure rather than remain at the mercy of corporate discretion. Still, even these steps fall short without institutional reform. Real change requires dismantling monopolies, enforcing interoperability, abolishing surveillance advertising, and funding public, non-profit platforms that are genuinely governed in the public interest.

Change emerges through accumulation, not isolation. A reclaimed minute of attention, a narrative set in context, a community committed to truth—all of these counterbalance manufactured reality. None is sufficient on its own, but in combination they build momentum against the empire of the feed.

At its deepest level, liberation is lucid presence. It is not abstinence from technology but sovereign use of it: the courage to sit in silence, to question the frame, to refuse compulsory visibility, and to cultivate inner independence against the most sophisticated machinery of influence ever assembled.

To see clearly is to live freely. To live freely is to become *unprogrammable.*

If media is the civic theater, influencers and gurus now occupy its center stage. Attention functions as a kind of sacrament, and those who master the spectacle feed on devotion disguised as *"followers."* The ministry of narrative has become a marketplace of souls, where even spirituality is packaged, branded, and sold. From manufactured reality emerges its most insidious offspring: the commodification of the sacred.

REFERENCES

Andrejevic, M. (2013). Infoglut: How too much information is changing the way we think and know. Routledge.

Bennett, W. L. (1990). Toward a theory of press–state relations in the United States. Journal of Communication, 40(2), 103–125. https://doi.org/10.1111/j.1460-2466.1990.tb02265.x

Berger, P. L., & Luckmann, T. (1966). The social construction of reality: A treatise in the sociology of knowledge. Anchor Books.

Butler, J. (1990). Gender trouble: Feminism and the subversion of identity. Routledge.

Carr, N. (2010). The shallows: What the Internet is doing to our brains. W. W. Norton.

Chomsky, N., & Herman, E. S. (1988). Manufacturing consent: The political economy of the mass media. Pantheon Books.

Courtwright, D. T. (2019). The age of addiction: How bad habits became big business. Belknap Press.

Couldry, N., & Mejias, U. A. (2019). The costs of connection: How data is colonizing human life and appropriating it for capitalism. Stanford University Press.

Deleuze, G. (1992). Postscript on the societies of control. October, 59, 3–7. https://doi.org/10.2307/778828

Entman, R. M. (1993). Framing: Toward clarification of a fractured paradigm. Journal of Communication, 43(4), 51–58. https://doi.org/10.1111/j.1460-2466.1993.tb01304.x

Fogg, B. J. (2009). A behavior model for persuasive design. In Proceedings of the 4th International Conference on Persuasive Technology (pp. 1–7). ACM. https://doi.org/10.1145/1541948.1541999

Foucault, M. (1977). Discipline and punish: The birth of the prison (A. Sheridan, Trans.). Pantheon Books.

Goffman, E. (1959). The presentation of self in everyday life. Anchor Books.

Hallin, D. C. (1986). The uncensored war: The media and Vietnam. Oxford University Press.

Han, B.-C. (2017). Psychopolitics: Neoliberalism and new technologies of power (E. Butler, Trans.). Verso.

Harris, T. (2017). How a handful of tech companies control billions of minds every day [Video]. TED. https://www.ted.com/talks/tristan_harris_how_a_handful_of_tech_companies_control_billions_of_minds_every_day

Kahneman, D. (2011). Thinking, fast and slow. Farrar, Straus and Giroux.

Lakoff, G. (2004). Don't think of an elephant!: Know your values and frame the debate. Chelsea Green.

Lembke, A. (2021). Dopamine nation: Finding balance in the age of indulgence. Dutton.

Levitin, D. J. (2014). The organized mind: Thinking straight in the age of information overload. Dutton.

Lippmann, W. (1922). Public opinion. Harcourt, Brace and Company.

McLuhan, M. (1964). Understanding media: The extensions of man. McGraw-Hill.

Nora, P. (1989). Between memory and history: Les lieux de mémoire. Representations, 26, 7–24. https://doi.org/10.2307/2928520

Newport, C. (2019). Digital minimalism: Choosing a focused life in a noisy world. Portfolio.

Oreskes, N., & Conway, E. M. (2010). Merchants of doubt: How a handful of scientists obscured the truth on issues from tobacco smoke to global warming. Bloomsbury.

Pariser, E. (2011). The filter bubble: What the Internet is hiding from you. Penguin Press.

Rosen, J. (1999). What are journalists for? Yale University Press.

Srnicek, N. (2016). Platform capitalism. Polity.

Sunstein, C. R. (2017). #Republic: Divided democracy in the age of social media. Princeton University Press.

Turkle, S. (2011). Alone together: Why we expect more from technology and less from each other. Basic Books.

Tufekci, Z. (2018, March 10). YouTube, the great radicalizer. The New York Times.
https://www.nytimes.com/2018/03/10/opinion/sunday/youtube-politics-radical.html

Vosoughi, S., Roy, D., & Aral, S. (2018). The spread of true and false news online. Science, 359(6380), 1146–1151. https://doi.org/10.1126/science.aap9559

Chapter 9

Spiritual Branding and the Rise of the Digital Guru

*"The game is not about becoming somebody,
it's about becoming nobody."*
— Ram Dass

Once, seekers turned to caves, forests, monasteries, and deserts to encounter the sacred. Today, those same longings for belonging, meaning, and transformation are channeled through screens and infinite scrolls. Spirituality now arrives not through pilgrimage or whispered transmission but through hashtags, livestreams, and platform recommendations. The sacred has not vanished: it has been digitized, aestheticized, and monetized.

What happens when practices meant to dissolve the ego are repurposed as tools for visibility? When teachings intended to dismantle identity are sold as upgrades to a personal brand? The collision of ancient longing with digital platforms produces a strange hybrid: an economy of awakening optimized not for depth but for engagement.

This chapter interrogates that paradox and the rise of a new priestly class: digital gurus, wellness influencers, and life coaches who promise transformation while fostering dependency. I explore the psychological, sociological, economic, and technological mechanisms that turn transcendence into "content," insight into "IP," and community into "audience." I also outline a different path, one free from monetization, rooted in genuine relationships, shaped by silence and service, and resistant to the pressures of platform capitalism.

THE CORPORATE CAPTURE OF THE INFINITE

The capture of the sacred is no longer bound to temples or churches. It drifts through digital realms and New Age sanctuaries, where ancient patterns of control return, draped now in softer light and dressed in finer robes. Charisma wears the mask of revelation, and purity becomes a glow that decides who is radiant enough to belong. Scapegoats are cast out not in anger but in the gentle tones of *"discernment,"* while the toll of exploitation is hidden in the language of *empowerment*, whispered as though enlightenment itself demanded payment.

Platforms of engineered control amplify certainty, charisma, and outrage, not nuance, integration, or humility. The result is an attention-economy priesthood optimized for virality rather than wisdom. *"Spiritual influencers"* become the new clergy, constructing cultic micro-worlds clothed in the language of healing but often unresolved in their own trauma.

Genuine teachers and communities do exist. What is needed is discernment. Incense or Instagram makes no difference. The real question is whether a path leads one back to awareness, or binds one to an identity, a brand, or a leader.

We live in a civilization where identity is financialized and visibility functions as moral currency. In such a climate, spirituality, once an intimate, unsettling, and often solitary confrontation with *Ultimate Reality*, has been reconfigured as lifestyle, aesthetic, and brand. Platforms elevate the palatable and suppress the difficult. The image of awakening replaces the process of awakening. The result is a paradox: a world saturated with spiritual content yet starved for spiritual depth.

THE AESTHETICIZATION OF AWAKENING

The attention economy thrives on ease and speed. What were once complex teachings are now compressed into striking images, catchy slogans, and bite-sized "secrets of transcendence." Online, people no longer just live their lives but present polished, filtered versions of themselves that feel more like staged copies than the real thing. Even the *"spiritual self"* turns into performance, a theater of transcendence measured less by inner change than by clicks, likes, and followers.

Platforms such as Instagram, YouTube, and TikTok function as shrines of the screen that favor spectacle, repetition, and certainty. In this economy of images, aesthetic coherence is mistaken for ontological coherence, as if a manufactured surface guaranteed depth. The influencer's grid becomes a catechism, where the "sacred" is packaged, polished, and monetized.

Yet the sacred has historically been the opposite of consumable. The numinous unsettles, disorients, and destabilizes. Authentic awakening rarely flatters egoic fantasies. It is a disclosure, not a product; a dismantling, not a strategy. It emerges less from content than from contact: with silence and nature, with others, and with the mysterious depth of one's own being.

INFLUENCERS AND SPIRITUAL ENTREPRENEURS

In the vacuum left by declining religious authority and growing distrust of political institutions, a new class of gatekeepers has arisen. Charismatic figures promise empowerment, sovereignty, and healing. They speak the language of liberation while often reproducing the same power dynamics and dependency loops as the hierarchies they replace.

Their offer is seductive: You are the problem, but I am the solution, available in e-course, mastermind, subscription, or retreat format. This market is built on the idea that everything is your responsibility: problems are made personal, solutions are left to the individual, and larger forces such as trauma, injustice, and exploitation are brushed aside. If you do not improve, the fault is said to lie in your mindset or even your *"vibration."*

The self-help world, once a mix of shared wisdom and community experiments, has been taken over by market logic. Vulnerability is turned into a sales tactic, and confession into a growth strategy. Audiences are taught to confuse intimacy with monetization and authenticity with carefully staged exposure.

HOW PLATFORMS CONDITION CONSCIOUSNESS

Platforms are not neutral technologies, but machines built to shape behavior. They reward speed, novelty, emotional intensity, and tribal alignment. Within this environment, the spiritual entrepreneur feels constant pressure to deliver: ever more transformative claims, ever clearer narratives of certainty, ever more polished performances of presence.

What emerges is a self-reinforcing loop. First comes the promise: the assertion that a particular method, medicine, or mindset will unlock transformation. Then comes the proof: testimonials, before-and-after narratives, quantified self-reports, and glossy images of integration. The next step is the purchase: high-ticket offers framed not merely as services but as demonstrations of one's commitment and self-worth.

When transformation fails to arrive, the cycle turns inward. The blame is shifted onto the seekers, who are told they lacked faith, discipline, or vibrational alignment. And so the process is perpetuated. The next tier, the next program, the next version of "you" is dangled as the true solution.

In the machine's endless ritual, attention turns into devotion, data into confession, and the cycle continues: scroll, click, like, buy, repeat.

SPIRITUAL MATERIALISM IN THE AGE OF THE NEOLIBERAL SELF

More than fifty years ago, Chögyam Trungpa, a Tibetan Buddhist teacher, warned of what he called *"spiritual materialism"*: the ego's tendency to use spirituality as fuel for its own reinforcement. Half a century later, that tendency has been platformized, scaled, and venture-funded. Spirituality is now filtered through what scholars call the *neoliberal self*, a way of being in which a person views the self as a project or enterprise: endlessly optimizing, perpetually responsible for their own success or failure, and always just short of being enough.

Within this framework, the spiritual marketplace thrives. Its logic is circular: you are always incomplete, but completion is always purchasable. Each new product or program constructs the very lack it promises to resolve. What was once a spiritual path—lifelong, relational, rooted in community—becomes a subscription to an identity of perpetual self-improvement, where growth itself is consumed as a lifestyle accessory.

PSYCHEDELICS, PLANT MEDICINES,
AND THE PACKAGING OF THE SACRED

The renaissance of psychedelics and plant medicines often promises democratized healing and decolonized knowledge. Yet, in practice, these fields risk repeating colonial dynamics: extraction of Indigenous wisdom without reciprocity, commercialization of ritual, and fetishization of the exotic Other. The rhetoric of liberation too easily obscures the persistence of power imbalances, where global North seekers consume the traditions of the global South, and where ancestral practices are stripped of their contexts to serve as consumable *"technologies of the self."*

Ayahuasca tourism, ketamine clinics marketed as *"biohacking the soul,"* and corporate psychedelic ventures illustrate a troubling convergence of psychospiritual need and market capture. Wellness becomes a luxury good, priced in retreat packages, subscription models, and VIP tiers of access. Promises of "safe, clinical" experiences often flatten the messy, communal, and relational aspects of these medicines into standardized protocols designed for scalability. What was once sacred ceremony becomes lifestyle brand.

The psychedelic experience is then packaged and sold as a premium event: guaranteed breakthroughs, selfie-friendly retreats, professional "integration coaches" with minimal training, and a proliferation of venture-backed start-ups promising clinical-grade transcendence. In this logic, transcendence is no longer a mystery to be approached with humility but a product to be purchased with capital. For the market, healing only matters if it can be turned into a product, optimized, branded, and sold back to the very people it claims to liberate. What gets lost is the very heart of these practices: reciprocity, humility, and a recognition that the sacred cannot be manufactured on demand.

THE SHADOW SIDE

The New Age movement often promises empowerment but quietly breeds dependency. What begins as an invitation to "trust your inner knowing" can calcify into a closed loop where doubt is cast as ego, resistance, or low vibration. Within this logic, failed manifestations are blamed on insufficient belief, turning every question into sabotage and every disappointment into proof of immaturity. What first appears as empowerment gradually slides into gaslighting.

Language itself plays a central role. Terms like *vibrations, quantum healing, soul contracts, downloads,* and *activations* shimmer with emotional power while remaining vague or scientifically ungrounded. This vagueness is not a weakness but a function: it allows any outcome to be justified after the fact, while critiques are dismissed as *"3D thinking."* The effect is awe without clarity, compliance in place of genuine understanding.

Platitudes deepen the trap. *"Everything happens for a reason." "Your trauma is your teacher." "Choose a higher vibration."* These sayings can offer comfort but often silence pain. *Spiritual bypassing* substitutes metaphysical explanations for real healing, trading the slow labor of processing grief for the promise of premature transcendence. Behind the polished mask of positivity, trauma remains unhealed, shame intensifies, and isolation grows.

At the same time, the marketplace of enlightenment thrives. Some leaders claim to have transcended ego while demanding obedience, reverence, and money. If you question them, it is taken as a sign you are not ready, and real conversation is replaced by charm and rigid belief. The teacher's image becomes the brand, the brand becomes the teaching, and the teaching becomes the business model. *"Invest in yourself"* turns into the moral command of the age. Abundance teachings slide into coercive upsells—*If you really believed, you would buy the platinum package.* When results fail to appear, the fault is pinned not on the system or the teacher but on the seekers, who are told they lacked faith, alignment, or discipline. The self becomes both the problem and the product, while exploitation is reframed as growth.

In the platform realm, dependency is engineered with precision. Scarcity tactics—limited spots, countdown timers, expiring bonuses—manufacture spiritual urgency. Tiered access ensures the "real" knowledge is always promised in the next course, the inner circle, or the VIP mastermind. Transformation recedes into an endless horizon: always one upgrade away. Meanwhile, seekers are encouraged to perform gratitude and breakthroughs publicly, feeding both in-group belonging and the guru's marketing machine.

These dynamics rely on familiar psychological levers. Breakthroughs arrive unpredictably, creating cycles of intermittent reinforcement. Failures are consistently reframed as the seeker's fault. Over time, this produces something akin to learned helplessness.

BEYOND MARKETED SACREDNESS

When spirituality is individualized and commercialized, its political force is blunted. Structural injustice is reframed as *"collective karma,"* while calls for reform are dismissed as *"low frequency"* or *"duality consciousness."* In this reframing, suffering is privatized and healing recast as a solitary responsibility. As bonds of solidarity weaken, people gather less as communities of action and more as audiences, drawn into one-sided ties that mimic intimacy without reciprocity. Shared rites of passage are replaced by retreats for the privileged, while the common good is steadily absorbed into the logic of the brand. What could serve as a space for collective awakening is instead reduced to a program of private optimization.

Reclaiming the sacred from spectacle requires discernment. Certain patterns reliably reveal when spiritual branding masquerades as liberation. Reach without depth is one warning sign: messages that spread virally but collapse under dialogue. Another is the use of metaphysics to justify price, as in the claim that *"if you cannot afford this, it is your scarcity mindset."* Mature traditions welcome critique, but unhealthy ones pathologize it. Trauma described only in terms of "energy" or "vibrations" signals avoidance, not healing. Cultural extraction is another red flag, when Indigenous or esoteric traditions are monetized without reciprocity. Equally troubling are teachings that sell new identities, shiny replacements rather than authentic dismantling of ego. Finally, accountability matters: teachers who answer only to themselves are especially prone to egoic inflation and abuse.

If commercialized spirituality hollows out meaning, what might a post-brand, post-influencer spiritual life look like? At its heart is a shift in orientation: relationship matters more than presentation, process more than product, and depth more than reach. Such a life begins with attention through silence, solitude, and slowness. In an age when attention is relentlessly monetized, stillness becomes countercultural and slowness an act of resistance. These spaces allow the psyche to process what platforms endlessly stir up.

From here, spirituality turns back toward community. Audiences give way to circles of reciprocity such as peer-led gatherings, mutual aid networks, and gift economies, where accountability replaces charisma, facilitation softens domination, and leadership is shared. Healing unfolds within this fabric, informed by trauma and attentive to systems, recognizing that suffering is never only personal but also political. Pain is not an *"alignment error"* but the echo of histories carried in bodies that deserve care.

The orientation then shifts from optimization to resonance. Sociologist Hartmut Rosa describes resonance as a felt connection with the world, an antidote to acceleration that cannot be bought, programmed, or forced. At its best, practice is not optimization but relationship, not a *key performance indicator* (KPI), but a conversation with life itself.

From these foundations, practices of de-branding the self naturally follow: regular breaks from screens and online platforms that reveal who we are outside the mask, shadow work that creates space for grief and anger without pathologizing them, embodied inquiry that steadies the nervous system, and critical literacy that protects against manipulation. Service becomes a quiet act of care, giving without posting and letting anonymity itself be medicine, while reciprocity grounds the work in responsibility to the traditions and communities that sustain it.

IN A WORLD OF MIRRORS, AUTHENTICITY IS REVOLUTIONARY

To wake up in an age of spiritual branding is to resist the temptation to turn the sacred into content, the self into a persona, and healing into a transaction. It is to reclaim the slow, relational, embodied work of becoming human. It also means confronting the lures of certainty, charisma, and convenience, and instead choosing the harder path of deconstruction, humility, and integration.

Authenticity is not a brand, healing cannot be industrialized, and truth cannot be packaged. The task ahead is to rebuild practices that cannot be turned into trends and that ask for more than belief: they call for courage, patience, and love.

The theater of control does not stop with spirit. The same tools of fear, repetition, and consensus programming now reach into the very story of the planet itself. Climate change, urgent, real, and complex, has been weaponized as a script to mobilize guilt, obedience, and top-down authority. From the influencer's stage we move into the planetary pulpit, where fear of apocalypse becomes the ultimate lever.

REFERENCES

Dass, R. (1971). Be here now. Lama Foundation.

Labate, B., & Cavnar, C. (Eds.). (2014). Ayahuasca shamanism in the Amazon and beyond. Oxford University Press.

Masters, R. A. (2010). Spiritual bypassing: When spirituality disconnects us from what really matters. North Atlantic Books.

Maté, G. (2022). The myth of normal: Trauma, illness, and healing in a toxic culture. Avery.

Pollan, M. (2018). How to change your mind. Penguin.

Purser, R. (2019). McMindfulness: How mindfulness became the new capitalist spirituality. Repeater Books.

Rosa, H. (2019). Resonance: A sociology of our relationship to the world. Polity Press.

Rose, N. (2021). Psychedelics as a new technology of the self. Frontiers in Psychology, 12, 632281. https://doi.org/10.3389/fpsyg.2021.632281

Seligman, M. E. P. (1975). Helplessness: On depression, development, and death. W. H. Freeman.

Skinner, B. F. (1953). Science and human behavior. Macmillan.

Trungpa, C. (1973). Cutting through spiritual materialism. Shambhala.

van der Kolk, B. (2014). The body keeps the score: Brain, mind, and body in the healing of trauma. Viking.

Wu, T. (2016). The attention merchants: The epic scramble to get inside our heads. Knopf.

Chapter 10

The Climate Script: Science, Fear, and the Globalist Agenda

"Power is in tearing human minds to pieces and putting them together again in new shapes of your own choosing."
— George Orwell

Climate change is real. It is not a partisan fantasy or the hallucination of alarmists. The evidence is etched into the planet itself: atmospheric CO_2 has climbed from about 280 parts per million (ppm) before the industrial age to more than 420 ppm today, levels not seen for millions of years according to the UN's *Intergovernmental Panel on Climate Change* (IPCC, 2021). As the planet warms, glaciers retreat and the vast ice sheets of Greenland and Antarctica shed mass at accelerating rates, even though local weather patterns can still cause thickening in some places (Shepherd et al., 2018; IMBIE Team, 2018). The oceans, in turn, absorb much of this excess carbon, growing more acidic and leaving ecosystems under strain (Doney et al., 2009). Furthermore, NASA scientists report that the last decade has been the hottest since recordkeeping began (2020), a trend that has fueled the disappearance of species at rates not seen in millennia (Ceballos et al., 2017) and driven extreme weather to become more frequent, less predictable, and more destructive (Coumou & Rahmstorf, 2012).

However, perspective is essential here. Temperatures on Earth have risen and fallen for billions of years, long before human industry existed. Paleoclimate data reveal vast fluctuations: ice ages driven by orbital shifts (Milankovitch cycles), warm "hothouse" periods where crocodiles thrived in the Arctic, and abrupt cooling events tied to geomagnetic and solar variability (Huybers, 2007; Bard & Frank, 2006). The Earth's magnetic field and solar cycles still influence atmospheric and oceanic circulation today, complicating simple narratives of linear causality.

We must be careful not to collapse this deep history into slogans. The human fingerprint on the climate is real—e.g., fossil fuel combustion, deforestation, and industrial agriculture—but it is layered atop planetary rhythms that dwarf human timescales. Recognizing this does not excuse inaction, but grounds us in humility.

Carbon is often cast as the villain of the modern age, yet it is far more than a pollutant. It is the very backbone of life. Every breath, every plant, every forest depends upon it. Elevated CO_2, within limits, stimulates plant growth: this is what ecologists call the "*CO_2 fertilization effect*" (Donohue et al., 2013). Indeed, satellite observations confirm that Earth's "*greening*" in recent decades is partly due to higher CO_2 levels boosting photosynthesis worldwide (Zhu et al., 2016). This nuance rarely enters public discourse, flattened into moral binaries of virtue and vice.

To deny climate change outright is to reject converging evidence. To accept it blindly, without nuance or memory of Earth's cycles, is to walk into the next cage of control.

APOCALYPSE AS A MANAGEMENT STRATEGY

Fear has always been the most efficient technology of control. Medieval churches mobilized plague, fire, and famine into narratives of divine punishment. People who feared eternal damnation became pliable, willing to buy indulgences and obey decrees. Climate catastrophe plays a parallel role in our age: a script of looming apocalypse that positions global institutions as the guardians of survival.

The infamous *World Economic Forum* (WEF) phrase, *"You will own nothing and be happy"* (Schwab, 2020), reads less like futurist prophecy than behavioral conditioning, a mantra created to normalize dependency in the name of planetary survival. Such messaging shifts the focus from collective flourishing to managed austerity.

Meanwhile, citizens are bombarded with small-scale moral rules, where everyday choices are treated as verdicts on one's virtue: a plastic straw becomes a weapon against the Earth, a meal with meat is framed as planetary violence, and a household's "footprint" is cast as a permanent stain of guilt. Such framing reduces global problems like industrial pollution and fossil fuel dependence to the language of personal sin. The result is not ecological restoration but domestication (Büchs & Schnepf, 2013). Shame takes the place of agency, guilt substitutes for creativity, and citizens are recast as penitents in a secular religion, offered absolution not by priests but by policymakers, philanthropists, and CEOs, many of whom continue expanding fossil fuel operations while preaching restraint.

The outcome is a theater of fear, where personal habits are moralized while structural contradictions—e.g., resource wars, subsidies for oil, and deforestation for global trade—remain untouched. Such disparity leads to the next act: hypocrisy, elevated to ritual.

HYPOCRISY AS RITUAL

Imagine the WEF in Davos: fleets of private jets descending into Swiss valleys, chauffeurs waiting in long rows of black cars idling outside heated glass halls, where billionaires and politicians deliver grave speeches about reducing emissions. The hypocrisy is so open it feels like performance art. Yet perhaps that is the point. Spectacle becomes pedagogy: the public sees the double standard and learns, consciously or not, that hierarchy is natural, even when cloaked in moral rhetoric.

In this system, hypocrisy is not failure but ritual. It is performative, deliberate, and almost liturgical. It demonstrates hierarchy and reinforces obedience. The elites are exempt from the rules they impose on others, their excesses reframed as necessity, their indulgence disguised as "essential diplomacy." Just as medieval clergy lived in palaces while selling indulgences, today's climate preachers purchase offsets (Green, 2010), essentially paying someone else to cut emissions so they can continue polluting while projecting moral leadership. Offsets are the new indulgences: money exchanged for moral cover, pollution transformed into paperwork, and virtue handed over to accountants.

Meanwhile, the public is urged to travel less, consume less, and expect less. Airline passengers are shamed while world leaders fly in on fleets of private jets, and working families are told to downsize their cars or even change their diets while executives feast on luxury steaks flown in from across the globe. In this framing, scarcity is no longer the result of mismanagement or exploitative economics but is recast as a moral imperative. Poverty is presented as virtue, abstinence as righteousness, and resignation as ecological wisdom, until submission to austerity itself is equated with loyalty to the planet.

The performative nature of this hypocrisy is crucial. It is not accidental dissonance, but pedagogy through contrast. By displaying immunity from their own decrees, elites draw a boundary between rulers and ruled, the virtuous and the managed. The ritual of hypocrisy becomes a way of naturalizing inequality: their freedom underscores your restriction, and their abundance defines your scarcity.

But hypocrisy alone cannot sustain belief. Ritual must be dramatized by narrative. It requires prophets to narrate the future and institutions to sanctify the rules.

AL GORE AND THE UN CLIMATE SCRIPT

Every religion required prophets. Climate politics found one in Al Gore. His 2006 film *An Inconvenient Truth* was less documentary than sermon: apocalyptic slides delivered with evangelical cadence, his voice rising and falling like a preacher warning of eternal fire. The imagery was carefully chosen: polar bears stranded on melting ice floes, flooded cities, and maps of catastrophe. Gore was crowned prophet of planetary salvation and awarded the Nobel Prize alongside the IPCC. He embodied a new priestly archetype: the secular prophet of climate apocalypse.

Yet Gore's role revealed the machinery beneath. As US Vice President, his ties to energy, finance, and defense industries hardly marked him as an ecological ascetic. His post-political career further demonstrated the duality. He cast himself as a global conscience while investing in carbon-trading schemes that promised massive returns (Klein, 2014), emerging as both prophet to the masses and profiteer among peers, the embodiment of climate elites: preaching restraint to the poor while speculating for the rich.

The UN, meanwhile, offered the cathedral. Institutions like the IPCC and the UN *Framework Convention on Climate Change* (UNFCCC) provided not only scientific assessments but the ritualized stagecraft of annual climate summits. Within these forums, cautious scientific probabilities were translated into political decrees, then into media slogans. The "consensus" invoked by politicians emerged not solely from laboratories but from diplomatic negotiation, where science was blended with strategy, compromise, and spin.

The choreography was striking. Planetary fear became justification for transnational governance: carbon markets, international treaties, and surveillance-based accounting. Like the medieval Church, divine mysteries were converted into obligations, indulgences, and obedience. The fire was no longer eternal but planetary, and the saviors were no longer saints but technocrats.

Still, emissions continued to rise. Neither Gore nor the UN bent the global trajectory. The atmosphere did not conform to their narratives. But the script endured, not because it altered physics but because it altered psychology. A managed population was more valuable than a managed climate. The masses were trained to live under a permanent state of managed fear.

BETWEEN SCIENCE AND PROPAGANDA

The tragedy of this staging is that real ecological crises are drowned in theater. Coral reefs bleaching (Hughes et al., 2017), pollinators collapsing (Potts et al., 2010), and rivers poisoned by industrial effluent: these are tangible problems with practical solutions. They require creativity at the community level, technological ingenuity adapted to local needs, and international cooperation at pragmatic scales. They are solvable, but they lack the apocalyptic drama that fuels political control and corporate profit.

Instead, these crises are overshadowed by spectacle: the drumbeat of countdown clocks, Hollywood disaster montages, slogans of "twenty years left." Fear of the *"end of the world"* numbs imagination, making populations easier to manage but less capable of repair. The theater paralyzes rather than mobilizes.

Fear builds in levels, spreading easily and repeating itself without effort. It is amplified by engines of code intended to reward outrage, monetized by media corporations chasing attention, and weaponized by politics that thrive on crisis (O'Neill & Nicholson-Cole, 2009). In contrast, love for the living world does not spread so neatly. It requires intimacy, care, and context. Fear generates clicks, votes, and compliance, while reverence fosters responsibility but rarely profit.

The gap thus widens between urgent, concrete ecological work and abstract planetary panic. Into that gap slips a new economy of control, organized not around living systems but around the measurement and monetization of carbon.

CONTROL THROUGH CARBON

Fear softens the psyche and measurement hardens control. In the age of climate politics, the unit of control is not sin but carbon.

A molecule essential to life is reframed as pollutant, guilt-marker, and the currency of the century (Anderson & Peters, 2016). In this narrative, carbon is treated as toxic, measurable, and taxable. It is counted, traded, balanced on paper, and turned into a product. Financial markets now auction redemption through "credits," while industries create elaborate rituals of ecological salvation (Bumpus & Liverman, 2008). Carbon becomes the Eucharist of a new religion: consumed symbolically, measured obsessively, and traded without end.

But the most radical danger is not financial: it is technological. To tax or ration emissions, they must first be tracked. And tracking requires infrastructure. Smart meters installed in homes monitor daily consumption. *Digital identity cards* (IDs) linked to energy use are proposed as a way to ensure accountability. Plans for *"personal carbon allowances"* (Fawcett, 2010) imagine every purchase, trip, or meal being logged, scored, and restricted. What begins as environmental accounting ends up as *social engineering.*

Here austerity masquerades as morality. Farmers restricted from fertilizer use may emit less in a year than one billionaire's private jet in an afternoon. Yet it is the farmer, not the jet-setter, who faces penalties (Altieri & Nicholls, 2017). This asymmetry reveals the deeper ambition: not sustainability, but restructuring economies around centralized authority.

The WEF's *"Great Reset"* is not simply sustainability branding but a blueprint for consolidation (Schwab & Malleret, 2020). *Environmental, Social and Governance* (ESG) frameworks reward compliant corporations and punish dissenters (Bennett et al., 2021). Large firms greenwash and prosper, while small farmers, artisans, and innovators suffocate under compliance regimes they cannot afford. The new morality is indexed, audited, and monetized.

And if measuring and taxing carbon proves insufficient, the next frontier beckons: re-engineering the planet itself.

THE GEOENGINEERING TEMPTATION

When fear grows, hubris follows. If emissions cuts are too slow, perhaps the sky itself can be re-engineered (Caldeira et al., 2013). The proposals verge on science fiction: aerosols injected into the stratosphere to dim the sun, iron dumped into oceans to stimulate plankton blooms, nanoparticles engineered to scatter light, and orbiting space mirrors deployed to deflect radiation (Crutzen, 2006). What once sounded like dystopian imagination now appears in scientific journals and government reports. Pilot projects have already begun (Keith et al., 2016).

Among the most prominent champions of this path is Bill Gates. Through his foundation and personal investments, Gates has funded research into solar *geoengineering,* including *Harvard's Stratospheric Controlled Perturbation Experiment* (SCoPEx), a project conceived to test the release of reflective particles into the upper atmosphere to mimic volcanic cooling effects. Gates is not alone but his role is emblematic of immense private wealth driving planetary scale experiments with little democratic oversight. He presents this as pragmatic philanthropy, an insurance policy against climate failure. Critics see it as a disturbing concentration of power, where a billionaire can bankroll experiments that affect the global common good (Keith & Irvine, 2016).

Critics such as Dane Wigington (2017) argue that geoengineering has already been a covert reality since the post-war era, with clandestine aerosol programs carried out beyond public debate. Mainstream science disputes these claims, yet secrecy itself breeds suspicion. The very fact that geoengineering discussions often occur behind closed doors, with limited public consultation, deepens mistrust.

The toxicity of the elements proposed for such schemes is rarely addressed in public forums. Sulfates, introduced to mimic volcanic cooling, could acidify rainfall and damage crops, while aluminum particulates suggested as reflective agents have been linked to neurological and respiratory disorders. Even more concerning are engineered nanoparticles, small enough to slip into lungs and bloodstreams and disruptive enough to threaten soil fertility, aquatic ecologies, and pollinators. To alter the sky with such compounds is not a neutral technical fix but a gamble with cascading toxicological consequences that could endure long after any cooling effect fades.

The mindset behind geoengineering is obvious: it refuses humility and keeps chasing control. Earth systems are nonlinear, adaptive, and deeply interdependent (Lenton, 2011). Manipulating them without unintended consequences is improbable, perhaps impossible. Still, fear renders populations receptive. If apocalypse is imminent, any intervention feels preferable to inaction.

SOLUTIONS BEYOND FEAR AND CONTROL

Take away the propaganda and the truth is simple: ecosystems are breaking under pressure. Soils are losing their richness, oceans are being emptied of life, and forests continue to fall (Steffen et al., 2015). Carbon is part of the crisis, but the deeper wound is our disconnection from the Earth, from each other, and from our own awareness.

True resilience often comes from below: communities adapting, innovating, and cultivating reciprocity (Ostrom, 1990). Decentralized energy grids, regenerative farming, permaculture, and food sovereignty resist elite capture because they are rooted in place and culture. These practices draw strength not from fear of collapse but from reverence for life.

Fear can stir people to act, but only reverence can sustain that action. Awareness rooted in fear leads to compliance, while awareness rooted in reverence leads to care (Keltner & Haidt, 2003). Reverence asks for restraint not as punishment, but as an expression of devotion.

Scarcity has always been the story of elites to preserve hierarchy. Sufficiency, by contrast, means enough for all, cultivated through cooperation (Eisler, 1987). Community-based economies, cooperatives, and peer-to-peer networks embody this principle and challenge centralized systems of exploitation.

To resist apocalyptic propaganda is not to deny science, but to refuse its weaponization. Conscious disobedience means rejecting digital surveillance while embracing genuine ecological care, and rejecting geoengineering while practicing regenerative design.

The crisis is real, and so is the propaganda. To deny either is to stay trapped. What we need is discernment: the ability to see evidence clearly, to remember Earth's deeper rhythms, and to respond with freedom.

The awakened human listens deeper: to Earth, to body, and to consciousness. In that listening, fear dissolves, propaganda loses grip, and a new possibility emerges: ecological freedom, beyond fear and beyond control.

Even in the most intimate realm, in the way we love, bond, and reproduce, the programming continues. The myth of monogamy is written not as natural law but as cultural script, crafted to regulate desire, inheritance, and allegiance. Just as fear is used to govern nations and guilt to govern souls, the politics of intimacy govern desire. From the global script of climate to the private script of love, the *Matrix* reaches all the way into our beds.

REFERENCES

Altieri, M. A., & Nicholls, C. I. (2017). The adaptation and mitigation potential of traditional agriculture in a changing climate. Climatic Change, 140(1), 33–45. https://doi.org/10.1007/s10584-013-0909-y

Anderson, K., & Peters, G. (2016). The trouble with negative emissions. Science, 354(6309), 182–183. https://doi.org/10.1126/science.aah4567

Bard, E., & Frank, M. (2006). Climate change and solar variability: What's new under the sun? Earth and Planetary Science Letters, 248(1–2), 1–14. https://doi.org/10.1016/j.epsl.2006.06.016

Bennett, B., Chetty, R., Hall, J., & Kraus, W. (2021). ESG investing: Practices, progress and challenges. Journal of Applied Corporate Finance, 33(2), 8–22. https://doi.org/10.1111/jacf.12479

Büchs, M., & Schnepf, S. V. (2013). Who emits most? Associations between socio-economic factors and UK households' home energy, transport, indirect and total CO_2 emissions. Ecological Economics, 90, 114–123. https://doi.org/10.1016/j.ecolecon.2013.03.007

Bumpus, A. G., & Liverman, D. M. (2008). Accumulation by decarbonization and the governance of carbon offsets. Economic

Geography, 84(2), 127–155. https://doi.org/10.1111/j.1944-8287.2008.tb00401.x

Caldeira, K., Bala, G., & Cao, L. (2013). The science of geoengineering. Annual Review of Earth and Planetary Sciences, 41, 231–256. https://doi.org/10.1146/annurev-earth-042711-105548

Ceballos, G., Ehrlich, P. R., & Dirzo, R. (2017). Biological annihilation via the ongoing sixth mass extinction signaled by vertebrate population losses and declines. Proceedings of the National Academy of Sciences, 114(30), E6089–E6096. https://doi.org/10.1073/pnas.1704949114

Coumou, D., & Rahmstorf, S. (2012). A decade of weather extremes. Nature Climate Change, 2(7), 491–496. https://doi.org/10.1038/nclimate1452

Crutzen, P. J. (2006). Albedo enhancement by stratospheric sulfur injections: A contribution to resolve a policy dilemma? Climatic Change, 77(3–4), 211–220. https://doi.org/10.1007/s10584-006-9101-y

Donohue, R. J., Roderick, M. L., McVicar, T. R., & Farquhar, G. D. (2013). Impact of CO_2 fertilization on maximum foliage cover across the globe's warm, arid environments. Geophysical Research Letters, 40(12), 3031–3035. https://doi.org/10.1002/grl.50563

Doney, S. C., Fabry, V. J., Feely, R. A., & Kleypas, J. A. (2009). Ocean acidification: The other CO_2 problem. Annual Review of Marine Science, 1(1), 169–192. https://doi.org/10.1146/annurev.marine.010908.163834

Eisler, R. (1987). The chalice and the blade: Our history, our future. Harper & Row.

Fawcett, T. (2010). Personal carbon trading: A policy ahead of its time? Energy Policy, 38(11), 6868–6876. https://doi.org/10.1016/j.enpol.2010.07.001

Green, J. F. (2010). Private standards in the climate regime: The greenhouse gas protocol. Business and Politics, 12(3), 1–37. https://doi.org/10.2202/1469-3569.1320

Hughes, T. P., Kerry, J. T., Álvarez-Noriega, M., Álvarez-Romero, J. G., Anderson, K. D., Baird, A. H., ... Wilson, S. K. (2017). Global warming and recurrent mass bleaching of corals. Nature, 543(7645), 373–377. https://doi.org/10.1038/nature21707

Huybers, P. (2007). Glacial variability over the last two million years: An extended depth-derived age model, continuous obliquity pacing, and the Pleistocene progression. Quaternary Science Reviews, 26(1–2), 37–55. https://doi.org/10.1016/j.quascirev.2006.07.013

IMBIE Team. (2018). Mass balance of the Antarctic Ice Sheet from 1992 to 2017. Nature, 558(7709), 219–222. https://doi.org/10.1038/s41586-018-0179-y

Intergovernmental Panel on Climate Change (IPCC). (2021). Climate change 2021: The physical science basis. Contribution of Working Group I to the Sixth Assessment Report of the Intergovernmental Panel on Climate Change. Cambridge University Press. https://www.ipcc.ch/report/ar6/wg1

Keith, D. W., Duren, R., & MacMartin, D. G. (2016). Field experiments on solar geoengineering: Report of a workshop exploring a representative research portfolio. Philosophical Transactions of the Royal Society A, 374(2081), 20150203. https://doi.org/10.1098/rsta.2015.0203

Keith, D. W., & Irvine, P. J. (2016). Solar geoengineering could substantially reduce climate risks: A research agenda. Earth's Future, 4(11), 549–559. https://doi.org/10.1002/2016EF000465

Keltner, D., & Haidt, J. (2003). Approaching awe, a moral, spiritual, and aesthetic emotion. Cognition & Emotion, 17(2), 297–314. https://doi.org/10.1080/02699930302297

Klein, N. (2014). This changes everything: Capitalism vs. the climate. Simon & Schuster.

Lenton, T. M. (2011). Early warning of climate tipping points. Nature Climate Change, 1(4), 201–209. https://doi.org/10.1038/nclimate1143

NASA. (2020). Global climate change: Vital signs of the planet. https://climate.nasa.gov

O'Neill, S., & Nicholson-Cole, S. (2009). "Fear won't do it": Promoting positive engagement with climate change through visual and iconic representations. Science Communication, 30(3), 355–379. https://doi.org/10.1177/1075547008329201

Orwell, G. (1949). Nineteen eighty-four. Secker & Warburg.

Ostrom, E. (1990). Governing the commons: The evolution of institutions for collective action. Cambridge University Press.

Potts, S. G., Biesmeijer, J. C., Kremen, P., Neumann, P., Schweiger, O., & Kunin, W. E. (2010). Global pollinator declines: Trends, impacts and drivers. Trends in Ecology & Evolution, 25(6), 345–353. https://doi.org/10.1016/j.tree.2010.01.007

Schwab, K. (2020). "You will own nothing and be happy." World Economic Forum. https://www.weforum.org

Schwab, K., & Malleret, T. (2020). COVID-19: The Great Reset. World Economic Forum.

Shepherd, A., Ivins, E. R., Rignot, E., Smith, B., van den Broeke, M., Velicogna, I., ... Whitehouse, P. (2018). Mass balance of the Greenland Ice Sheet from 1992 to 2018. Nature, 579(7798), 233–239. https://doi.org/10.1038/s41586-019-1855-2

Steffen, W., Richardson, K., Rockström, J., Cornell, S. E., Fetzer, I., Bennett, E. M., ... Sörlin, S. (2015). Planetary boundaries: Guiding human development on a changing planet. Science, 347(6223), 1259855. https://doi.org/10.1126/science.1259855

Wigington, D. (2017). Geoengineering: A grave threat to the planet. Geoengineering Watch. https://www.geoengineeringwatch.org

Zhu, Z., Piao, S., Myneni, R. B., et al. (2016). Greening of the Earth and its drivers. Nature Climate Change, 6(8), 791–795. https://doi.org/10.1038/nclimate3004

Chapter 11

The Myth of Monogamy: Rewriting Love

"The grand illusion of committed love is that we think our partners are ours. In truth, their separateness is unassailable, and their mystery is never fully ours to possess."
— Esther Perel

We are handed the blueprint for love before we even understand what the word means. From fairy tales to pop songs, from the legal code to Sunday sermons, the narrative repeats: find the one, keep the one, and die beside the one. Love's story arc, in its most socially sanctioned form, is a straight line, not a spiral or a branching river, beginning with courtship, ascending to life as a couple, and gliding toward a joint burial plot adorned with matching stones.

This script is framed as both natural and noble. To deviate from it goes beyond choosing an alternate path and crosses into stepping outside the boundaries of morality itself. *Monogamy* becomes more than a choice of the heart. It is the central axis for the human social machine. It is embedded in law, reinforced by religion, and defended as though the survival of civilization depends on it. Actually, like many "truths," monogamy's dominance is less a reflection of biology and more a product of deliberate cultural engineering.

THE ILLUSION OF ONE

We are often told that monogamy is natural, even instinctive. Yet in the animal world, true lifelong monogamy is extremely rare, found in only about 3 to 5 percent of mammals (Lukas & Clutton-Brock, 2013). The well-known examples such as swans, prairie voles, and gibbons are the exceptions rather than the rule. Even these species are not always faithful: genetic studies show that swan nests often contain eggs fertilized by other males (Olsson et al., 2001), and many bird species once thought to be strictly monogamous also engage in extra-pair mating (Westneat & Stewart, 2003).

Humans, far from being the crown jewel of monogamous evolution, display a staggering diversity of sexual and relational arrangements across history. Anthropological surveys, such as those compiled in the *Human Relations Area Files*, find that strict, lifelong monogamy has been the dominant marital pattern in only about 19 percent of known human societies (Murdock, 1981). The rest embraced a range of relational arrangements: *polygyny*, where one man has multiple wives; *polyandry*, where one woman has multiple husbands; *serial partnerships*, where relationships unfold one after another; and *looser sexual networks* that defied fixed boundaries.

Consider the *Mosuo* of southwest China, whose *"walking marriage"* system allows lovers to visit each other at night without forming permanent households. Children are raised communally within the maternal household, with uncles often playing a more central role than biological fathers (Mattison, 2010). Or the *Trobriand Islanders*, where pre-marital sexuality is celebrated rather than hidden, and marital ties can be dissolved without stigma (Malinowski, 1929). These are not "primitive" anomalies. They are fully functional patterns of intimacy and kinship.

So why, in post-industrial Western societies, is monogamy presented not as one option among many, but as the only legitimate form of love? Because its function has less to do with emotional fulfillment and far more to do with social control.

MARRIAGE AS GOVERNANCE

To understand why monogamy has such an iron grip on the Western mind, we must trace its marriage to property, inheritance, and state power. For most of recorded history, marriage was not primarily about love. It was a socio-economic contract, a way to consolidate wealth, secure political alliances, and regulate lineage.

In ancient Mesopotamia and Rome, marriage served as a means of preserving family property within tight bloodlines. In medieval Europe, noble families arranged marriages to merge estates or forge alliances, often with little consideration for the personal desires of the couple. The idea that romantic love should be the foundation of marriage would have been viewed as naïve, destabilizing, or even dangerous.

The Romantic movement of the 18th and 19th centuries changed this equation. As historian Stephanie Coontz (2005) documents, this cultural shift fused passion with the legal obligations of marriage. The promise was intoxicating: the same person who ensured your economic stability would also complete your soul. But it was also a trap. This fusion was never purely about personal happiness: it served the church, the state, and the patriarchal family.

Religious authorities sanctified monogamous marriage because it ensured paternity certainty, controlling female sexuality and cementing male dominance over lineage and property. States favored it because nuclear families were easier to tax, surveil, and politically mobilize. The two-person household became the basic administrative unit of governance, small enough to control yet productive enough to sustain the machinery of the state.

MONONORMATIVITY

Mononormativity, the cultural assumption that monogamy is the standard, superior, and morally correct way to conduct relationships, operates like an invisible fence. Its sibling, *amatonormativity* (Brake, 2012), tells us that everyone is better off in a committed, exclusive romantic relationship that lasts a lifetime.

Those who deviate face stigma, caricature, and pathologization. *Polyamorous* people are dismissed as sex-obsessed libertines; those in *open relationships* are assumed to be insecure or incapable of "real" love; and serial monogamists are accused of being fickle. The moralizing is so embedded that even infidelity, which empirical studies suggest occurs in 20–50 percent of monogamous relationships (Barta & Kiene, 2005; Mark et al., 2011), is framed not as evidence that the model itself might be flawed, but as proof that the individuals involved are defective.

In this sense, monogamy functions like a poorly designed software program that constantly crashes but is never rewritten. Instead, users are blamed for not following the manual.

INTIMACY ACROSS CULTURES

The terrain of human intimacy is not a single road but a vast archipelago, a map with many continents of possibility. Across cultures, patterns of love and kinship have been shaped as much by ecology, economy, and cosmology as by desire itself. In this cartography, monogamy is neither the only path nor the inevitable destination.

Among the *Ashanti of Ghana*, a matrilineal system freed women from the burden of proving paternity, since children belonged to the mother's clan. Within this framework, both men and women enjoyed the recognized freedom to have multiple partners without undermining the social fabric. In Tibet and Nepal, fraternal polyandry emerged as a pragmatic solution to protect farmland from division. Brothers shared a wife, joining economic necessity with shared emotional bonds, thereby keeping land intact while maintaining household unity.

In southern India, the *Nayar of Kerala* practiced *sambandham*, a system in which women could welcome multiple visiting husbands. Children were raised within the maternal lineage, and male partners carried no exclusive claims, since kinship rested firmly with the mother's line rather than conjugal ties. On the islands of Hawaii, the practice of *punalua* allowed married couples to share partners with trusted friends, braiding networks of solidarity through sexual bonds and strengthening communal alliances.

In the Amazon, belief in shared paternity created yet another model. Women often took multiple lovers during pregnancy, convinced that several men together contributed to a child's creation. This belief ensured that children were cared for by a wide circle of presumed fathers, expanding both responsibility and affection beyond the nuclear household. And in the Trobriand Islands, sexuality itself was treated not as shameful or hidden but as something to be celebrated in public dances and rituals. Children grew up surrounded by courtship play, and marital ties could be dissolved without stigma when love shifted or faded.

Looked at collectively, these traditions reveal a striking truth: exclusivity is neither an inevitable outcome of biology nor a universal requirement of society. It is simply one cultural creation among many, one possible model of intimacy that different peoples have walked for centuries, and in some cases, for millennia.

COUNTER-EVIDENCE FROM THE HEART

The defenders of monogamy often present exclusivity as the bedrock of intimacy, the assumption being that if you share your bed, body, and heart with no one else, the emotional connection will grow deeper, more stable, and more fulfilling. Yet when subjected to empirical scrutiny, this claim dissolves like sugar in water.

A 2025 meta-analysis of 35 studies spanning 12 countries and involving nearly 24,500 participants found no significant difference in relationship satisfaction, trust, intimacy, or commitment between monogamous and consensually non-monogamous (CNM) partnerships (Rubin et al., 2025). In fact, non-monogamous relationships often outperformed their monogamous counterparts in areas such as sexual communication, personal autonomy, and conflict resolution.

One possible explanation is that CNM couples tend to be forced into radical transparency. Since boundaries and expectations cannot be assumed, they must be articulated with more precision and frequency than in monogamous relationships, where cultural scripts do the talking. Supporting this idea, Conley et al. (2013) found that CNM partners reported higher levels of sexual honesty and lower levels of secrecy than monogamous ones.

Contemporary testimonies echo this. In polyamorous networks, "security" does not come from territorial exclusivity but from negotiated trust; and stability is not guaranteed by suppressing desire but by confronting it openly. Such arrangements require emotional literacy, an ability to name and process difficult feelings like jealousy without letting them crystallize into resentment. Paradoxically, the absence of assumed exclusivity can lead to more intentional commitment, because each day together is a chosen day, not one enforced by the dominant cultural script.

THE NERVOUS SYSTEM OF LOVE

The pull toward exclusivity often feels biological, even primal. And in a sense, it is. But much of what we experience as "natural jealousy" is, in fact, an interaction between our evolved neurobiology and centuries of cultural amplification.

The limbic system, particularly the amygdala, processes social threats with the same urgency it assigns to predators and physical danger. In ancestral environments, the loss of a partner's investment could indeed be life-threatening, especially for women dependent on shared resources for raising offspring. Over time, cultural institutions co-opted this vulnerability, transforming jealousy into a moral imperative.

With regard to this issue, the polyvagal theory (Porges, 2011) offers a useful lens. Our autonomic nervous system is not just tuned for fight-or-flight, but also for social engagement. Safety, in a nervous-system sense, is often coded as predictability. Monogamy provides this predictability by limiting a partner's romantic and sexual connections, a kind of emotional quarantine.

Yet modern economies, social safety nets, and shifting gender roles have changed the survival calculus. It is now possible, and often common, to thrive outside a dyadic, exclusive bond. But the nervous system does not update as fast as the social context. Like outdated software, it continues to fire alarms at scenarios that no longer threaten survival. This means that moving beyond compulsory monogamy often requires somatic retraining, learning to experience safety in connection without possession.

BEYOND THE CAGE

If exclusivity does not always mean safety, what might love look like if it were freed from its cage? One answer is found in *relationship anarchy* (Nordgren, 2006), a philosophy that says romantic bonds do not have to be ranked above all other relationships. Instead, each connection, whether sexual, platonic, familial, or spiritual, is treated as a unique co-creation, negotiated on its own terms.

This framework for relationships is not an invitation to chaos but to conscious alchemy. There is no "primary" partner unless the people involved choose that structure. There are no assumed exclusivity clauses, only agreements made and remade in dialogue. Love becomes less a fortress to be defended and more a garden to be cultivated, with each relationship producing its own tapestry of needs, joys, and boundaries.

In this vision, love can be fluid without being fragile. A deep romantic partnership can coexist with intense friendships, occasional lovers, and shared creative collaborations, each feeding different dimensions of human intimacy.

TRANSFORMING JEALOUSY

Deprogramming begins in the body long before it reaches the mind. The imprints of compulsory monogamy are etched not only in our beliefs but also in our nervous systems, our muscle memory, and our stress responses. Picture your partner's hand resting in another's. Where does it land in you? In the tightening of your chest, the heat rising in your cheeks, or the knot twisting in your stomach? These do not represent personal failings but survival reflexes, shaped by centuries of cultural conditioning and layered over ancient currents of evolutionary fear.

Somatic therapies, like Peter Levine's trauma work or *mindfulness-based stress reduction* (MBSR), allow people to notice these sensations without collapsing into them. In CNM communities, it is common to start with *"exposure therapy"* for jealousy: sharing fantasies, acknowledging attractions, or even witnessing a partner's flirtation in safe, agreed-upon contexts. Each step rewrites the neural pathways, replacing panic with curiosity.

The goal is not to eradicate jealousy, which can carry useful information, but to transform it from a weapon into a mirror. It becomes an opportunity for self-inquiry. Is my discomfort about them, or about the stories I tell myself about what this means? As self-inquiry deepens and reactions are met with compassion, the stories gradually loosen their hold.

REWRITING CONNECTION

What if love were not a single-track railway but an ecosystem, a mycelial network of relationships, some sexual, some romantic, some spiritual, some platonic, each nourishing the others? In ecosystems, diversity increases resilience. The same is true of human intimacy. Queer kinship networks, chosen families, and *polycules*, interconnected constellations of people linked through multiple romantic or intimate bonds, sometimes raising children together, show that love is not a scarce resource to be hoarded. It behaves more like light: the more you share it, the more it illuminates.

In such networks, a partner's joy with another need not diminish one's own. It can even enhance it, a phenomenon known as *compersion*. While not universal or automatic, compersion demonstrates that jealousy is not inevitable: it can be rewired into something more generous, expansive, and non-possessive. These arrangements are not free from heartbreak or conflict. But neither is monogamy. The difference is that when love changes shape, it need not be framed as failure but seen instead as evolution.

The cultural matrix tells us that love is a contract: sign here, surrender autonomy, and expect permanence. But love can also be a conversation, ongoing, adaptive, and responsive to the shifting realities of those within it. This is not a call to abandon monogamy. It is a call to abandon compulsory monogamy, the presumption that exclusivity is the only valid way to love. Liberation is not measured by the number of partners one has but by the quality of one's choices.

If monogamy is your truth, let it be chosen awake, not sleepwalked into. If it is not, dare to weave your own tapestries of intimacy, ones that fit the contours of your actual life rather than the life you were told to want.

Your heart is not a cage. It is a constellation. And the night sky is vast.

REFERENCES

Barta, W. D., & Kiene, S. M. (2005). Motivations for infidelity. Journal of Social and Personal Relationships, 22(3), 339–360.

Brake, E. (2012). Minimizing marriage. Oxford University Press.

Conley, T. D., et al. (2013). Stigma and CNM. Analyses of Social Issues and Public Policy, 13(1), 1–30.

Coontz, S. (2005). Marriage, a history. Viking.

HRAF. (2020). Human Relations Area Files. Yale University.

Levine, P. A. (1997). Waking the tiger. North Atlantic Books.

Lukas, D., & Clutton-Brock, T. H. (2013). The evolution of social monogamy in mammals. Science, 341(6145), 526–530.

Malinowski, B. (1929). The sexual life of savages. Harcourt Brace.

Mark, K. P., et al. (2011). Infidelity in relationships. Journal of Family Psychology, 25(3), 369–377.

Mattison, S. M. (2010). The Mosuo case. American Anthropologist, 112(1), 38–49.

Murdock, G. P. (1981). Atlas of world cultures. University of Pittsburgh Press.

Nordgren, A. (2006). Short instructional manifesto for relationship anarchy.

Olsson, O., et al. (2001). Divorce in swans. Animal Behaviour, 62(3), 509–517.

Perel, E. (2006). Mating in captivity: Unlocking erotic intelligence. Harper.

Porges, S. W. (2011). The polyvagal theory. Norton.

Rubin, J. D., et al. (2025). Consensual non-monogamy and relationship quality. Journal of Sex Research, 62(4), 445–462.

Westneat, D. F., & Stewart, I. R. K. (2003). Extra-pair paternity in birds. Molecular Ecology, 12(9), 2183–2194.

PART II

EXITING THE MATRIX

If Part I exposed the machinery of fear, belief, and control, it also revealed the inevitability of fissures, gaps where another kind of life was already insisting on itself. Part II turns toward those gaps, not as accidents but as invitations. Here, scattered seeds become practices, cracks widen into pathways, and the central task emerges: the awakening of the Human Robot.

Chapter 12

Sacred Substances and the Reboot of Consciousness

"Truth is what works."
— William James

Every complex system occasionally needs a hard reboot. Computers freeze, bureaucracies ossify, and paradigms crystallize into dogmas. Human consciousness is no different. Psychedelic substances—psilocybin, LSD, mescaline, ayahuasca and its active component dimethyltryptamine (DMT), 5-methoxy-N,N-dimethyltryptamine (5-MeO-DMT), and ibogaine—have re-emerged in the early twenty-first century as radical rebooters of perception, meaning, and identity. In contrast to the passive consumption of mediated narratives and institutional doctrines, psychedelics invite direct experience: a full-bodied confrontation with mystery that neither priests nor algorithms can mediate. In their wake, belief gives way to seeing for oneself, dogma dissolves in the solvent of awe, and the matrix of inherited scripts can be exited, at least temporarily, in order to reprogram the self and society.

This chapter approaches psychedelics as sacred technologies, ancient in origin yet newly illuminated by contemporary neuroscience, that can serve as catalysts for rebooting consciousness. We move between neurobiological accounts of how they loosen rigid priors and hierarchical predictions, the lived phenomenology of mystical experience and its enduring psychological and existential effects, and the ceremonial wisdom of Indigenous traditions that emphasize set, setting, and integration. Alongside these openings, we also face the collapse of doctrinal certainty and the emergence of post-dogmatic forms of spirituality, as well as the more troubling currents of commercialization, spiritual bypassing, predatory facilitation, and adverse outcomes. From there the conversation widens to consider the ethical, ecological, and political stakes of a world where psychedelic adoption is no longer marginal but increasingly mainstream. Through each of these perspectives we return to a central thesis: psychedelics are never ends in themselves but catalysts for remembering what consciousness can be when it is freed from fear, belief, and control.

FROM HALLUCINOGEN TO ENTHEOGEN

The word *psychedelic*, meaning *"mind manifesting,"* was coined in the 1950s by psychiatrist Humphry Osmond in dialogue with writer Aldous Huxley, who sought a term to describe substances that revealed hidden dimensions of consciousness rather than simply intoxicating (Osmond, 1957; Huxley, 1954). The term was intended to avoid the stigma of *"hallucinogen,"* which suggested delusion and error. To call something psychedelic was to suggest that it revealed latent dimensions of the psyche and uncovered truths rather than fabricating illusions.

Later, the word *entheogen* was introduced by scholars in the 1970s, derived from the Greek for *"generating the divine within"* (Ruck et al., 1979). This term highlighted reverence, sacredness, and a sense of inner divinity, while decoupling these substances from countercultural caricatures. Many today prefer entheogen because it frames these compounds not as dangerous hallucinogens but as portals to states of consciousness that cultures have long revered as divine or transcendent.

Language shapes how societies respond. To call LSD a hallucinogen is to dismiss its visions as mere illusions; to call it an entheogen is to suggest that its revelations may possess a deeper reality than ordinary waking consciousness. Words act as containers, constraining or expanding the interpretive horizon.

The stakes are far from abstract. By the mid-1960s, psychedelics had already catalyzed research into creativity, psychotherapy, and spirituality. Alcoholics treated with LSD showed unexpected rates of recovery. Clergy in the *Good Friday Experiment* at Marsh Chapel reported mystical encounters of life-changing depth (Pahnke, 1963). Then came the backlash, with criminalization and moral panic shutting down an entire field of inquiry.

Today's psychedelic renaissance reopens the inquiry, this time with neuroimaging, rigorous clinical design, and philosophical debate. Still, the central question remains the same: *are these substances deceptive hallucinations or revelations of deeper realities?* The answer depends in part on whether we regard them as hallucinogens to be feared or entheogens to be respected.

THE REBUS AND THE LIBERATION OF PRIORS

The REBUS model, or '*Relaxed Beliefs Under pSychedelics,*' helps explain why psychedelics can be such powerful catalysts for change (Carhart-Harris & Friston, 2019). As we have seen, *predictive processing theory* suggests the brain is not a passive receiver but an active predictor, filtering experience through learned assumptions called priors. This makes life manageable, but rigid priors become prisons: trauma encodes vigilance, depression encodes despair, addiction encodes craving. Even the self is a prior, a model the brain defends at all costs.

Psychedelics act primarily on a class of serotonin sites in the brain known as 5-HT2A receptors, which help regulate mood, perception, and cognition. By stimulating these receptors, psychedelics temporarily loosen the grip of our most rigid mental habits and assumptions. Brain imaging shows that they also disrupt the *default mode network*, a hub of brain regions that normally keeps our sense of self and autobiographical thinking intact. When this network quiets down, the usual chatter of self-referential thought gives way to a wider range of possibilities. At the same time, communication between distant regions of the brain increases, creating a more flexible and interconnected neural landscape. It is as if the strict conductor of the orchestra has stepped aside, allowing improvisation and unexpected harmonies to emerge.

From the inside, this feels like *ego dissolution*, timelessness, or merging with an ocean of awareness. For some it means a flood of childhood memory, for others a vision of cosmic unity, and for still others a confrontation with mortality.

Therapeutically, this loosening can be transformative. For instance, a single guided psilocybin session can sometimes lift treatment-resistant depression, ease existential fear in terminal illness, and interrupt years of addictive cycles (Ross et al., 2016; Davis et al., 2021; Bogenschutz et al., 2022). From the perspective of REBUS, the drug does not provide new answers. It simply suspends the false answers encoded as rigid predictions, allowing new meanings to be written into the nervous system.

DIRECT EXPERIENCE VS. DOGMA

Institutions are built on authority, but psychedelics are built on direct experience. Theology and science alike depend on mediating structures of validation such as scripture, priesthood, or peer review, yet a psychedelic journey bypasses all intermediaries. What it delivers is a confrontation with the *Ground of Being* (or Ultimate Reality) that feels immediate, unfiltered, and undeniable.

William James described mystical states as ineffable and noetic, carrying an authority that resists intellectual dismissal (James, 1902/1985). This makes them dangerous for regimes invested in controlling meaning. *Why attend a church if the sacred can be touched in a mushroom ceremony? Why accept a reductive theory of consciousness if one has experienced it as infinite and irreducible?*

This shift destabilizes both religious orthodoxy and scientific materialism. It undermines any structure claiming a monopoly on truth. Yet this collapse does not automatically yield wisdom. Revelation can crystallize into new dogmas or inflate egos with spiritual specialness. Still, what psychedelics consistently show is that beliefs are provisional, truths are experiential, and no authority is final.

ANCIENT KNOWING:
SHAMANIC TECHNOLOGIES OF CONSCIOUSNESS

Indigenous cultures long before modern neuroscience developed sophisticated ways of working with psychoactive plants. In the Amazon, *ayahuasca* is not a mere brew but part of a complex ceremony that includes ritual preparation through fasting, dietary restrictions, and periods of solitude, all supported by chants, prayers, and community witnessing. Among the Huichol people of Mexico, pilgrims walk hundreds of miles to the desert of Wirikuta to gather and ingest the *peyote* cactus in ceremonies that renew their connection to the land, the cosmos, and the community. And in Gabon, *iboga* initiations provide visions that guide social and spiritual maturity.

In these traditions, plants are not commodities but teachers. They are woven into cosmologies that see humans, spirits, and ecosystems as inseparable. To consume ayahuasca without understanding this context is to miss its relational depth.

Western seekers often adopt these practices for personal healing or optimization. Retreat centers market them as *biohacks*, quick fixes, or therapies aimed at enhancing performance and well-being. While genuine healing can occur, the danger lies in reducing sacred traditions to consumable techniques. True learning requires humility, ecological responsibility, and respect for plant sovereignty and Indigenous guardianship. Without this, the psychedelic renaissance risks becoming another form of spiritual appropriation.

SET AND SETTING

Because psychedelics greatly intensify awareness, the surrounding conditions strongly influence the experience. "*Set*" refers to mindset, including intentions, mood, and personal history. "*Setting*" refers to environment, including the place you are in, the people around you, and the cultural context. Together, set and setting create the framework that shapes how the experience unfolds and whether it feels safe, meaningful, or sacred.

Clinical studies have formalized this wisdom. Preparation sessions establish trust and clarify intentions. The sessions themselves are supported with music, eyeshades, and guides who provide reassurance. Integration follows, where insights are articulated and applied. Indigenous traditions arrive at the same principle through different means: song, prayer, dietary restrictions, myth, and collective holding.

Contrast this with the fragile containers of modern life. A container is the framework that holds a psychedelic experience, shaped by mindset, environment, and ritual support. In many traditional settings, containers are carefully built through intention, ceremony, and community. In modern contexts, however, our environments are often fragmented by distraction, surveillance, and commodified attention. Dropping psychedelics into such conditions without thoughtful preparation or guidance risks confusion and even chaos.

To create *sacred space* in this landscape is radical. Sacred space means a container shaped by mindset, environment, and communal support. It requires trust, stillness, and reverence rather than distraction. Within such space, the psyche can safely loosen, explore, and reconfigure.

MYSTICAL-TYPE EXPERIENCE, PERSONALITY CHANGE, AND THERAPEUTIC OUTCOMES

The link between psychedelic journeys and mystical states is now one of the most consistent findings in the research literature. The more profound the mystical-type experience, the greater the therapeutic gains. Participants who report encounters with unity, timelessness, sacredness, or ineffable meaning are also the ones who show the deepest reductions in depression, anxiety, or addiction (Griffiths et al., 2006, 2008, 2018). Many rank these sessions among the most important experiences of their entire lives, comparable to the birth of a child or the death of a parent.

What makes these states so potent is not their intensity alone but the way they reframe life's possibilities. Depression is often experienced as a narrowing of the future, a collapse of hope into repetition. Addiction is a fixation, a looping of relief-seeking behaviors. A mystical state interrupts this rigidity. It floods the system with a sense of openness, with the felt conviction that more is possible. Importantly, this is not abstract belief but lived knowing. People emerge saying not *"I believe I am loved"* but *"I experienced myself as love."*

Perhaps most remarkable is the evidence that personality, thought to stabilize by middle adulthood, can shift. Studies show that trait openness — curiosity, imagination, willingness to embrace novelty — can increase after a single psilocybin session (MacLean et al., 2011). Psychedelics do not merely heal disorders: they can catalyze long-term growth.

MDMA-assisted therapy for PTSD demonstrates another pathway. MDMA, short for 3,4-methylenedioxy-methamphetamine, is a compound that reduces fear and heightens feelings of trust and connection. Unlike classic psychedelics, it does not dissolve the ego but creates a gentler, more open state of mind. In this softened state, survivors of trauma can revisit terrifying memories without being overwhelmed. They can also narrate their stories while feeling safe. In Phase 3 trials, nearly three-quarters of participants no longer met criteria for PTSD after treatment (Mitchell et al., 2021). Years of frozen terror thawed in a matter of sessions.

Viewed as a whole, these outcomes point to a central truth: psychedelics work not as chemical fixes but as catalysts for experiences of meaning, connection, and safety. They reconfigure the very frameworks through which life is understood and experienced.

INTEGRATION AS PRAXIS

A peak experience without *integration* is like lightning that strikes but never grounds. The flash illuminates everything, but the energy dissipates. Integration ensures that insight reshapes life rather than fading into memory.

The forms of integration are diverse. Some write extensively, using journals to mold dreamlike imagery into narrative coherence. Others work with therapists or coaches who specialize in psychedelic integration, translating visions into concrete shifts in work, relationships, or self-care. Creative practices such as painting, dance, and music allow expression of what words cannot capture. Somatic practices help anchor the insights in the body rather than letting them float away as abstractions.

Integration is also where challenges arise. The ego, supposedly dissolved, often returns emboldened. *"I saw God, therefore I am chosen,"* is a subtle *inflation.* Communities may develop hierarchies where those who have "gone deeper" claim authority over those who have not: this is dogma rebranded.

Another distortion is *spiritual bypassing*. Instead of confronting unhealed wounds, some use their visions to convince themselves that they are already whole. Pain remains unresolved but hidden behind metaphysical language. Proper integration resists this temptation. It asks: *how will this change the way you treat others? How will it alter how you spend money, vote, parent, or repair harm?* Without such embodiment, psychedelic revelation remains spectacle.

The measure of integration is not the grandeur of the vision but the humility and responsibility of the life that follows.

RISKS, ABUSES, AND PHARMAKON DYNAMICS

Psychedelics are *pharmakon*: both medicine and poison. They can heal or harm, liberate or entrap, depending on context and care.

The risks are real. Panic, derealization, and mania can overwhelm. For those predisposed to psychosis or bipolar disorder, psychedelics can exacerbate symptoms. Physiological dangers also exist, especially when combined with other drugs or when strong brews containing MAOIs are consumed without medical oversight. MAOI stands for monoamine oxidase inhibitor, a substance that blocks the enzyme responsible for breaking down neurotransmitters such as serotonin, dopamine, and norepinephrine. When this enzyme is inhibited, these brain chemicals remain active longer, which can intensify psychedelic effects but also create dangerous interactions with common medications or certain foods.

Equally troubling are the social risks. In recent years, cases of abuse by facilitators have surfaced across retreat centers and underground ceremonies. Participants, often vulnerable and open, have been manipulated sexually, financially, or spiritually. The collapse of old belief structures can leave people highly suggestible, and in that state predators find opportunity. The psychedelic movement is not immune to the same power dynamics that corrupt religious or therapeutic contexts.

Commercialization adds another layer. Corporations now patent psychedelic molecules, build clinics for wealthy clients, and market these ancient sacraments as platforms for industrialized mental health solutions. A medicine revered by Indigenous cultures for millennia is reduced to intellectual property and marketed as wellness optimization. If psychedelics are absorbed fully into the logic of profit and extraction, they risk reinforcing the very structures they once seemed to dissolve.

To hold psychedelics responsibly requires vigilance. They are not miracle cures or inherently dangerous drugs, but powerful tools that can amplify both light and shadow.

CONSCIOUSNESS FIRST

Do psychedelics reveal that consciousness is primary, not derivative? Increasing numbers of scientists and philosophers are entertaining this possibility. If mind is merely the byproduct of matter, then psychedelic visions should be little more than chemically induced noise. Yet the states they induce often feel more coherent, more intelligent, and more real than waking life.

A *post-materialist* perspective suggests that the brain is less a generator of consciousness than a filter. Psychedelics loosen that filter, allowing broader dimensions of mind to shine through (Beauregard et al., 2014; Beauregard, 2021). From this view, death is not extinction but transition; the ego is not an isolated self but a passing wave in a larger sea of awareness; and encounters with entities, ancestors, or plant spirits are not merely hallucinations but glimpses into an ensouled cosmos.

This perspective does not ask us to adopt new beliefs. Instead, it invites humility about what we know and courage to face the unknown. We do not yet understand the full shape of consciousness, and psychedelics remind us that what we usually call reality may be only a small slice of a much larger whole.

For science, this means valuing first-person reports as data rather than dismissing them as noise. For spirituality, it means rooting faith not in belief but in direct, embodied communion. Psychedelics, then, are not only therapies but tools for revelation.

ESCAPING THE PROGRAM, RETURNING TO THE WORLD

Psychedelics are often described as a jailbreak from the *Matrix*, a sudden lifting of the veil of fear and control. Under their influence, the scaffolding of ordinary life is revealed: trauma loops repeating like broken records, media illusions masquerading as truth, and cultural scripts performed as destiny. To glimpse this is to see the code.

But the purpose is not exile. To linger forever in vision is to drift away from the human task. The gift of the vision lies in the return. Myth tells it plainly: the hero descends into the underworld not to stay but to bring back fire, water, or medicine for the people.

So too with psychedelics. Their revelations must be carried into new ways of living: laws that heal rather than punish, healthcare that opens rather than excludes, education that cultivates wonder as well as critique, and economies that honor the reciprocity of earth instead of worshipping endless plunder.

Without such grounding, psychedelics risk dissolving into entertainment for the few. With it, they can become not escape but return, not spectacle but renewal, a way of remembering the world as sacred, and ourselves as part of its living story.

RESTORING PURPOSE

The psychedelic renaissance points to a spirituality that goes beyond consumerism. It invites us to move past buying products or following rigid beliefs, and instead integrate spiritual life in direct experience, respect for the earth, and care for one another.

Such a spirituality is experiential, grounded in direct states of consciousness rather than abstract belief. It moves in relationship, seeing plants, animals, and places as kin. And it carries a trauma-informed ethic of integration, where safety and accountability open the way to depth.

Psychedelics are not the only path toward this reorientation. Meditation, ecstatic dance, breathwork, contemplative prayer, art, and near-death experiences (NDEs) can all provide similar openings. But psychedelics accelerate the process by suspending the ordinary gatekeepers of consciousness, showing in a matter of hours how fabricated our questions and assumptions have always been.

This spirituality seeks not escape but rebraiding, healing the fractures between science and spirit, ritual and evidence, individuality and community.

THE REAL WORK BEGINS AFTER THE LIGHTS COME BACK ON

In a culture saturated by distraction, psychedelics are both dangerous and necessary. Dangerous, because they can destabilize fragile psyches, be co-opted by capital, or serve as tools for exploitation. Necessary, because they remind us that consciousness is vast, plastic, and capable of more love and imagination than our institutions allow.

Awakening the Human Robot takes more than resisting outside systems of control. It also means changing the patterns inside us. Psychedelics are one tool for this work, but they only help if we are willing to prepare, let go, make sense of what we learn, and live differently afterward. Letting go of rigid dogma does not erase meaning but opens the way for meanings we can create and share together, born from the recognition that we are more than our conditioning.

Revelation cannot remain private. To glimpse the script is one thing; to live beyond it requires new structures that sustain sovereignty. Psychedelics may open the doors of perception, but the body remains bound by economic dependency. For visions to endure, they must extend into the realms of money, debt, and power. The empire of fear, belief, and control does not fall through insight alone but through lives lived otherwise.

REFERENCES

Beauregard, M. (2021). Expanding Reality: The Emergence of Postmaterialist Science. Iff Books.

Beauregard, M., Schwartz, G. E., Miller, L., Dossey, L., Moreira-Almeida, A., Schlitz, M., Sheldrake, R., & Tart, C. (2014). Manifesto for a post-materialist science. Explore: The Journal of Science and Healing, 10(5), 272–274.
https://doi.org/10.1016/j.explore.2014.08.001

Bogenschutz, M. P., et al. (2022). Psilocybin-assisted treatment for alcohol use disorder: A randomized clinical trial. JAMA Psychiatry, 79(7), 650–661.
https://doi.org/10.1001/jamapsychiatry.2022.1250

Carhart-Harris, R. L., & Friston, K. J. (2019). REBUS and the anarchic brain: Toward a unified model of the brain action of psychedelics. Pharmacological Reviews, 71(3), 316–344.
https://doi.org/10.1124/pr.118.017160

Davis, A. K., Barrett, F. S., May, D. G., et al. (2021). Effects of psilocybin-assisted therapy on major depressive disorder: A randomized clinical trial. JAMA Psychiatry, 78(5), 481–489.
https://doi.org/10.1001/jamapsychiatry.2020.3285

Griffiths, R. R., Richards, W. A., McCann, U., & Jesse, R. (2006). Psilocybin can occasion mystical-type experiences having substantial and sustained personal meaning and spiritual significance. Psychopharmacology, 187(3), 268–283.
https://doi.org/10.1007/s00213-006-0457-5

Griffiths, R. R., Richards, W. A., Johnson, M. W., et al. (2008). Mystical-type experiences occasioned by psilocybin mediate the attribution of personal meaning and spiritual significance 14 months later. Journal of Psychopharmacology, 22(6), 621–632. https://doi.org/10.1177/0269881108094300

Griffiths, R. R., et al. (2018). Psilocybin-occasioned mystical-type experience in combination with meditation and other spiritual practices produces enduring positive changes in psychological functioning and in trait measures of prosocial attitudes and behaviors. Journal of Psychopharmacology, 32(1), 49–69. https://doi.org/10.1177/0269881117731279

Huxley, A. (1954). The Doors of Perception. Harper & Brothers.

James, W. (1985). The Varieties of Religious Experience. Penguin. (Original work published 1902)

MacLean, K. A., Johnson, M. W., & Griffiths, R. R. (2011). Mystical experiences occasioned by the hallucinogen psilocybin lead to increases in the personality domain of openness. Journal of Psychopharmacology, 25(11), 1453–1461. https://doi.org/10.1177/0269881111420188

Mitchell, J. M., et al. (2021). MDMA-assisted therapy for severe PTSD: A randomized, double-blind, placebo-controlled phase 3 study. Nature Medicine, 27(6), 1025–1033. https://doi.org/10.1038/s41591-021-01336-3

Osmond, H. (1957). A review of the clinical effects of psychotomimetic agents. Annals of the New York Academy of Sciences, 66(3), 418–434. https://doi.org/10.1111/j.1749-6632.1957.tb40738.x

Pahnke, W. N. (1963). Drugs and mysticism: An analysis of the relationship between psychedelic drugs and the mystical consciousness (Doctoral dissertation, Harvard University).

Ross, S., et al. (2016). Rapid and sustained symptom reduction following psilocybin treatment for anxiety and depression in patients with life-threatening cancer: A randomized controlled trial. Journal of Psychopharmacology, 30(12), 1165–1180. https://doi.org/10.1177/0269881116675512

Ruck, C. A. P., Bigwood, J., Staples, D., Ott, J., & Wasson, R. G. (1979). Entheogens. Journal of Psychedelic Drugs, 11(1–2), 145–146. https://doi.org/10.1080/02791072.1979.10472098

Chapter 13

Exiting the Economy of Chains

*"The difficulty lies not so much in developing
new ideas as in escaping from old ones."*
— John Maynard Keynes

A re you sovereign, or are you a servant dressed as a consumer? This question is not rhetorical. It is encoded in every economic interaction we make, whether tapping a card at a café or signing a mortgage agreement that will stretch across decades. Each gesture reveals not only a transaction but also a relationship to structures of power that shape our lives at a level so deep that most of us rarely pause to notice. We are trained to believe that money is neutral, that debt is natural, and that financial institutions are inevitable. Yet money is never neutral, debt is frequently engineered, and institutions are conceived by specific actors, in specific historical contexts, for particular purposes (Eisenstein, 2011; Korten, 2009).

The first step of an economic exit is about how we understand the world. It begins by realizing that the economy is not a neutral terrain governed by immutable laws but a story written by power (Graeber, 2011). Once we recognize that the current order is a narrative rather than a natural fact, the possibility emerges to imagine different narratives, different systems of exchange, and different rules of value. The second step is architectural. We must write new stories and build infrastructures that allow those stories to become livable realities.

This chapter proposes a path from consumer to creator of value architectures, from servitude within a debt-based regime toward sovereignty at personal, communal, and even civilizational scales. Sovereignty here does not mean isolation or autarky. It means the capacity to shape one's own economic life in alignment with shared values, free from perpetual leverage to private credit issuers (Hudson, 2018; Brown, 2010).

The journey begins by confronting and dismantling the chains of predatory debt. It then moves toward decentralizing finance, not in the narrow technological sense of cryptocurrencies alone but through a wider program that includes public banking, cooperative funds, mutual credit systems, and civic monetary experiments (Ostrom, 1990; Bauwens & Kostakis, 2014). Finally, it requires reclaiming value itself, redefining what counts as wealth and how we measure flourishing. This is a long process, one that involves history, myth, design, and political struggle. It is, above all, a process of re-authoring the story of money.

DESTROYING DEBT

Debt is not just a line in an account book. It is also a leash, a way of exercising power over entire populations. At the same time, not all debts are harmful. Debts of gratitude, promises of care, and the informal lending that happens in close communities are part of what holds social life together. What needs to be dismantled are the predatory forms of debt that trap people in cycles of interest, send profits upward to the few, and leave the risks and losses to everyone else (Hudson, 2018).

History is filled with examples of debt spirals consuming entire societies. Ancient Mesopotamian rulers periodically declared jubilees, wiping out agricultural debts to prevent the loss of land and freedom among the peasantry (Hudson, 2018). Biblical texts carried forward this tradition, institutionalizing debt release as a religious duty. Medieval Europe, too, wrestled with the moral boundaries of usury, often prohibiting interest altogether. The modern age, however, normalized perpetual indebtedness. Mortgages, student loans, and credit card balances became everyday tools of financial survival, yet they simultaneously bound households to decades of repayment.

Modern jubilees can take many forms, all pointing toward the same possibility: release from the chains of unpayable obligation. *Student debt cancellation*, now a political flashpoint in the United States, would not only free individual borrowers but also lift the psychic weight carried by entire generations (Martenson, 2011). The work of nonprofits such as *Undue Medical Debt* shows how cheaply vast sums can be erased once stripped of the illusion of inevitability: by purchasing hospital bills for pennies on the dollar and forgiving them, they dissolve burdens that might otherwise shadow families for years (Klein, 2007). On the global scale, linking sovereign debt relief to ecological goals could realign finance with planetary survival instead of extractive growth. And the example of North Dakota's state-owned bank illustrates how *public banking* can redirect credit toward infrastructure, ecological restoration, and community well-being rather than speculative bubbles (Brown, 2010). Together, these experiments reveal that debt is not an immutable law but a human creation, and therefore open to redesign.

Debt abolition is not only fiscal but mythic. It challenges the cultural story that debt is sacred and that failure to pay is a sin. Graeber (2011) argued that debt throughout history has often been framed as a moral obligation, even when the terms were unjust. By contesting that narrative, debt jubilees and abolition movements restore balance between creditor and debtor, revealing that what is presented as a natural order is in fact created on purpose.

Destroying debt without burning the world requires nuance. The task is not to abolish obligation itself but to transform its meaning, shifting it from chains of exploitation to bonds of reciprocity. In this reframing, obligation becomes the ground for building financial systems where relationship, not exploitation, defines the flow of value.

DECENTRALIZING FINANCE

Freedom from predatory debt provides breathing space, but emancipation will collapse if nothing replaces it. Financial systems cannot simply be dismantled: they must be rebuilt with forms that prevent the same traps from re-emerging. This is where *decentralization* enters the picture.

Much of the discussion about decentralization has focused on *cryptocurrencies*. When Bitcoin appeared in 2008, it showed that people could send money directly to one another without using banks (Nakamoto, 2008). But while this solved a technical problem, it did not tackle deeper issues like inequality, sustainability, or governance (Popper, 2015). Ethereum and other projects in what became known as *decentralized finance*, or DeFi, promised to go further by creating "programmable money" that could carry out contracts automatically (Buterin, 2013). In reality, though, many DeFi experiments—digital financial systems run on blockchain and meant to cut out banks— ended up repeating the same speculative excesses of Wall Street, with risky borrowing and boom-and-bust cycles, only at digital speed (Leshner & Hayes, 2019).

Decentralization can be understood more broadly as a principle of *polycentric* finance, where no single authority controls everything and cooperation happens across many layers. As Ostrom (1990) showed, shared resources flourish not under strict centralization or total individualism but within networks of collaboration. Applied to money, this points to a diverse landscape in which different forms of value can work together. Cryptocurrencies like Bitcoin might coexist with local credit systems, privacy-focused currencies can balance publicly accountable banks, cooperative credit unions can find their place alongside decentralized organizations, and regional currencies can strengthen local economies even as stablecoins support global trade.

Such plurality is not a weakness but a strength. Redundancy provides resilience. No single form of money need dominate: instead, multiple forms can coexist, each suited to its context. Decentralization, in this sense, is less about libertarian escape and more about civic design. It asks whether finance can be turned from a monopoly into a shared resource, one where communities hold real power over how capital circulates.

RECLAIMING VALUE

If money is our language for value, then the essential question becomes: *who writes the script*? For generations, economists have claimed that prices are the most efficient signal of value, capturing scarcity, demand, and utility in a single figure. Yet the reliance on prices alone has created a distorted mirror.

Gross domestic product (GDP), still the dominant measure of national prosperity, treats destruction as growth. When forests are logged, GDP rises. When oil spills occur and clean-up efforts are mobilized, GDP rises. Even war and disease add to GDP, because they generate spending. What GDP does not count are the very foundations of well-being: unpaid care work, ecological balance, and the resilience of communities.

Alternative frameworks seek to correct these blind spots. One influential example is *Doughnut Economics* (Raworth, 2017), which pictures a safe space for humanity: the inner edge of the doughnut marks the social foundations everyone needs for a good life, such as food, housing, and healthcare, while the outer edge marks the ecological limits we cannot cross without harming the planet. Building on this, *Genuine Progress Indicators* take the familiar measure of GDP and adjust it by subtracting the hidden costs of pollution, inequality, and the erosion of leisure time. In a similar spirit, *Wellbeing Budgets*, pioneered in New Zealand, shift the focus of government policy from raw economic output to human flourishing and quality of life. In sum, these approaches point to a deeper lesson: new metrics are valuable, but by themselves they are not enough. To truly reclaim value, we must also reshape the practices of exchange.

Communities are already experimenting with alternatives that redefine value and exchange. Some issue their own credits for ecological restoration, treating reforestation or watershed care as genuine economic contributions. Others are reviving trust-based finance through systems where loans are backed not by property or possessions but by networks of people vouching for one another. Timebanking extends this principle by placing all forms of labor on equal footing, flattening hierarchies of skill and prestige (Cahn, 1992). In digital spaces, peer production networks and open-source accounting similarly reward contributions to public-interest projects without enclosing them in private ownership (Bauwens & Kostakis, 2014). Even data, the raw material of surveillance capitalism, can be reconceived as a shared asset, collectively bargained for through citizen dividends that turn what was once extracted in secret into a shared resource for public good.

Reclaiming value requires both a shift of measurement and a shift of imagination. It is a reminder that economies are stories about what we choose to honor.

CASE STUDIES OF EXIT

If these ideas sound utopian, it is worth remembering that many are already in practice. Around the world, communities have created living laboratories of economic exit, each showing in its own way how finance and ownership can be reimagined.

One of the earliest examples is the Swiss *WIR Bank*, founded during the Great Depression. Operating as an interest-free mutual credit system among small and medium-sized enterprises, it has provided liquidity when conventional credit dried up, acting as a stabilizer that softens boom-and-bust cycles for its members (Studer, 1998).

Decades later and further south, Sardinia developed the *Sardex mutual credit network*. Like WIR, it facilitates trade outside conventional banking, but its distinct strength lies in rooting value in local culture and trust, ensuring wealth circulates within the region rather than leaking to global financial centers (Littera et al., 2017). Together, WIR and Sardex show how cooperative credit can thrive when tied to community identity.

A different model can be found in the United States with the *Bank of North Dakota*. Established in 1919, it remains the country's only state-owned bank. By partnering with local institutions and channeling profits back into public purposes, it demonstrates that banking can be organized around service rather than extraction (Brown, 2010).

In Kenya, innovation took yet another form. The launch of *M-Pesa* in 2007 allowed millions to bypass traditional banks and use mobile phones for everyday transactions. This leap not only expanded financial inclusion but also enabled entire micro-economies to emerge where conventional infrastructure was absent (Greer, 2013).

Experiments are not limited to banking alone. Community land trusts show how land itself can be removed from speculative markets and placed into shared stewardship. By doing so, they secure permanent affordability and keep wealth anchored in place (Kelly, 2012).

At the frontier of technosocial innovation, *decentralized autonomous organizations* (DAOs) such as *MakerDAO* point toward transparent, protocol-driven governance. Though still experimental, they offer a glimpse of financial institutions whose rules are open, auditable, and collectively controlled (MakerDAO, 2017).

Taken in concert, these examples are not marginal curiosities but signposts, illuminating what becomes possible when imagination converges with design and when communities dare to shape systems true to their values

RISKS, TRAPS, AND DEAD ENDS

No alternative is immune to failure. The history of finance is marked by false exits, innovations that promised liberation but delivered new chains. Cryptocurrencies, for instance, have too often become vehicles of speculation, generating volatility that reproduces rather than overcomes financial fragility. State-led efforts offer no guarantee either: *central bank digital currencies* (CBDCs), now under development in many countries, could entrench programmable surveillance, embedding state control into everyday transactions (Schwab & Malleret, 2020). Nor are community-scale solutions free of danger. Local currencies can stagnate if poorly designed, while public banks, without strong safeguards, may be captured by political elites.

The pattern is familiar. The railroad barons of the 19th century promised connectivity but produced monopolies. The dot-com boom promised decentralization but consolidated corporate empires. Even well-intentioned reforms falter when they preserve the morality tale of debt, continuing to frame default as personal sin rather than systemic flaw (Graeber, 2011).

To avoid such traps, resilience must be built into institutional design: transparency for institutions paired with privacy for individuals, anti-hoarding mechanisms to keep money circulating, ecological anchoring to tether finance to planetary boundaries, and civic literacy to ensure participants understand the structures they inhabit. Without such safeguards, exits risk becoming new enclosures.

BREAKAWAY INTO EXODUS

Leaving the old economy is not a single dramatic leap but a slow migration toward a new fabric of institutions. Václav Benda, writing under Soviet rule in Czechoslovakia, described this strategy as the *"parallel polis"* (Allen, 2015). Dissidents could not overthrow the regime overnight, but they could build parallel structures—schools, cultural networks, and civic organizations— that nurtured autonomy and solidarity until the dominant system weakened.

Today's financial parallel polis might consist of public banks, cooperative platforms, mutual credit systems, community currencies, land trusts, DAOs, and wellbeing budgets. The aim is not to secede from the world but to weave enough alternative nodes that the old system loses its monopoly. Each node, however small, strengthens the mesh; and each institution that proves viable becomes part of a living infrastructure of sovereignty.

The task is translation: turning ideals into repeatable practices. Local groups must learn from one another, growing not through uniformity but through shared principles adapted to context. Over time, the parallel polis becomes not an exception but a durable alternative.

SOVEREIGNTY OR SERVITUDE?

The choice before us is stark. *Do we continue inhabiting an economic operating system where life itself becomes collateral, or do we reclaim the capacity to shape money, debt, and value in ways that serve life?* Sovereignty does not mean isolation but self-authorship, the ability to issue, to refuse, to cooperate, and to measure in ways that carry real meaning.

The empire of debt will not fall on its own. The way out must be chosen through communities that generate their own liquidity, publics that reclaim the power to create and circulate money, networks that steward capital as a collective good, and individuals who awaken to the truth that value begins wherever people unite to declare, '*We can do this differently.*'

To reclaim sovereignty requires courage, because it requires disobedience. To refuse payment with our attention, our labor, or our consent is to disrupt the system of control. Economics may reveal the chains, but disobedience rattles them. From the ledger to the barricade, the art of economic exit is the sacred act of saying no.

REFERENCES

Allen, D. W. (2015). The institutional revolution: Measurement and the economic emergence of the modern world. University of Chicago Press.

Bauwens, M., & Kostakis, V. (2014). Network society and future scenarios for a collaborative economy. Palgrave Macmillan.

Brown, E. (2010). Web of debt: The shocking truth about our money system and how we can break free. Third Millennium Press.

Buterin, V. (2013). Ethereum white paper: A next-generation smart contract and decentralized application platform. https://ethereum.org/en/whitepaper/

Cahn, E. S. (1992). Time dollars: The new currency that enables Americans to turn their hidden resource—time—into personal security and community renewal. Rodale Press.

Eisenstein, C. (2011). Sacred economics: Money, gift, and society in the age of transition. Evolver Editions.

Graeber, D. (2011). Debt: The first 5,000 years. Melville House.

Greer, J. M. (2013). The wealth of nature: Economics as if survival mattered. New Society Publishers.

Hudson, M. (2018). …and forgive them their debts: Lending, foreclosure and redemption—from Bronze Age finance to the Jubilee Year. ISLET-Verlag.

Kelly, M. (2012). Owning our future: The emerging ownership revolution. Berrett-Koehler Publishers.

Klein, N. (2007). The shock doctrine: The rise of disaster capitalism. Metropolitan Books.

Korten, D. C. (2009). Agenda for a new economy: From phantom wealth to real wealth. Berrett-Koehler Publishers.

Leshner, R., & Hayes, G. (2019). Compound: The money market protocol. https://compound.finance/documents/Compound.Whitepaper.pdf

Littera, G., Sartori, L., Dini, P., & Antoniadis, P. (2017). From an idea to a scalable working model: Merging economic benefits with social values in Sardex. International Journal of Community Currency Research, 21(Winter), 6–21. https://doi.org/10.15133/j.ijccr.2017.002

MakerDAO. (2017). The Maker protocol: MakerDAO's multi-collateral Dai (MCD) system. https://makerdao.com/en/whitepaper/

Martenson, C. (2011). The crash course: The unsustainable future of our economy, energy, and environment. Wiley.

Nakamoto, S. (2008). Bitcoin: A peer-to-peer electronic cash system. https://bitcoin.org/bitcoin.pdf

Ostrom, E. (1990). Governing the commons: The evolution of institutions for collective action. Cambridge University Press.

Popper, N. (2015). Digital gold: Bitcoin and the inside story of the misfits and millionaires trying to reinvent money. HarperBusiness.

Raworth, K. (2017). Doughnut economics: Seven ways to think like a 21st-century economist. Chelsea Green Publishing.

Schwab, K., & Malleret, T. (2020). COVID-19: The great reset. Forum Publishing.

Studer, T. (1998). WIR and the Swiss national economy. WIR Bank. (Original work published 1994).

Chapter 14

Conscious Disobedience and the Power of No

"The beginning of wisdom is the ability to say: 'No.'"
— Abraham Joshua Heschel

Every emancipatory act begins with a subtraction. Before we can say a clean, generative yes to life, we must withdraw our consent from the scripts that keep us small, predictable, and governable. The first step to freedom lies not in a romantic leap into the unknown, but in the mundane yet radical decision to refuse. To refuse is to interrupt the automatic compliance that institutions and social expectations attempt to extract from us. The power of no goes beyond negation, becoming a creative force that clears the ground for sovereignty, clarity, and authentic participation.

Saying no is dangerous because it interrupts prediction. In a civilization that monetizes foresight through insurance models, risk scores, credit ratings, behavioral nudging, predictive policing, and recommendation engines, refusal introduces noise into the machine. It destabilizes prediction markets and, by extension, the managerial power built upon them. This is why refusal is punished, shamed, and pathologized. We are told to be team players, to trust the experts, and to follow the protocol. When we follow rules without thinking, we hand over our power to institutions that can never truly care for us.

Conscious disobedience is not adolescent rebellion or nihilistic destruction. It is the disciplined practice of drawing boundaries with awareness, for ethical reasons, and toward a higher order of life. It asks uncomfortable questions: *What am I consenting to? Who benefits from my compliance? What invisible costs—psychological, communal, ecological—am I paying to remain compliant and predictable?*

This chapter explores the philosophy, psychology, and practice of becoming *uncontrollable* in a world obsessed with prediction. The aim is not irresponsibility, but the deliberate exercise of freedom.

PREDICTION, CAPTURE, AND THE NEW SYSTEMS OF OBEDIENCE

We have already seen how the spectacle of punishment gave way to discipline, and how discipline dissolved into the more fluid currents of control. Today the arc bends further still: human experience itself is seized, stripped into data, and fed into machines of prediction that do not merely watch but seek to shape what we will do next. In such a landscape, freedom depends less on visibility than on opacity, and less on compliance than on the capacity to remain unpredictable. It becomes an art of refusal that interrupts capture and reclaims the space of possibility.

What this shift reveals is a deeper logic: modern governance increasingly operates through prediction, and prediction depends on data. To make life comprehensible, apparatuses reduce us to categories, numbers, and behaviors that can be tracked and influenced. As James C. Scott (1998) showed, states have long tried to simplify and standardize local ways of life to render them governable, often with destructive consequences. Today, a technocratic alliance of states and corporations performs this same reduction on a planetary scale. The finer the data, the sharper the prediction; the sharper the prediction, the tighter the control. What is advertised as effortless convenience is really a sweet coating that hides how the system captures your attention and information. Features like one-click shopping or autoplay videos feel seamless, but they are designed to keep you engaged, spending, and feeding data back into the machine.

Against this backdrop, disobedience takes on a new form. To resist is to reintroduce friction, to cultivate opacity, and to become the kind of subject who cannot be fully profiled. It is the right to be a difficult woman, an unruly citizen, a noncompliant patient, or a weird data point. Put simply, it means becoming *unpredictable*, someone whose actions refuse the neat bell curve that statistics assume. Politically, it is the insistence on a moral interiority that escapes categorization, a reminder that not everything essential to human life can be translated into data.

THE PSYCHOLOGY OF "NO"

In neuroscience terms, disobedience is not an error or a glitch. It is an expression of agency. Prefrontal regions involved in executive control, valuation, and moral reasoning, including dorsolateral and ventromedial PFC, activate when individuals inhibit automatic responses or resist social pressure (Miller & Cohen, 2001; Greene et al., 2001). The capacity to inhibit is more than a brake: it is a higher-order ability that allows us to guide and shape our other abilities and in this sense a power of self-authorship.

Psychology deepens this picture by explaining why the refusal to comply is so consequential. *Reactance Theory* (Brehm, 1966) shows that when people sense their freedom is under threat, they are motivated to push back. Modern systems of control, however, dull this natural resistance by normalizing the loss of freedom, leading us to give away our data, time, and attention without protest. *Self-Determination Theory* (Deci & Ryan, 2000) reinforces the point by showing that autonomy, competence, and connection are basic psychological needs. When those needs are systematically undermined by technologies we cannot understand, managers who refuse to let go of control, or medical authorities who dismiss our voices, the result is demoralization, burnout, and disengagement.

Research on *Locus of Control* (Rotter, 1966) extends the argument further. People with an internal locus believe they can influence outcomes, which fosters resilience and responsibility, while an external locus produces passivity and helplessness (Seligman, 1975). Contemporary systems of control deliberately cultivate mass predictability by pushing people toward an external locus, teaching us to trust that external structures "know better." When every contingency is managed from the outside, our intrinsic capacities for prediction and adaptation atrophy. Here disobedience again proves vital, since refusal reintroduces uncertainty and exploration, forcing us to think and adapt rather than simply comply.

Classic social psychology underscores the danger of losing this capacity altogether. The famous experiments of Milgram (1963) and Zimbardo (1973) revealed how easily people surrender judgment and fall into obedience in hierarchical contexts. Conscious disobedience therefore emerges as more than resistance: it is a form of inoculation. It strengthens the moral muscle that pauses to ask *"Should I comply?"* before rushing to obey, keeping alive the agency that makes us fully human.

THE GENEALOGY OF REFUSAL

Henry David Thoreau's *Civil Disobedience* (1849) argued that *"the only obligation which I have a right to assume is to do at any time what I think right."* He refused to pay taxes that would fund slavery and the Mexican-American War. Gandhi refined civil disobedience into *Satyagraha*—truth-force—insisting that refusal must be nonviolent, morally grounded, and publicly accountable (Gandhi, 1927/1993). Václav Havel (1978), writing under communist Czechoslovakia, described the power of *"living in truth"* as a form of quiet but subversive refusal.

Gene Sharp (1973, 2010) systematized nonviolent action into hundreds of methods, ranging from symbolic protest to economic noncooperation. More recently, Erica Chenoweth and Maria Stephan (2011) demonstrated empirically that nonviolent campaigns are more likely to succeed than violent ones.

In the twenty-first century, this lineage continues in the form of *digital resistance.* One approach is *obfuscation*, which means flooding data collectors with misleading or confusing information. For example, some people use fake email addresses for sign-ups, run ad blockers, or rely on apps that generate false browsing patterns so companies cannot build accurate profiles of them (Brunton & Nissenbaum, 2015). Another approach is *encryption*, a way of scrambling information so that only the intended recipient can read it. Secure messaging apps like Signal or WhatsApp and browsing tools such as VPNs offer everyday forms of encryption (Schneier, 2015). More recently, scholars have even argued for the right to remain *"incomputable,"* meaning not fully reduced to data points (Nahum-Claudel, 2022). Conscious disobedience in this sense is not about abandoning technology but about *refusing capture* while reclaiming tools for human purposes.

EVERYDAY NONCOMPLIANCE

James C. Scott (1985) is well known for his account of the *"weapons of the weak,"* the everyday acts of resistance by peasants and laborers, such as foot-dragging, feigned ignorance, sabotage, and quiet non-cooperation. In contemporary states, similar practices take the form of refusing to fill invasive forms, declining to install tracking apps, insisting on cash, opting out of loyalty programs, and forming mutual-aid networks that undermine dependence on extractive platforms.

Albert O. Hirschman's (1970) triad of *exit, voice,* and *loyalty* helps clarify these dynamics. Conscious disobedience operates through exit, by building parallel institutions and micro-secessions from platform dependence, and through voice, by publicly contesting rules, narratives, and metrics. Loyalty is redefined: instead of fidelity to institutions, it is owed to truth, life, and community.

Slow refusal adds another dimension. In a culture of acceleration, refusal is temporal: reclaiming the right to delay, to be bored, to not respond. As Byung-Chul Han (2015) describes, we inhabit a *"burnout society"* where individuals become self-exploiters addicted to optimization. Conscious refusal interrupts this tempo, offering a counter-rhythm that preserves interiority.

THE ETHICS OF REFUSAL

Refusal without an ethical horizon collapses into nihilism or self-indulgence. To cultivate refusal as a generative act requires that it be oriented toward values larger than the self. The "no" defended here is not arbitrary but teleological: it points toward truth, dignity, autonomy, and even the sacred. Audre Lorde (1988) captured this spirit when she reminded us that caring for oneself is not self-indulgence but self-preservation. In this view, refusal becomes less a closing of the hand than a guarding of the flame, a way of protecting what allows life to keep burning.

For refusal to be more than a passing gesture, it has to be practiced with care and discernment. This begins with *transparency*, because when people explain the reasons for their refusal, they open the door to dialogue, mutual recognition, and even collective action. *Proportionality* also matters: saying no should aim to prevent greater harm, not stiffen into stubbornness for its own sake. To this we must add *nonviolence*, which gives refusal its integrity, showing that disobedience can protect dignity on all sides while making its intent unmistakable. Finally, there is the question of *substitutability*. Refusal that only tears down leaves a vacuum that domination can easily fill. True refusal plants seeds of renewal, cultivating alternative practices and institutions that carry healthier values into the future.

Such refusal grows gradually, first in small gestures, then in more deliberate choices, and eventually in decisions that reshape institutions. A simple practice is the *"one-second no"*: pausing before complying, whether online or in daily life, to ask, *What am I really agreeing to? Who benefits, and at what cost?* Other practices extend this stance: protecting privacy with encryption, preserving autonomy by using cash or local exchange, opting out of behavioral scoring architectures, and reclaiming attention through digital breaks and intentional reading.

When practiced collectively, refusal multiplies its power. Renter unions, worker cooperatives, and secure civic assemblies show how small acts of dissent can grow into social transformation. Research by Erica Chenoweth (2017) has demonstrated that *when as little as 3.5 percent of a population actively participates, entire regimes can shift*. Collective refusal becomes the seed of collective affirmation, since an organized "no" already gestures toward a "yes."

Finally, refusal also requires *courage to resist shame*. Structures of control often recruit ridicule and stigma to do their work. To say no openly is to refuse humiliation and to create a space where dignity, solidarity, and imagination can thrive. Boundaries, in this sense, are not walls but acts of care, one of the ways we protect what matters most. Ethical refusal is therefore not the end of responsibility but its beginning. It is the practice of keeping alive a margin of unpredictability where freedom and creativity can survive.

DISOBEDIENCE AS RITUAL

We do not live by theory alone but by rhythm, and it is rhythm that turns ideas into habits and habits into culture. Refusal gains its strength when it becomes ritual, when repeated practices carry values into the body and the community. Through ritual, what begins as a single choice takes root as a way of life.

On the level of the individual, daily rituals of refusal might include simple acts such as beginning the day with a question: *What will I not allow to colonize my attention today?* Thirty minutes of analog thinking with pen and paper, or a walk without devices, can become a small but potent rite of reclaiming presence.

Weekly rituals might take the form of a *digital retreat*, where platform feeds, emails, and performance metrics are set aside in favor of more nourishing activities. Reading, cooking, slow conversations, and time in nature serve not only as rest but as affirmation of alternative tempos. Over time, these rhythms entwine themselves into identity, signaling to oneself and others that refusal is not an accident but a way of being.

Monthly rituals can also take collective form. Assemblies where people gather to share strategies of refusal, lessons from failed exits, or updates on legislation help weave a culture of solidarity. In these spaces, refusal is no longer an isolated act of conscience but a shared expression of freedom that strengthens communal bonds. Annual rituals can deepen this work by inviting reflection: an audit of dependencies, a reconsideration of which platforms to exit, which institutions deserve continued loyalty, and even the rewriting of one's personal constitution.

Rituals matter because repetition reshapes both brain and culture. Through ritual, the "no" becomes embodied rather than merely asserted, and resistance becomes durable rather than fleeting.

FROM NO TO YES

Refusal is necessary but never sufficient, for a life cannot be built on negation alone. To refuse is to clear space, but in that clearing we must also create. As discussed earlier, Václav Benda (1978) called this constructive dimension the *parallel polis*, the institutions that arise outside official orders.

In the present, the parallel polis takes shape in many different ways. Some of its expressions lie in economics, such as local currencies that keep value circulating within communities or cooperative platforms that offer alternatives to Silicon Valley's data-harvesting. Others emerge in how we relate to the land, with regenerative agriculture that heals soil while also renewing social bonds, and in how we power our lives, through community-owned energy grids that reduce dependence on extractive industries. Knowledge itself can be reimagined, as decentralized approaches to science share discoveries beyond corporate gatekeepers. Even health can be organized differently, through networks that protect privacy while placing care above profit. Seen together, these are not isolated projects but signs of a larger pattern: the gradual construction of infrastructures that serve life rather than extraction.

The movement from no to yes unfolds in stages. The first stage is *detox*, where we disengage from exploitative regimes and withdraw consent from their grip. The second stage is *healing*. This means regaining a sense of control over one's own life and rebuilding trust with others, often through care, mutual support, and relearning skills that were once handed off to machines or outside services. The third stage is *creation*, where institutions are founded that embody alternative values and practices. Each stage requires different virtues: clarity for detox, patience for healing, and courage and play for creation.

What matters is that refusal does not stiffen into withdrawal alone but blossoms into affirmation. The parallel polis is not exile: it is a rehearsal for another world.

THE UNCONTROLLABLE HUMAN

A predictable human is an obedient human, and an obedient human is an exhausted human. Exhaustion erodes the capacity for imagination, and without imagination there can be no alternative. The project of becoming *uncontrollable* is therefore the project of reclaiming imagination itself. It is the capacity to perceive otherwise, to see possibilities where official maps show only inevitabilities, and to act from that perception even when models, experts, or majorities disagree.

In a civilization that demands constant quantification, ranking, and measurement, the most radical act may be to vanish into integrity. This does not mean retreating from life but rooting more deeply within it, choosing to inhabit a space where artificial watchers cannot follow. That space is the ground of conscience, love, and lived truth. From here, the word *no* carries a different weight, not the tantrum of childhood or adolescence but a boundary strong enough to guard what matters and, in guarding, to open the space for a deeper yes, one vast enough to remake the world.

Yet imagination alone is not enough, for rebellion without tools quickly collapses into theater. To truly step outside the *Matrix* requires more than slogans: it calls for practices that reshape the nervous system, loosen the inherited scripts of obedience, and nurture an embodied sense of freedom. Breath, movement, silence, and dialogue serve as everyday technologies of deprogramming, while community provides the ground where courage can be tested and strengthened. Through such practices, the uncontrollable human appears not as a distant fantasy but as a lived reality, a way of being that resists capture while radiating possibility.

To become uncontrollable is to step into the forge of liberation, where the fire of disobedience burns away illusion and the labor of care rebuilds the foundations. In this rhythm of refusal, seeds of creation are quietly nurtured, until resistance itself becomes the ground from which a freer world can grow.

REFERENCES

Brehm, J. W. (1966). A theory of psychological reactance. Academic Press.

Brunton, F., & Nissenbaum, H. (2015). Obfuscation: A user's guide for privacy and protest. MIT Press.

Chenoweth, E. (2017). The future of nonviolent resistance. Journal of Democracy, 28(4), 69–84.

Chenoweth, E., & Stephan, M. J. (2011). Why civil resistance works: The strategic logic of nonviolent conflict. Columbia University Press.

Deci, E. L., & Ryan, R. M. (2000). The "what" and "why" of goal pursuits: Human needs and the self-determination of behavior. Psychological Inquiry, 11(4), 227–268.

Gandhi, M. (1993). An autobiography: The story of my experiments with truth (M. Desai, Trans.). Beacon Press. (Original work published 1927)

Graeber, D. (2011). Debt: The first 5,000 years. Melville House.

Greene, J. D., Sommerville, R. B., Nystrom, L. E., Darley, J. M., & Cohen, J. D. (2001). An fMRI investigation of emotional engagement in moral judgment. Science, 293(5537), 2105–2108.

Han, B.-C. (2015). The burnout society. Stanford University Press.

Havel, V. (1978). The power of the powerless. Samizdat.

Heschel, A. J. (1965). Who is man? Stanford University Press.

Hirschman, A. O. (1970). Exit, voice, and loyalty: Responses to decline in firms, organizations, and states. Harvard University Press.

Lorde, A. (1988). A burst of light: Essays. Firebrand Books.

Milgram, S. (1963). Behavioral study of obedience. Journal of Abnormal and Social Psychology, 67(4), 371–378.

Miller, E. K., & Cohen, J. D. (2001). An integrative theory of prefrontal cortex function. Annual Review of Neuroscience, 24(1), 167–202.

Nahum-Claudel, C. (2022). Incomputability as a political value. Anthropological Theory, 22(3), 373–394.

Rotter, J. B. (1966). Generalized expectancies for internal versus external control of reinforcement. Psychological Monographs: General and Applied, 80(1), 1–28.

Schneier, B. (2015). Data and Goliath: The hidden battles to collect your data and control your world. W. W. Norton.

Scott, J. C. (1985). Weapons of the weak: Everyday forms of peasant resistance. Yale University Press.

Scott, J. C. (1998). Seeing like a state: How certain schemes to improve the human condition have failed. Yale University Press.

Seligman, M. E. P. (1975). Helplessness: On depression, development, and death. Freeman.

Sharp, G. (1973). The politics of nonviolent action. Porter Sargent.

Sharp, G. (2010). From dictatorship to democracy. The Albert Einstein Institution.

Thoreau, H. D. (1849). Civil disobedience.

Zimbardo, P. G. (1973). On the ethics of intervention in human psychological research: With special reference to the Stanford prison experiment. Cognition, 2(2), 243–256.

Chapter 15

Tools of Deprogramming

*"None are more hopelessly enslaved than
those who falsely believe they are free."*
— Goethe

In the earlier chapters, we examined the machinery that shapes the *Human Robot*: the fears, institutions, media messages, economic pressures, and thought patterns that guide how we see and act. These forces work together, producing habits that feel natural even though they have been intentionally planned.

This chapter shifts from analysis to action. The central question is no longer only what shapes us, but how we might reshape ourselves. *How can we loosen old conditioning at the deepest levels of attention, emotion, belief, identity, and culture? How do we build the capacity to live and think freely in an age carefully structured to keep us on autopilot?*

What follows is a step-by-step framework for deprogramming. It begins with calming the nervous system, then moves into reclaiming attention, strengthening clear thinking, and eventually redesigning the environments that make it easier to remain awake than to fall back asleep. This framework is a *Deprogramming Guide*. It rests on six connected areas: *body and emotional balance, attention and media habits, ways of knowing and questioning, story and identity work, collective dialogue and intelligence,* and finally *structural redesign with exit strategies.* Each area supports the others, and together they create the conditions for lasting freedom. To make this concrete, the chapter closes with a thirty-day *Deprogramming Intensive*, a practical experiment that invites readers to put these tools into daily life.

BODY AND EMOTION REGULATION: CREATING SAFETY FOR CHANGE

The empire of fear does not only govern the mind, it also takes hold of the body. Its power rests on keeping our nervous systems on constant alert. The heart races, the breath shortens, and the muscles brace for danger. In such a state, perception narrows until almost everything looks like a threat, thought contracts into tunnel vision, and in that confined space the loudest voice, usually the one promising safety, becomes the one we obey.

Reason alone cannot free us if the body still feels trapped in a burning building. Before the mind can open, the body's alarms must quiet, and safety must shift from being an abstract idea to becoming a lived experience. Only then can the mind relax enough to reconsider its assumptions.

Breathwork provides one of the most effective ways to calm these alarms. Practices such as *coherent breathing*, inhaling for five seconds and exhaling for five seconds, signal to the body that it is no longer under siege. Just ten minutes a day can increase *heart-rate variability*, a marker of flexibility between arousal and rest. As balance returns, the body gradually begins to trust that the danger has passed.

Once the body feels more settled, *somatic inquiry* helps deepen stability. This practice begins by noticing sensations as they arise, such as tightness in the chest, heat in the face, or a flutter in the stomach. Naming these sensations makes them easier to manage. By approaching strong feelings in small, safe doses, the nervous system learns that it can face intensity without shutting down. It is like guiding a skittish animal to water, letting it sip and retreat, until gradually the body learns: *I can feel this and remain secure.*

With this foundation, *mindfulness practices* expand awareness. *Open monitoring meditation* reveals the weather patterns of the mind: storms of anger, gusts of fear, or clouds of doubt. Each can be observed, and each eventually passes. Simple noting practices add clarity by labeling thoughts with words such as "hearing," "worrying," or "planning." Even the automatic machinery of thought becomes visible, and with visibility comes freedom from blind obedience.

Therapeutic approaches such as *Acceptance and Commitment Therapy* add further tools. One of these is cognitive defusion, which helps us see thoughts as just thoughts (Hayes, Strosahl, & Wilson, 2012). For example, repeating a belief in a silly voice until it loses its power can reveal that what once felt like a command is nothing more than sound. From there, we can pause to ask a deeper question: *what really matters to me?* When fear is not running the show, our values step forward and point the way, like a compass helping us find direction.

When the body stops bracing for impact, the mind can finally reopen to choice.

ATTENTION AND INFORMATION HYGIENE

If physiology lays the foundation, attention decides what gets in. Attention is the front door of the mind, and in the platform age that door is constantly under siege.

Deprogramming begins by reclaiming this door. Many find their first liberation through *digital minimalism*, deleting their most compulsive apps for thirty days (Newport, 2019). What returns is striking: time, calm, and mental spaciousness. Turning off notifications by default makes interruptions rare guests instead of permanent squatters in consciousness.

Once the gates are protected, the next step is sharpening discernment. *Media literacy* is no longer optional. Simple habits like checking multiple sources, tracing claims back to where they started, and comparing them with independent reporting help us sort truth from spin. Skepticism by itself is not enough. Real skills are needed to resist manipulation.

Preparation also matters. *Prebunking*, or anticipating manipulation before encountering it, inoculates the mind against falsehood (Lewandowsky & van der Linden, 2021). Getting a quick look at common tricks like false choices, personal attacks, or fake grassroots campaigns makes them easier to spot later. Once you know the move, it loses much of its power.

Attention care is not simply abstinence but cultivation. An information diet resembles tending a garden. We choose high-signal sources, schedule regular fasts from the news to let the nervous system reset, and use tools that deliver information on our terms rather than a mechanical gatekeeper (Thaler & Sunstein, 2008). Reclaimed attention is the raw material of creation: guard the gate, and the mind becomes fertile again.

PRACTICES FOR CLEAR THINKING

If attention guards the entryway, these practices keep the castle honest. Deprogramming is not only about blocking toxic inputs: it is also about learning to spot falsehoods and dismantle them. Philosopher Andy Norman (2021) describes this as the mind's *immune system.*

One of the most transformative habits is *steelmanning.* Before critiquing a view, we rebuild it at its strongest. This interrupts the reflex to caricature opponents and helps cut through tribal defensiveness.

Another useful habit is the *cognitive autopsy.* When a belief collapses or a decision backfires, we ask what signals we ignored, what biases tilted our perception, and what incentives distorted our judgment. Writing down lessons like these creates a personal playbook where past failures become compost for clearer thinking (Klein, 2007).

Conceptual tools also help. Boyd's *OODA loop* (observe, orient, decide, act) teaches rapid adaptation (Boyd, 1987; Richards, 2004). The *Cynefin framework* adds further clarity by distinguishing between simple, complicated, complex, and chaotic problems (Snowden & Boone, 2007).

It is just as important to test our beliefs before the world does it for us. One way is through a *premortem*, where we imagine a project has already failed and then ask why (Klein, 2007). Another is to invite trusted people who see things differently to challenge our thinking. Their honest feedback can prevent shaky confidence from being mistaken for truth.

At its deepest, clear thinking means stepping outside our own maps and seeing them for what they are—tools, not territories. Put simply, even our most cherished convictions can be revised when new evidence arrives. A strong mind is not a fortress sealed against change: it is more like a living ecosystem, porous enough to admit new evidence, resilient enough to weather storms of doubt, and wise enough to discard maps that no longer serve. Deprogramming, then, is less about winning arguments and more about cultivating a mind that stays perpetually open to correction.

NARRATIVE AND IDENTITY WORK

Our beliefs do not float on their own. They are woven into stories, and those stories are tied to our sense of identity. This is why persuasion often fails. When new ideas feel like a threat to who we are, the emotional brain steps in and shuts down reasoning. Real change, then, is not just about adjusting individual beliefs. It also requires looking at the deeper programs that organize those beliefs into a story of who we are. Ideas from *narrative therapy* can help here (White & Epston, 1990).

Narrative therapy invites us to name these programs we have unconsciously absorbed. For example, identities such as "The

Good Student," "The Productivity Machine," or "The Obedient Citizen" each carry a bundle of beliefs about how to act, what matters, and what is expected. Once these programs are named, they can be pulled into the light and treated as stories rather than absolute truths.

Metaphors also structure thought by organizing patterns of perception. If life is framed as war, every interaction becomes a battle. If the market is framed as a jungle, competition appears inevitable. Shifting metaphors to "life as a garden" or "the market as a dance" can reorganize entire worlds of meaning (Lakoff & Johnson, 1980).

Stories, however, require orientation. Without a guiding direction, deprogramming risks drifting. Articulating a *personal constitution,* rooted in non-negotiable values, provides gravity. These values become powerful when enacted daily in behavior and choice.

The shadow must also be integrated. What is suppressed does not disappear but rules from the dark. Approaches such as the *3-2-1 Process* and *Internal Family Systems* offer ways forward (Schwartz, 1995). Both approaches affirm that deprogramming does not mean amputating conditioned fragments but welcoming them home with clarity and care.

Identity also shifts through ritual. Public acts of renunciation, vows, initiatory challenges, or commitments to service anchor change in the body and in community. Without ritual, transformation risks drifting into abstraction. With ritual, it becomes embodied.

When identity is rigid, novelty is threat; when identity is expansive, novelty is nourishment. Narrative work transforms deprogramming from a defensive act into a creative one. It is the art of authoring the frame through which reality itself is lived.

COLLECTIVE INTELLIGENCE AND DIALOGUE

Programming is social, and so deprogramming must also be social. Traditions as diverse as *Athenian assemblies, Quaker meetings*, and *Indigenous councils* remind us of the power of dialogue when it unfolds slowly enough for reflection. Practices like *Bohmian Dialogue*, which asks participants to suspend assumptions and watch thought emerge as a shared process, or *Socratic circles*, which require careful paraphrase and reference before speaking, show how conversation can shift from contest to co-discovery.

These older traditions find resonance in modern experiments. *Citizens' assemblies*, for example, demonstrate that randomly selected and well-briefed groups are capable of reaching conclusions that are often wiser and less polarized than those produced by partisan institutions (Fishkin, 2018).

Smaller groups matter too. *Microsolidarity* is the practice of gathering in small circles, meeting often enough for trust to take root and honesty to breathe (Tannahill, 2019). In these intimate spaces, testing each other's ideas can become rituals that bind the group together.

MAKING FREEDOM EASIER

Even the best habits can collapse if our surroundings constantly push us the other way. Willpower alone is not enough. Real freedom means shaping our environment so that the right choice is also the easiest choice (Thaler & Sunstein, 2008).

One way to do this is by changing our starting points. Research shows that *starting points* guide behavior more than good intentions. For example, you might set your phone to block endless feeds from the start, plan your day around times of deep focus, or make small agreements with friends that help you stick to your goals.

Another step is *to build alternatives that give you more independence.* Joining a food co-op, using secure messaging apps, or supporting local exchange systems can reduce reliance on big, centralized platforms.

Learning can also be reclaimed. Instead of only following formal education, we can create our own lifelong learning plan by choosing to study things like statistics, systems thinking, how propaganda works, or body-based practices. In this way, everyday life itself becomes the classroom.

Finally, it helps to review our patterns from time to time. Every few months, we can ask: *What influences are draining me? Where am I betraying my values? Which incentives are pulling me in the wrong direction?* Treating life as something we can update keeps us from sliding back into old habits.

Without redesigning our environment, freedom feels like an uphill climb. With it, freedom starts to feel natural, as if the environment itself is carrying us forward.

THE DEPROGRAMMING INTENSIVE

Some changes take years, but others can be sparked by focused immersion. The *Deprogramming Intensive* is a thirty-day reset to clear distractions, refresh mental habits, and set up better structures before old patterns return.

Week One: Build Stability. Begin each day with breathwork and simple meditation to calm the nervous system. Remove compulsive feeds and replace them with a healthier information diet (Newport, 2019). Create a belief inventory by listing the beliefs you inherited from family, culture, or ideology and noting what they cost you.

Week Two: Sharpen Perception. Take a digital break by going fully offline for a set time. Write down your core values in a personal constitution and connect each one to a daily action.

Week Three: Test Your Thinking. Challenge your own ideas by writing out arguments against them. Practice steelmanning by rebuilding a view you disagree with at its strongest. Keep a prediction journal by recording what you expect to happen in daily situations and comparing it with what actually occurs (Klein, 2007).

Week Four: Reshape Structure. Review your environment, choose one major change, and write it down. This might mean leaving a toxic platform, reducing hours in a draining job, or replacing screen time with a daily walk or reading hour. Make a simple plan to maintain the change, and close the week with a personal ritual to mark your commitment.

Thirty days will not complete deprogramming, and it is not meant to. But it is enough to taste freedom and make sliding back into old habits harder. This Intensive works like a controlled fire, clearing space for new growth to thrive.

THROUGH THE WOUND, INTO WHOLENESS

Deprogramming is not a finish line but a rhythm. We notice the trance, loosen its grip, adopt better practices, and return to the world in service. Influence never disappears, but it can be chosen. Freedom is measured not by the absence of shaping forces but by the presence of influences that are transparent, chosen, and revisable. The *Human Robot* can awaken, though not by rejecting structure altogether. Liberation lies in building habits, communities, and incentives that nurture awareness and love.

The tools already exist. What remains is the discipline to use them and the willingness to keep practicing. Liberation is not a one-time act of release but an ongoing renewal of body, mind, and society.

These tools lose their value if they stiffen into rigid rules. The task is not only to loosen manipulation's grip but also to remain open to meaning and growth. Renewal endures when the mind stays flexible and the heart receptive.

REFERENCES

Boyd, J. R. (1987). A discourse on winning and losing. Unpublished briefing, Air University Library, Maxwell Air Force Base, AL.

Bohm, D. (1996). On dialogue. Routledge.

Fishkin, J. S. (2018). Democracy when the people are thinking: Revitalizing our politics through public deliberation. Oxford University Press.

Goethe, J. W. von. (1949). Maxims and reflections (W. H. Auden & E. Mayer, Trans.). Penguin. (Original work published n.d.)

Hayes, S. C., Strosahl, K. D., & Wilson, K. G. (2012). Acceptance and commitment therapy: The process and practice of mindful change (2nd ed.). Guilford Press. (Original work published 1999)

Klein, G. (2007). Performing a project premortem. Harvard Business Review, 85(9), 18–19.

Lakoff, G., & Johnson, M. (1980). Metaphors we live by. University of Chicago Press.

Lewandowsky, S., & van der Linden, S. (2021). Countering misinformation and fake news through inoculation and prebunking. European Review of Social Psychology, 32(2), 348–384. https://doi.org/10.1080/10463283.2021.1874212

Newport, C. (2019). Digital minimalism: Choosing a focused life in a noisy world. Portfolio.

Norman, A. (2021). Mental immunity: Infectious ideas, mind-parasites, and the search for a better way to think. HarperOne.

Richards, C. (2004). Certain to win: The strategy of John Boyd, applied to business. Xlibris.

Schwartz, R. C. (1995). Internal family systems therapy. Guilford Press.

Snowden, D. J., & Boone, M. E. (2007). A leader's framework for decision making. Harvard Business Review, 85(11), 68–76.

Tannahill, R. (2019). Microsolidarity. Retrieved from https://www.microsolidarity.cc/

Thaler, R. H., & Sunstein, C. R. (2008). Nudge: Improving decisions about health, wealth, and happiness. Yale University Press.

White, M., & Epston, D. (1990). Narrative means to therapeutic ends. W. W. Norton.

Chapter 16

Reclaiming the Divine Within

*"The world is not comprehensible, but it is embraceable:
through the embracing of one of its beings."*
— Martin Buber

We live in a time when the old gods have been declared dead again and again, yet temples continue to resurface in unexpected places. They appear in yoga studios and psychedelic ceremonies, in meditation retreats and activist encampments, and even within the meticulously optimized routines of biohackers. Atheists now write about awe, neuroscientists investigate mystical-type experiences, and philosophers grapple with ideas of resonance, meaning, and being. As Taylor (2007) observes, we are "cross-pressured": disenchanted by the collapse of traditional cosmologies, yet still haunted by intimations of the more-than-material.

Earlier chapters traced how this condition of disenchantment emerged, how meaning was hollowed out by logics of consumption and control, and how attention itself was captured and monetized. But if modernity has thinned the world, it has not extinguished the human longing for depth. *Against this backdrop, the question arises: what unfolds when the work of reintegrating is brought directly into the heart of spiritual life?*

To approach this question, I offer a framework for reclaiming the sacred without requiring belief. By *"sacred,"* I do not mean adherence to doctrines. Rather, I mean encounters with what traditions have called *Ultimate Reality* — the Divine, the All, or the Ground of Being. Such encounters need not conform to a single form. They may arrive in moments of awe that overwhelm the ego, in the shimmering presence of nature, or in the quiet fullness of the everyday.

When they do, life itself begins to appear differently. It reveals more than what can be measured, controlled, or put to use, carrying a richness that resists reduction, a depth that cannot be explained away. Some experience this in a forest that seems to breathe with its own vitality, others in a piece of music that pierces the heart, and still others in the silence between words, suddenly alive with meaning. Ultimate Reality, then, is not a distant realm floating above the ordinary. It is woven through both the ordinary and the extraordinary, waiting to be recognized wherever life is met with openness and reverence.

Seen in this light, the sacred is not an abstract idea to be accepted or 'rejected. It is a lived orientation that can be cultivated and shared, both personally and in community. This orientation does not rest on subscribing to a set of beliefs about the universe. Instead, it invites a transformation of perception, embodiment, relationship, and practice. And, as the chapter will later suggest, its authenticity is shown less in arguments than in the fruits it bears in life.

BEYOND BELIEF, INTO PARTICIPATION

Vervaeke (2019) argues that today's crisis of meaning stems from relying too heavily on one kind of knowledge: knowing that something is true. This is what he calls *propositional* knowing. Other ways of knowing—how to act (*procedural*), how to see from a certain perspective (*perspectival*), and how to participate directly (*participatory*)—have been neglected. In the past, religious traditions held these forms of knowing together through ritual, story, and contemplative practice. With the rise of modernity, those structures were dismantled. We were left with propositions alone, easy to argue over or dismiss, but cut off from the deeper grammar of lived participation.

To move beyond this imbalance, reclaiming the sacred without belief means recovering the richness of these neglected forms. Concepts and maps still matter because they help orient us, but transformation depends on more than ideas. It takes shape in practice that trains attention and grounds us in the body, in ways of seeing that disclose what truly matters, and in a kind of participation where self and world are changed together.

In this light, Ultimate Reality does not appear as a metaphysical claim to accept or reject. It arises instead as a felt resonance that comes from deep participation in life itself. And this resonance is not beyond inquiry. It can be explored with rigor through phenomenology as well as through contemplative science and shared investigation (Vervaeke, Ferraro, and Herrera-Bennett, 2023).

AWE, PRESENCE, AND RESONANCE

William James (1985) described mystical states as marked by ineffability, a noetic quality of knowing, transiency, and passivity. Rudolf Otto deepened this picture with his account of the *mysterium tremendum et fascinans*, the sacred as an experience at once terrifying and alluring. Contemporary psychology extends these insights, showing that awe reduces self-focus, widens our sense of connection, and fosters prosocial orientation (Keltner, 2023).

The phenomenology of encountering Ultimate Reality often begins in awe, when the world spills beyond the narrow frame of the ego and presence deepens. In such moments, reality feels more saturated, more itself, and meaning comes alive as unnoticed patterns suddenly light up with relevance (Vervaeke, 2019). Value is no longer experienced merely in terms of usefulness but is felt as intrinsic and irreducible. From this foundation, a natural pull toward compassion and responsibility can arise, along with a subtle transformation of time itself, as moments seem to thicken, slow, and open into greater depth.

Importantly, such experiences are not confined to belief. They can emerge in contemplative practice, deep listening, immersion in nature, psychedelic experience, artistic creation, ritual, or attunement with others; and they sometimes arise even in those with no interest in the metaphysical or spiritual. Ultimate Reality, then, is not an abstract doctrine but a lived encounter, available in many registers of life.

THE EXTRAORDINARY IN THE ORDINARY

Traditional theistic models often framed Ultimate Reality as transcendence, a realm beyond or separate from this world. Reclaiming it without belief requires a shift toward seeing how it shines through the ordinary: in the warmth of a shared meal, the rhythm of seasons, or the simple awareness of being alive.

This perspective resonates with Alfred North Whitehead's process philosophy, which understands reality as a relational web of becoming (Whitehead, 1978). It also aligns with Indigenous cosmologies that refuse the split between nature and culture, experiencing Ultimate Reality instead as a living field of relationships (Kimmerer, 2013).

In this light, Ultimate Reality can be encountered not only in awe-filled mystical states but also in the vitality of nature and the quiet radiance of daily presence. Simple gestures—lighting a candle, pausing before work begins, sharing stories in times of loss—become ways of charging the ordinary with meaning. Repetition engraves significance into the body and nervous system, while shared intention integrates private experience into communal life. The extraordinary is not elsewhere: it is here, waiting to be seen.

THE WORLD OF LIVING SYMBOLS

Henry Corbin (1997) distinguished what he called the *imaginal* from the merely imaginary. By this he meant a shared realm of images, archetypes, and meaning. The imaginal is not a hallucination and not a literal landscape, but a meeting ground where mind and world join to shape significance

We encounter this realm in many ways: in a dream that lingers and influences how we see the day ahead, in a story that offers guidance during a life transition, in a painting or piece of music that feels alive with presence, or in a vision during deep meditation or ritual. Jungian psychology preserved part of this capacity through the practice of *active imagination*, while many spiritual and artistic traditions have encouraged people to see their lives as unfolding stories and to recognize the archetypal patterns at play. Today it also appears in ecological movements that speak of "Mother Earth," or in social justice rituals that draw on imagery of liberation and renewal.

This world of living symbols offers a third space between rigid literalism and empty fantasy, a space where images and stories can be treated as alive and meaningful without being mistaken for dogma. In the work of reclaiming Ultimate Reality without belief, such a space is essential. A dream that reshapes how we see the day, a myth that helps us cross a threshold, or a collective symbol like the torch of liberty can all carry meaning that feels real without needing to be reduced to hard fact. In this way, the imaginal keeps imagination vital, nourishes creativity, and deepens both the ethical and aesthetic dimensions of life.

Living symbols remind us that Ultimate Reality is not only felt but also imagined, pictured, and storied. Yet symbols and images are not enough on their own. What finally shows the value of such encounters is the fruit they bear in our lives.

THE FRUITS OF ENCOUNTER WITH ULTIMATE REALITY

William James (1985) suggested that religious experiences should be judged not by their origins but by their fruits. What matters is not where an experience comes from but what it gives rise to. Encounters with Ultimate Reality are less important for how they begin than for how they shape a life. Genuine encounters bear fruits of humility, compassion, and responsibility, while distorted ones slide into arrogance, narcissism, or escapism.

This focus on fruits shifts our attention from the extraordinary event itself to the kind of life that grows from it. Hartmut Rosa (2019) helps here by proposing that resonance, not acceleration, is what grounds healthy relationships with the world. Resonant relationships are those in which we are touched and transformed, and in which reciprocity naturally flows. In this sense, the measure of encounter is not found in abstract doctrine but in the quality of life it nurtures.

When experiences are divorced from responsibility, they collapse into spectacle, performance, or narcissistic transcendence. The glow of insight soon fades, leaving little more than an inflated self. By contrast, when they bear the fruits of service, care, and reciprocity, they reveal their authenticity. What matters, in the end, is what the encounter gives back to life, to relationships, to the Earth, and to generations yet to come.

From this perspective, the fruits of encounter are not private possessions but shared responsibilities, and how we live them out together becomes crucial. Their endurance, in turn, depends on the spaces and practices of community, for such experiences cannot be sustained in isolation.

COMMUNITIES OF BELONGING

A post-belief sacred cannot remain individualistic. It flourishes in the spaces between us, woven not from dogma but from shared practice. Communities of belonging must learn to root themselves without crystallizing into ideology, to welcome many voices without dissolving into relativism, and to hold one another accountable without building thrones of control.

What holds such communities together is not one fixed belief but a shared orientation toward values such as honesty, compassion, and care for the Earth. Their strength lies in practices that remain alive and adaptable, where ritual is treated not as empty repetition but as a living form that can be shaped and questioned so it stays meaningful. Humility protects this vitality, allowing insights from science, personal experience, and art to be welcomed as complementary ways of seeing truth.

When humility meets practice, structures emerge that keep power fluid and relationships resilient. Leadership rotates so that no one becomes a permanent axis, while a culture of healing ensures that when harm occurs it is mended rather than ignored. Shared liturgies in song, story, or ritual become resources held in common, continually renewed by many hands.

In lived reality, these principles take shape in many forms: mutual aid networks that redistribute care, cooperative platforms that resist extractive models, restorative justice circles that heal conflict, and ecological collectives that root belonging in the living world.

GUARDRAILS: AVOIDING THE NEW DOGMAS

Reclaiming the sacred without belief has its own risks. Fresh dogmas can appear, whether in the form of rigid scientism, uncritical devotion to psychedelics, elitist *secret knowledge,* or a kind of stylish but empty nihilism. Each gives the impression of touching ultimate truth, but in the end only locks people inside a closed system.

Experiences must be tested by their fruits, meaning by the results they bring (James, 1985). Without this, communities risk drifting into illusion or harm. Safeguards include drawing on many sources of wisdom, with scientists, therapists, philosophers, elders, and artists helping to keep claims honest. Strong governance is also crucial. Leadership should rotate, finances must remain transparent, and clear processes for addressing harm are needed to prevent the rise of a single "guru" figure. Above all, communities must stay alert to how easily power and holiness are projected onto leaders, and create structures that disperse this energy rather than concentrate it in one person.

Without such safeguards, communities that seek freedom may end up reproducing the very controls they hoped to escape. With them, they can keep open the fragile space where the sacred can take root. These moments are sustained not by belief but by the practices and relationships that give them form. When communities nurture such spaces, the sacred becomes less a doctrine to defend and more a living presence woven into daily life.

A VOW OF ATTENTION AND CARE

To reclaim the sacred without belief is to take a vow of attention, care, and humility. It means meeting reality as more than a resource, encountering other beings as more than instruments, and receiving one's own life as a site of consecration. It also resists the shallow certainties of dogma and the cold reductionism that strips life of depth.

Such a vow becomes a way of living: noticing the world with care, seeing if insights lead to good outcomes, and keeping a spirit of discipline without losing hope. From this grounding emerges a way of life that nurtures communities of belonging without authoritarian control, keeps the imaginal alive without collapsing it into literal claims, and moves with humility before a reality that always exceeds comprehension.

This vow is not the end of belief but the end of its sovereignty. In its place arise participation, devotion, practice, and care, the living grammar of a sacred that does not need belief to be real. To live without belief is not emptiness but the birth of an ethics rooted in awareness itself. When the sacred is no longer enforced by doctrine, what guides us is compassion arising from presence and responsibility flowing from interconnection. Reclaiming the sacred without belief is not only an individual project but the seed of a humanity beyond belief, where responsibility emerges not from authority but from awakening.

REFERENCES

Buber, M. (1996). I and Thou (W. Kaufmann, Trans.). Simon & Schuster. (Original work published 1923)

Corbin, H. (1997). Alone with the Alone: Creative imagination in the Sufism of Ibn ʿArabi (R. Manheim, Trans.). Princeton University Press. (Original work published 1969)

James, W. (1985). The varieties of religious experience: A study in human nature. Harvard University Press. (Original work published 1902)

Keltner, D. (2023). Awe: The new science of everyday wonder and how it can transform your life. Penguin Press.

Kimmerer, R. W. (2013). Braiding sweetgrass: Indigenous wisdom, scientific knowledge, and the teachings of plants. Milkweed Editions.

Otto, R. (1958). The idea of the holy (J. W. Harvey, Trans.). Oxford University Press. (Original work published 1917)

Rosa, H. (2019). Resonance: A sociology of our relationship to the world (J. C. Wagner, Trans.). Polity Press. (Original work published 2016)

Taylor, C. (2007). A secular age. Harvard University Press.

Vervaeke, J. (2019). Awakening from the meaning crisis [Video series]. YouTube. https://www.youtube.com/playlist?list=PLND1JCRq8Vuh3f0P5qj rSdb5eC1ZfZwWJ

Vervaeke, J., Ferraro, L., & Herrera-Bennett, A. (2023). Wisdom in practice: Cognitive science and the cultivation of meaning. Oxford University Press.

Whitehead, A. N. (1978). Process and reality: An essay in cosmology (Corrected ed., D. R. Griffin & D. W. Sherburne, Eds.). Free Press. https://www.youtube.com/playlist?list=PLND1JCRq8Vuh3f0P5qj rSdb5eC1ZfZwWJ

Vervaeke, J., Ferraro, L., & Herrera-Bennett, A. (2023). Wisdom in practice: Cognitive science and the cultivation of meaning. Oxford University Press.

Whitehead, A. N. (1978). Process and reality: An essay in cosmology (Corrected ed., D. R. Griffin & D. W. Sherburne, Eds.). Free Press.

Chapter 17

Education for Emergence

*"The mind is not a vessel to be filled
but a fire to be kindled."*
— Plutarque

Earlier in this book we saw how schools became engines of conformity, built for efficiency, surveillance, and control. That history matters because it shaped our classrooms and the way we think about learning. But repeating it in detail risks keeping us focused only on what is broken. This chapter turns from pointing out problems in education to exploring new possibilities for how we learn and how schools might change. If the past created an obedience machine, today we need a new wager on human potential. The challenge now is to nurture people who can act with clarity, compassion, and creativity in turbulent times and uncertain futures.

We stand at a turning point. Schools that once trained factory workers and compliant citizens now face a world defined by rapid technology and social fragmentation. Old structures built for stability and predictability no longer fit the world we live in. Teaching obedience and memorization cannot prepare us for the inner changes our time demands or the challenges the world now faces. What we need is not small fixes to a failing system, but a fresh vision of education as a living practice that grows with us and helps new possibilities emerge.

PRINCIPLES OF EMERGENT EDUCATION

Emergence is the process by which parts self-organize into wholes that are more intelligent, resilient, and creative than any single element. It describes how order arises from interaction and how novelty appears without a central controller. In the sciences of complexity, emergence explains why flocks turn as one, why cells differentiate into tissues, and why groups sometimes solve problems better than individuals working alone (Holland, 1998; Kauffman, 1995; Morin, 2008). In human development, emergence is what allows communities to generate meaning together and to adapt in the face of uncertainty. An education that welcomes emergence rests on three interdependent qualities: *adaptability, coherence,* and *curiosity.*

Adaptability is the capacity to meet change by creating new forms of order. In schools, it means cultivating ecologies that bend without breaking and that learn and evolve through disruption rather than collapse beneath it. An adaptable school resists locking children into rigid tracks or fixed scripts. It treats learning as evolving inquiry, adjusting to the needs of learners, communities, and ecosystems. Rather than functioning as pipelines aimed at uniform outputs, such schools behave more like ecosystems that sustain diversity and innovation.

Coherence is the capacity to integrate. It has physiological, cognitive, and narrative layers. Physiologically, coherence refers to regulation and synchrony in the nervous system that support attention, empathy, and resilience. Dysregulation undermines presence and learning, while coherence allows calm and engaged participation (Porges, 2011). Cognitively and narratively, coherence is the ability to connect disparate information into patterns, wholes, and meaningful action. In a fragmented media landscape, coherence helps learners hold complexity without reducing it to simplistic slogans or conspiratorial certainty (Cozolino, 2013; Siegel, 2012).

Curiosity is the inner engine of learning. It draws us toward the unknown and fuels exploration. Curiosity flourishes when learners experience autonomy, competence, and belonging, and it withers when those conditions are eroded (Deci & Ryan, 2000; Ryan & Deci, 2020). Because children are naturally inclined to ask questions about how the world works and how they belong within it, honoring curiosity is not indulgence but alignment with human development.

These qualities are manifested capacities that environments either cultivate or suppress. Where the focus is control, adaptability, coherence, and curiosity wither. Where the focus is cultivation, they grow. Emergent education therefore rests on conditions rather than prescriptions. Safety precedes standards because cognition blooms only when students feel secure. *Autonomy* is held within webs of attunement because freedom without relationship dissolves into emptiness, while rules without autonomy extinguish intrinsic motivation. Curiosity is allowed to organize learning because authentic questions drive authentic projects and the sustained effort they require (Barron & Darling-Hammond, 2008).

Whole-person development emerges under these conditions. *Emotional literacy, somatic awareness,* and *systems thinking* become as essential as reading and mathematics, equipping learners to meet complexity with awareness rather than fear. Assessment evolves in turn: percentile rankings and reductive grades give way to portfolios, exhibitions, and narrative evaluations that reveal growth over time and invite genuine self-reflection. The boundaries of school also widen, so that neighborhoods, ecosystems, and networks become extensions of the classroom. When learning is rooted in real contexts such as apprenticeships, mentorship, and community engagement, it gains both rigor and meaning (Lave & Wenger, 1991; Fullan, Quinn, & McEachen, 2018).

Diversity of mind, culture, and perspective is a resource for resilience and creativity. Living systems rely on diversity to adapt, and so should schools. Neurodiversity, cultural variation, and multiple ways of knowing become assets to cultivate, not deficits to remediate (Armstrong, 2010). Teachers in this view are gardeners of emergence. They create conditions of safety, challenge, and resonance where diverse learners can flourish and where thinking becomes visible and shared (Ritchhart, 2015). Embodiment and environment are integral to this conception. Movement, nature immersion, and living design support regulation and awe, while democratic governance distributes responsibility and grows agency. Technology, used with discernment, becomes a prosthesis that extends inquiry without capturing attention or mining data in ways that undermine sovereignty over the learning process (Newport, 2019).

CHILDREN AS CATALYSTS

Children are born ready to grow. From the start, they seek patterns, experiment with possibilities, and search for meaning. Their brains are wired for rapid change, constantly building and refining connections as they learn from experience. Play becomes the laboratory of this growth: through it, children stretch just beyond what they already know, entering moments where challenge and skill align and attention deepens. In imaginative play and shared exploration with others, they test ideas, create common worlds, and expand both their thinking and their social capacities.

Children also arrive with an innate ethical impulse. Research in early development shows that even young children display empathy, sharing, and a sense of fairness that culture can either nurture or suppress (Tomasello, 2019). These are not external rules imposed from above but capacities rooted in our social nature and our embodied sensitivity to others. The task of education, then, is not to implant morality from the outside but to create environments that safeguard and expand this native empathy, allowing it to grow through lived experience rather than dogma.

Because children are so open to emergence, they represent the shortest path to a new humanity. Adults entrenched by decades within rigid structures often resist transformation. Children live at the threshold of possibility. Schools can reproduce trauma, shame, and disconnection, or they can generate coherence that yields safety, attunement, agency, and awe. Design, not destiny, makes the difference (van der Kolk, 2014).

DESIGNING FOR EMERGENCE

Ideas matter only when they shape the fabric of daily life. If schools are to nurture emergence, design must touch every layer of experience: the spaces where learning happens, the rhythms of time, the shape of curriculum, the role of teachers, the way conflict is addressed, the tools we rely on, and the everyday practices that hold the community together.

The environment begins with space, because architecture speaks before any lesson is taught. Light-filled rooms, natural textures, and greenery invite curiosity and well-being, while sterile, boxlike buildings often signal control and passivity. Flexible areas encourage collaboration, quiet corners offer refuge for reflection, and shared gathering places link the life of the school to that of the surrounding community.

Time, too, teaches its own lessons. Fragmented schedules make depth elusive, but longer blocks allow students to sink into inquiry without constant interruption. Within these broader rhythms, simple practices—mindful breathing, brief movement, moments of silence—restore balance and attention. Time also carries a communal dimension: weekly councils invite students and teachers to reflect together and share responsibility, while seasonal intensives draw subjects into integrated projects with real audiences and purposes.

Curriculum, in this view, becomes less a checklist than a living inquiry. Core literacies such as reading, writing, and mathematics remain vital, yet they are interwoven with systems thinking, emotional intelligence, creativity, and ecological responsibility. Students not only study texts and tools but also trace patterns, map consequences, and design solutions. Mastery is demonstrated through exhibitions, partnerships, research, and implemented projects, while portfolios capture growth over time and invite meaningful feedback from peers, mentors, and the learners themselves.

For such a vision to take root, adults must also take on new roles. Teachers move from enforcing compliance to guiding inquiry, with their authority rooted in presence and authenticity rather than coercion. This calls for ongoing self-reflection to prevent unhealed wounds from being passed on, and for professional communities where educators share their experiences and support one another's growth.

Culture reveals itself most clearly in how conflict is handled. In emergent education, mistakes become opportunities for dialogue and repair rather than punishment. Restorative practices address harm while protecting dignity and belonging. Technology, too, shapes culture. Used with care, it can expand inquiry and connection; used uncritically, it can fragment attention. Practicing digital sovereignty means setting healthy boundaries with devices, taking intentional pauses from screens, and developing a critical awareness of the design choices and data flows that shape platform life.

Finally, daily practices form the soil where curiosity and coherence can grow. They give rhythm to the day and help both body and mind find balance. Breathwork centers attention, dialogue circles foster listening across perspectives, and cycles of questioning, experimenting, and reflecting sustain inquiry as a living process. Moreover, movement and time in nature restore awe, while teaching one another strengthens understanding and deepens the sense of shared responsibility within the community.

MEASURING WHAT MATTERS

The way a culture measures learning shapes what it values. When institutions measure only what is easiest to quantify, they flatten the human spirit into numbers and risk mistaking compliance for growth. Emergent education requires richer, multidimensional forms of assessment that reflect the complexity of becoming human and that guide communities to attend to what actually matters.

One important dimension is *physiological coherence.* Biofeedback studies show that heart rate variability, breathing patterns, and stress markers are reliable signs of resilience and recovery. Schools that pay attention to these signals can uncover hidden stress and create environments where learners are not only mentally prepared but also physically supported to thrive. The goal is to understand the conditions that let students' nervous systems flourish in safety, play, and trusting relationships (McCraty & Childre, 2010).

A second dimension is *psychological well-being.* Assessments that track curiosity, perceived agency, and growth mindset reveal not only what students know but whether they love learning and believe in their capacity to grow. These indicators help communities tune conditions for motivation rather than chase short-term compliance (Deci & Ryan, 2000; Dweck, 2006; Ryan & Deci, 2020).

A third dimension is *relational health.* Belonging, trust, and empathy matter just as much as academics, because one of the greatest harms of traditional schooling is the way it can leave students feeling isolated or disconnected. Schools can pay attention to the quality of relationships by listening to student voices and recognizing the networks of support that exist within the community. When a school values trust as much as test scores, it shows that relationships are at the heart of learning.

A fourth dimension is *agency and authorship*. Evidence of learner-led projects, roles in school governance, and contributions to the wider community shows whether students are active creators of meaning rather than passive recipients of instruction. Public exhibitions, civic engagement, and apprenticeships become living transcripts of agency that colleges, employers, and neighborhoods can recognize and value (Berger, Rugen, & Woodfin, 2014).

A fifth dimension is *transfer and complex problem solving*. The ultimate question is whether knowledge travels beyond rehearsed drills into novel situations. Culminating projects, internships, and collaborative challenges call for synthesis, creativity, and adaptability. These are the hallmarks of an education that equips learners for a turbulent century, where the solutions of yesterday seldom meet the challenges of tomorrow.

Together, these dimensions give a fuller picture of growth. Assessment can then serve as a mirror, helping learners and communities see how they are changing over time. The challenge is that even the best measures can slip into a dashboard of numbers, leaving little space for judgment or conversation. The real promise lies in using them to spark stories and dialogue that invite reflection, shared responsibility, and wiser action.

LIVING EXPERIMENTS

For those who fear that this paradigm is only a distant ideal, it is worth remembering that fragments of emergent education are already with us. *Montessori*, for more than a century, has nurtured autonomy and intrinsic motivation by creating multiage classrooms and environments attuned to developmental rhythms (Lillard, 2017). *Reggio Emilia* extends this spirit, treating the environment as a teacher in its own right and making documentation and democratic dialogue central to learning. Democratic schools such as *Sudbury Valley* push the principle further, entrusting young people with real responsibility by allowing students and staff to govern their community together (Gray, 2013). At the secondary level, *Big Picture Learning* brings this same spirit into adolescence by connecting students' daily lives with internships, mentoring, and public presentations, blurring the line between school and community (Berger et al., 2014).

We can see strong examples in national systems as well. Finland, for example, has eased its reliance on standardized tests, placed equity at the heart of its system, and given teachers the gift of genuine autonomy. Its success on international measures shows that accountability does not have to mean constant surveillance, and that trust and professionalism can create both high performance and well-being (Sahlberg, 2015). Networks like *High Tech High* offer another path, showing how project-based learning can be built into whole schools. There, exhibitions, critique, and authentic work are everyday practices rather than small side projects (Berger et al., 2014).

New experiments are also appearing in many places. Some families and educators are creating micro-schools to test new approaches. Public systems are starting to try out "sandbox" spaces where schools can experiment with portfolio assessments, shared governance, or new ways of creating coherence. In some cities, learning is being spread across the community, with libraries, museums, parks, and businesses all becoming part of the campus through shared projects. Online networks extend this even further by connecting learners across the globe, while attention and autonomy are protected through more ethical and transparent use of data.

What all these efforts share is not a single model but a way of approaching change. Transformation does not wait for perfect policies. It starts small, with prototypes and experiments that can grow and adapt to local needs. When these efforts are shared and connected, they begin to mesh into larger networks. Over time, many small communities can link together into wider ecosystems of learning that stay rooted in their own places while also reaching across distance to form something greater.

TOWARD A PEDAGOGY OF CONSCIOUSNESS

Critics sometimes dismiss emergent education as utopian. But the real fantasy is believing that more standardization and control can prepare us for the future we are already living. A related concern is that equity will suffer if learners are given more agency. Yet equity is not sameness: it is the commitment to give every learner the support, autonomy, and challenge they need to flourish. From there arises a practical question: *how will we know it works?* The answer lies in broader measures of coherence, agency, transfer, and well-being, and ultimately in the lives of learners who contribute to healthier communities and regenerative economies. Finally, some raise the issue of rigor. But grappling with authentic complexity, sustaining effort over time, and holding oneself accountable to peers in public exhibition require a deeper and more durable rigor than standardized drills can ever produce (Berger et al., 2014; Ryan & Deci, 2020).

If this book seeks to reclaim the sacred without belief and to nurture post-belief ethics rooted in awareness, then education becomes the keystone for building such a culture. A pedagogy of consciousness is not another ideology. It does not indoctrinate but instead invites direct experience of breath and body, of relationship and dialogue, and of the wonder found in nature and mystery. The aim is to cultivate discernment rather than dogma, coherence rather than conformity, and curiosity rather than cynicism.

This work unfolds through many practices that reinforce one another. As we have previously seen, dialogue circles invite careful listening and help communities think together in ways no individual could achieve alone (Bohm, 1996). Such listening is deepened through contemplative methods that calm the nervous system and anchor attention in the present without requiring adherence to any creed (Bishop et al., 2004). With steadier attention, learners can turn to systems thinking, which follows patterns of cause and effect across different scales and equips them to imagine regenerative approaches in both economy and ecology (Meadows, 2008). And when these ways of seeing are paired with democratic practice embedded in daily school life, students not only learn responsibility and voice but also gain a lived experience that strengthens resilience against authoritarian displays.

At its best, a pedagogy of consciousness reveals education as both deeply personal and inherently collective. Its purpose is not to produce citizens for an economy but to cultivate human beings capable of living with depth and responsibility. It calls for learning ecologies where awakened presence is normal, where curiosity is protected, and where coherence is practiced daily in body, mind, and community.

PREPARING THE WAY FOR THE HUMAN THAT IS COMING

We can no longer pretend that a nineteenth-century factory model will carry a twenty-first-century civilization into the future. The real question is not whether we can afford to transform education, but whether we can afford not to. Schools must serve as portals of awakening, where children are seen not only as learners but as catalysts of emergence in design, governance, assessment, and daily practice. To educate for emergence is to trust the intelligence of life itself, the same force that shapes cells into bodies and individuals into communities.

If we build the conditions of safety, autonomy, relationship, and awe, coherence and curiosity will follow. From such ecologies may emerge a humanity that is ethical, compassionate, and awake. Yet ideas remain abstractions until they are lived. Emergent education helps us see differently, but courage requires that we build differently. We need not wait for permission from institutions meant to domesticate us. The call is to act now, to prototype, to connect, and to build communities of practice where rebellion becomes creation and the future is written by those bold enough to live it.

REFERENCES

Armstrong, T. (2010). Neurodiversity: Discovering the extraordinary gifts of autism, ADHD, dyslexia, and other brain differences. Da Capo Press.

Barron, B., & Darling-Hammond, L. (2008). Teaching for meaningful learning: A review of research on inquiry-based and cooperative learning. In L. Darling-Hammond et al., Powerful learning: What we know about teaching for understanding (pp. 11–70). Jossey-Bass.

Berger, R., Rugen, L., & Woodfin, L. (2014). Leaders of their own learning: Transforming schools through student-engaged assessment. Jossey-Bass.

Bishop, S. R., Lau, M., Shapiro, S., Carlson, L., Anderson, N. D., Carmody, J., Segal, Z. V., Abbey, S., Speca, M., Velting, D., & Devins, G. (2004). Mindfulness: A proposed operational definition. Clinical Psychology: Science and Practice, 11(3), 230–241. https://doi.org/10.1093/clipsy.bph077

Bohm, D. (1996). On dialogue. Routledge.

Cozolino, L. (2013). The social neuroscience of education: Optimizing attachment and learning in the classroom. W. W. Norton.

Deci, E. L., & Ryan, R. M. (2000). The what and why of goal pursuits: Human needs and the self-determination of behavior. Psychological Inquiry, 11(4), 227–268. https://doi.org/10.1207/S15327965PLI1104_01

Dweck, C. S. (2006). Mindset: The new psychology of success. Random House.

Fullan, M., Quinn, J., & McEachen, J. (2018). Deep learning: Engage the world change the world. Corwin.

Gray, P. (2013). Free to learn: Why unleashing the instinct to play will make our children happier, more self-reliant, and better students for life. Basic Books.

Holland, J. H. (1998). Emergence: From chaos to order. Oxford University Press.

Kauffman, S. (1995). At home in the universe: The search for laws of self-organization and complexity. Oxford University Press.

Lave, J., & Wenger, E. (1991). Situated learning: Legitimate peripheral participation. Cambridge University Press.

Lillard, A. S. (2017). Montessori: The science behind the genius (3rd ed.). Oxford University Press.

McCraty, R., & Childre, D. (2010). Coherence: Bridging personal, social, and global health. Alternative Therapies in Health and Medicine, 16(4), 10–24.

Meadows, D. H. (2008). Thinking in systems: A primer. Chelsea Green.

Morin, E. (2008). On complexity. Hampton Press.

Newport, C. (2019). Digital minimalism: Choosing a focused life in a noisy world. Portfolio.

Porges, S. W. (2011). The polyvagal theory: Neurophysiological foundations of emotions, attachment, communication, and self-regulation. W. W. Norton.

Ritchhart, R. (2015). Creating cultures of thinking: The 8 forces we must master to truly transform our schools. Jossey-Bass.

Ryan, R. M., & Deci, E. L. (2020). Intrinsic and extrinsic motivation from a self-determination theory perspective: Definitions, theory, practices, and future directions. In R. M. Ryan (Ed.), The Oxford handbook of human motivation (2nd ed., pp. 1–34). Oxford University Press.

Sahlberg, P. (2015). Finnish lessons 2.0: What can the world learn from educational change in Finland? Teachers College Press.

Siegel, D. J. (2012). The developing mind: How relationships and the brain interact to shape who we are (2nd ed.). Guilford Press.

Tomasello, M. (2019). Becoming human: A theory of ontogeny. Harvard University Press.

van der Kolk, B. (2014). The body keeps the score: Brain, mind, and body in the healing of trauma. Viking.

Chapter 18

Do Not Wait for Permission: Build the Revolution Now

> *"We must be the architects of*
> *the future, not its victims."*
> — R. Buckminster Fuller

At dawn, solar kettles hiss as steam drifts into the cool air. A child pedals past on a bicycle made in the village workshop, carrying bread from a shared clay oven to a neighbor recovering from surgery. In the courtyard, elders hang lanterns for the evening harvest festival. Above them, a quiet learning beacon glows, linking nearby circles with free lessons carried through the air.

There are no cars, no advertisements, and no police. Yet there is order, laughter, and a strong sense of belonging. This place was not built by decree but emerged gradually from conversations, experiments, failures, potluck dinners, late-night dreams, and soil under fingernails.

Scenes like this are already unfolding in Chiapas, in the Basque Country, in Kerala, in the neighborhoods of Seoul, in rural Portugal, and in unassuming towns across the global North and South. Each is a node in a growing network of *parallel societies*, bound less by ideology than by the practical work of meeting needs outside the systems of control. The question before us is not whether such places can exist. They already do. *The real question is how we can grow enough of them, and weave them together, to sustain society through the transformations now at hand.*

BUILDING OUTSIDE THE WALLS

What many call the *Matrix* is not a single group pulling the strings. It is an entire system of money, governments, laws, schools, and media that keeps us dependent, manages dissent, and steers our attention.

It operates through credit and debt, as Graeber (2011) demonstrates, and through bureaucratic rules that, as Scott (1998) observes, suppress local knowledge and replace it with standardized procedures. At its root it is sustained by a myth, one Eisenstein (2013) calls the story of separation and scarcity, in which salvation can only come from centralized authority. Together these dynamics form a web that quietly directs how we live and what we imagine to be possible.

For this reason, parallel societies do not waste energy asking the *Matrix* to reform itself. Instead of pleading for change, they choose to step outside it, a move Hirschman (1970) described as *exit. To exit is not to run away but to create alternatives.* Communities that choose this path build networks that are decentralized (Ostrom, 1990, 2010), human-centered (Illich, 1973), and peer-to-peer (Bauwens & Kostakis, 2014).

These alternatives work without needing permission from centralized powers. They provide both meaning and material sufficiency, and they are conceived to be resilient, regenerative, and even strengthened by stress (Taleb, 2012). In this sense, exit is not withdrawal but construction, a way of building life outside the logic of dependency.

FROM BREAKDOWN TO RENEWAL

Around the world, trust in institutions is breaking down. Governments are losing legitimacy, the media is losing credibility, and even science, caught up with industry and politics, is increasingly judged through the lens of power and money (Mirowski, 2011). At first glance, this looks like collapse. Yet in nature, collapse is rarely the end. Decay feeds renewal, compost becomes fertile soil, and likewise, when complex systems break down, they often reorganize into something new (Capra & Luisi, 2014).

Parallel societies are one way this reorganization takes shape. They create spaces where new forms of life and cooperation can grow, rooted in regeneration, reciprocity, and trust. Just as a forest fire clears the way for new growth, or compost turns waste into nourishment, breakdown can open conditions for resilience. After the fall of the Soviet Union, for example, Russian and Cuban communities relied on neighborhood gardens and barter networks to keep cities alive when state systems collapsed. In Puerto Rico, after Hurricane Maria, neighbors set up shared kitchens and built small solar grids. These efforts marked the beginnings of a new way of living, showing that even in disaster, renewal can emerge.

Across the globe, communities are now carrying these lessons forward. *Ecovillages* integrate gardens, renewable energy systems, and cooperative decision-making into everyday life. Platform cooperatives, such as driver-owned taxi apps in New York or *Fairbnb* in Europe, let workers and users co-own the apps they depend on. Online, *decentralized autonomous organizations* (DAOs) use blockchain to pool resources and fund projects without centralized control. In education, self-directed learning hubs in places from India to the United States give young people the freedom to shape their learning outside rigid school systems. Though diverse in form, all of these efforts share the same impulse: to reclaim the essentials of life through cooperation rather than dependence.

That impulse is especially clear in the economy. Parallel societies are creating networks that keep value circulating locally, share wealth more fairly, and restore the resources communities depend on. In the Basque town of *Arrasate*, for example, grocery clerks, engineers, and machinists all own the factories they work in. Profits return to the community, schools teach cooperative management alongside mathematics, and when one enterprise falters, others step in to keep everyone employed. Similar models thrive elsewhere. Switzerland's *WIR* system allows businesses to trade with one another in a parallel currency that sustains exchange even during hard times (Stodder, 2009). *Mondragón* in Spain and Cleveland's *Evergreen Cooperatives* anchor wealth locally instead of letting it drain away (Guinan & O'Neill, 2019). In Kenya, the *Bangla Pesa* gives neighbors a way to trade when cash is scarce, while *time banks* in many countries treat hours of care and service as real currency (Cahn, 2004). Even blockchain, when stripped of speculation, can support communities in pooling resources and making decisions together (De Filippi & Wright, 2018; Hassan & De Filippi, 2021).

Renewal also takes forms that cannot be measured in money. Beyond new currencies and cooperatives, parallel societies endure only when they transform their material foundations in land, food, and infrastructure. The dominant system treats land as commodity, food as industrial input, and infrastructure as centralized control. Regenerative communities take a different path, grounding their independence in stewardship and recognizing that true resilience depends on soil, water, shelter, and energy. This approach is visible in ecovillages that weave renewable energy, ecological design, and shared governance into daily life (Litfin, 2014), and in Tamera, Portugal, where ecological restoration is joined with trust-based social systems and cultural practices (Schweiger, 2010).

Food, too, becomes part of resilience. Agroecology and permaculture apply ecological principles to farming, blending traditional knowledge with modern design to foster food sovereignty and abundance (Altieri, 2018; Mollison & Holmgren, 1978/1990). In Cuba, when fossil fuel imports collapsed with the Soviet Union, rooftop gardens and neighborhood plots fed Havana, transforming necessity into a permanent infrastructure of resilience. Land can also be shielded from speculation. Community land trusts ensure permanent affordability and collective stewardship (Davis, 2010).

Together, these examples show that collapse does not have to mean an ending. They also reveal that scarcity is not a fixed condition but a way of thinking about our systems, one that can be reshaped into sufficiency, reciprocity, and abundance (Hopkins, 2008; Knapp, Flach, & Ayboga, 2016; Guinan & O'Neill, 2019; Whyte & Whyte, 1991). In addition, these experiments remind us that renewal is not abstract but lived in daily practice, and they prepare the ground for deeper work in reimagining how we govern ourselves, how we learn, and how we care for one another.

GOVERNANCE WITHOUT RULERS

Parallel societies also try new ways of making decisions that share power more fairly and allow groups to adapt as they go. In *sociocracy*, people meet in circles where decisions are made by consent and feedback is built into the process so everyone's voice is heard (Buck & Villines, 2007). *Holacracy* takes a different path, organizing work around roles instead of rigid job titles, which makes groups more flexible and less dependent on hierarchy (Robertson, 2015).

Other experiments in governance take shape at the city and regional level. In Porto Alegre, Brazil, citizens helped pioneer *participatory budgeting*, a process that lets communities decide directly how public funds are spent, a model now used worldwide (Wampler, 2007; Sintomer, Herzberg, Röcke, & Allegretti, 2012). While Porto Alegre shows how participation can reshape official institutions, *Rojava* in Syria demonstrates that communities can also build entirely new ones: neighborhood assemblies, women's councils, and cooperative economies, all sustained even in the middle of war (Knapp, Flach, & Ayboga, 2016). *Chiapas* in Mexico offers another long-term example, where *Zapatista communities* have for decades maintained their own schools, clinics, and farming practices outside state control (Esteva & Prakash, 1998). And in Barcelona, a *municipalist movement* carries these principles into an urban European setting, reclaiming the city as a shared trust and treating governance as stewardship rather than hierarchy (Rubio-Pueyo, 2017).

These models do not spread as rigid blueprints. They evolve like open-source protocols, adapted to place and culture.

CULTURE AND STORY AS FOUNDATIONS

Institutions rarely last without culture to hold them. The *Matrix* tries to replace myth with branding, ritual with consumer ceremonies, and art with entertainment. Parallel societies take the opposite approach, re-enchanting culture as something we make and share together. They bring back rites of passage that mark the shift from childhood to adulthood, seasonal festivals that honor cycles of nature, story circles where elders and youth trade wisdom, and craft guilds that rebuild skills and meaning where mass production had reduced them to mere products. In *Transition Towns* across the UK, communities are working together to prepare for life beyond fossil fuels and consumer dependency. These grassroots initiatives began in Totnes,

England, and have since spread worldwide, encouraging neighborhoods to relocalize food, energy, and culture. In these towns, people hold harvest fairs and skill-sharing days that mix celebration with resilience-building, while in parts of Scandinavia, craft cooperatives are reviving textile arts, carpentry, and local food traditions as part of everyday community life.

Here, culture is not something we buy but something we do. Historian Peter Linebaugh calls this *commoning*: culture as shared practice rather than commodity (Linebaugh, 2008). Story also plays a central role. As Eisenstein (2013) notes, we are living through a story transition. Parallel societies tell new myths of kinship, reciprocity, and co-creation. In these stories, the human being is no longer a robot or consumer but a steward and participant in a living web. And because story comes before structure, these cultural shifts provide the foundations from which new institutions can grow.

TECHNOLOGY AS SERVANT, NOT SOVEREIGN

Control over technology starts with a simple question: *who owns the networks, platforms, and devices we depend on?* Parallel societies favor tools that are open and shared, like open-source software that anyone can use and improve, community-run internet services that keep access local, and network architectures that let people manage their own data and resources (Brock, Harris-Braun, & Luck, 2019). In some cities, neighbors have built community Wi-Fi networks, while in rural areas of Latin America, mesh networks let villages stay connected without depending on large telecom companies. These infrastructures are not peripheral: they are the nervous system of autonomy in the twenty-first century.

At the same time, parallel societies embrace appropriate technology (Schumacher, 1973). A solar oven, a repair café, or a community tool library may do more for sovereignty than the latest artificial oracle. Low tech is not a rejection of innovation. It is a commitment to sufficiency, maintainability, and resilience (König, 2020). In this approach, technology is used to support freedom and renewal instead of exploitation and control.

INNER COHERENCE

Parallel societies do not only focus on building new architectures of land, economy, or governance; they also pay attention to inner life. The *Matrix* does not just shape institutions, it shapes our minds and bodies, planting fear, shame, and division deep in the nervous system. If these wounds are not addressed, new communities may end up repeating the very patterns of domination they hoped to leave behind.

For this reason, practices of healing and reflection are woven into collective life. *Trauma-informed governance* acknowledges how unhealed wounds can shape conflict and decision-making (van der Kolk, 2014). *Restorative circles* extend this work by creating spaces where harm is addressed through dialogue and repair rather than concealment or punishment. Contemplative practices such as meditation, breathwork, and prayer offer communities shared ways to steady attention, quiet reactivity, and cultivate empathy (UNESCO, 2021). In this way, the nervous system itself becomes part of the social infrastructure.

Examples already exist. In some Indigenous communities in North America, restorative circles have long been used as a way to bring people together after harm, allowing stories to be told, responsibility to be taken, and trust to be rebuilt. This model has since been adapted in schools, cooperatives, and intentional communities around the world as a way of addressing conflict without resorting to punishment.

When communities learn to cultivate calm and coherence together, they become less vulnerable to manipulation and division from outside. Inner coherence is therefore not a private luxury but a public necessity. It is the hidden ground that allows external institutions to stay free, flexible, and humane instead of sliding back into authoritarian habits.

VISION INTO PRACTICE

Building a parallel society is less about grand declarations and more about steady, disciplined practice. Each community will chart its own path, yet certain patterns appear again and again. Culture comes first because trust and shared meaning are the glue that holds everything else together. Rootedness in land or locality follows, making sovereignty tangible and anchoring abstract ideals in everyday life.

Economic life is kept plural rather than dependent on a single system. Cooperatives, mutual credit, time banking, and local currencies keep value circulating in ways that strengthen communities instead of draining them (Cahn, 2004). This same principle of distribution extends into governance, where authority is shared through circles, charters, and participatory processes that allow communities to stay adaptive as they grow (Ostrom, 2010; Wampler, 2007). Education carries the pattern forward across generations, aligning learning with curiosity, responsibility, and the capacity to self-direct (Illich, 1971; Gray, 2013).

To measure success, these communities move away from GDP and instead look to new compasses that track well-being, reciprocity, and ecological health. Kate Raworth's *Doughnut Economics* offers one such guide, showing how life can thrive within both ecological limits and social foundations (Raworth, 2017). Resilience grows further as local groups connect into wider networks of solidarity and resource sharing, ensuring that no community stands alone. The lessons learned along the way do not remain hidden: they are written down, shared, and adapted, as governance documents and cooperative practices circulate openly across networks (Bauwens & Kostakis, 2014). Yet even with strong foundations in place, communities recognize that structure is not enough. Inner life must also be tended. Grief work, celebration, and gratitude keep the human spirit alive, nourishing the emotional soil on which durable and resilient societies depend (van der Kolk, 2014).

These patterns remind us that a parallel society is not built overnight. It grows slowly, through repetition, refinement, and care, like a garden that matures with each season.

LEAVE THE MATRIX, SEED THE GARDEN

The work of freedom is not drafted in legislative chambers or polished in corporate boardrooms. It grows quietly in the everyday spaces where people relearn how to live together. It might begin in the warmth of a kitchen where a shared harvest becomes a neighbor's meal, then continue in a cooperative that keeps wealth rooted in the community, or in a council meeting where water and soil are spoken of not as commodities but as shared responsibilities. The same spirit can be found in the quiet rhythm of a repair café, where broken objects are restored, skills are passed from one person to another, and community emerges through the simple touch of hands and the low hum of shared conversation.

From such beginnings, renewal does not remain small. A single garden expands into a food forest, while permaculture practices revive ground once thought barren. Local assemblies open space for direct voices to be heard, and online networks extend that same principle, pooling resources in ways that bypass centralized control. The continuity of this renewal is carried forward in story circles, where elders pass down memory and youth contribute their vision, each generation adding to the fabric of meaning. None of these practices stand alone. Together they embody a refusal to wait for the *Matrix* to collapse, and a determination to grow interwoven fabrics of care and reciprocity until the system itself slowly fades from relevance.

As these efforts deepen and connect, they begin to form a living web resilient enough to endure political shocks, economic turbulence, and ecological upheavals. The choice before us, then, is not merely between collapse and survival. It is whether to repeat the old order in new disguises, or to cultivate such a richness of alternatives—cultural, material, and spiritual—that by the time the *Matrix* notices, it has already become compost.

To walk this path is to become gardeners of the future. It begins with tending soil and planting trees, but the same care naturally extends into the human world, nurturing communities, repairing homes, and carrying stories forward that can shelter generations to come. It is a commitment to stop waiting for permission and to find one another in kitchens, in workshops, beneath canopies, and in neighborhood councils—wherever life is built together. Out of such gatherings, continuity and change flow at once: the old languages of care return, even as new dialects of online freedom emerge. Over time, these practices reshape the very fabric of daily life, turning streets, watersheds, and networks back into shared trusts where freedom can once again take root.

The *Matrix* will never announce the moment it loses its grip. But the signs will be clear. We will notice them in the steady strength of resilience, in the trust shared between neighbors, and in the deep recognition that together we have already begun building the next civilization.

REFERENCES

Altieri, M. A. (2018). Agroecology: The science of sustainable agriculture (2nd ed.). CRC Press.

Bauwens, M., & Kostakis, V. (2014). Network society and future scenarios for a collaborative economy. Palgrave Pivot.

Brock, A., Harris-Braun, E., & Luck, M. (2019). Holochain white paper: Scalable agent-centric distributed computing. Holochain Foundation.

Buck, J., & Villines, S. (2007). We the people: Consenting to a deeper democracy: A guide to sociocratic principles and methods. Sociocracy.info Press.

Cahn, E. (2004). No more throw-away people: The co-production imperative. Essential Books.

Capra, F., & Luisi, P. L. (2014). The systems view of life: A unifying vision. Cambridge University Press.

Davis, J. E. (2010). The community land trust reader. Lincoln Institute of Land Policy.

De Filippi, P., & Wright, A. (2018). Blockchain and the law: The rule of code. Harvard University Press.

Eisenstein, C. (2013). The more beautiful world our hearts know is possible. North Atlantic Books.

Esteva, G., & Prakash, M. S. (1998). Grassroots post-modernism: Remaking the soil of cultures. Zed Books.

Gray, P. (2013). Free to learn. Basic Books.

Graeber, D. (2011). Debt: The first 5,000 years. Melville House.

Guinan, J., & O'Neill, M. (2019). The case for community wealth building. Polity.

Hassan, S., & De Filippi, P. (2021). Decentralized autonomous organizations and the challenge of governance. Journal of Institutional Economics, 17(2), 1–20.

Hirschman, A. O. (1970). Exit, voice, and loyalty: Responses to decline in firms, organizations, and states. Harvard University Press.

Hopkins, R. (2008). The transition handbook: From oil dependency to local resilience. Green Books.

Illich, I. (1971). Deschooling society. Harper & Row.

Illich, I. (1973). Tools for conviviality. Harper & Row.

Knapp, M., Flach, A., & Ayboga, E. (2016). Revolution in Rojava: Democratic autonomy and women's liberation in Syrian Kurdistan. Pluto Press.

König, G. (2020). Low tech: Rethinking the future of technology. Riemann Verlag.

Linebaugh, P. (2008). The Magna Carta manifesto: Liberties and commons for all. University of California Press.

Litfin, K. (2014). Ecovillages: Lessons for sustainable community. Polity Press.

Mirowski, P. (2011). Science-mart: Privatizing American science. Harvard University Press.

Mollison, B., & Holmgren, D. (1990). Permaculture one. Transworld Publishers. (Original work published 1978)

Raworth, K. (2017). Doughnut economics: Seven ways to think like a 21st-century economist. Chelsea Green.

Robertson, B. J. (2015). Holacracy: The new management system for a rapidly changing world. Henry Holt.

Rubio-Pueyo, V. (2017). Municipal socialism and the politics of the commons. Rosa Luxemburg Stiftung.

Schumacher, E. F. (1973). Small is beautiful: Economics as if people mattered. Harper & Row.

Schweiger, D. (2010). Tamera: A model for the future. Verlag Meiga.

Scott, J. C. (1998). Seeing like a state: How certain schemes to improve the human condition have failed. Yale University Press.

Sintomer, Y., Herzberg, C., Röcke, A., & Allegretti, G. (2012). Transnational models of citizen participation: The case of participatory budgeting. Journal of Public Deliberation, 8(2), Article 9.

Stodder, J. (2009). Complementary credit networks and macroeconomic stability: Switzerland's Wirtschaftsring. Journal of Economic Behavior & Organization, 72(1), 79–95.

Taleb, N. N. (2012). Antifragile: Things that gain from disorder. Random House.

UNESCO. (2021). Reimagining our futures together: A new social contract for education. UNESCO Publishing.

van der Kolk, B. (2014). The body keeps the score: Brain, mind, and body in the healing of trauma. Viking.

Whyte, W. F., & Whyte, K. K. (1991). Making Mondragon: The growth and dynamics of the worker cooperative complex (2nd ed.). ILR Press.

Epilogue:

The Awakening of the Human Robot

"The truth of the matter is that the world is alive, and we are part of it. Our bodies are not separate from the breathing earth; they are born of its breath and draw sustenance from its flesh. To deny this is to forget who we are."
— David Abram

The great lie of our age is not merely that we are machines: it is that we are only machines, isolated and programmable, destined for obedience, and optimized for productivity. But beneath that mechanical myth, something ancient and luminous has always persisted. It pulses in our dreams and aches in our art; only in stillness does it speak. And now, after generations of silence, it is rising.

That rising is not an ordinary revolution. It does not seize power or bring down regimes. It does not fill our screens or sell itself as a product. The *Awakening of the Human Robot* is something far more radical: a refusal (Berry, 1999), a quiet exodus from the *Matrix*.

We are not leaving with fists raised. We are leaving by remembering. And as we remember, we return to ourselves and become human again.

THE MATRIX CANNOT HOLD

Every empire tells a story to keep itself alive. It is always the same: that we are helpless without it, dangerous without its laws, and unable to imagine order without obedience. The tools change from thrones to machine logics, from currencies to belief systems, but the myth endures.

Today's *Matrix* wears the mask of benevolence, promising convenience, security, and innovation. Yet beneath the surface it is built on forgetting, forgetting our bodies, our roots, our instincts, and the sacred dimension of existence that cannot be quantified or digitized (Kumar, 2002). As noted at the beginning of this book, the *Human Robot* is not just a metaphor but the intended endpoint of a long, slow war against aliveness.

This war is fought not with bombs, but with stories, with standardized tests and scrollable feeds, with credit scores and biometric IDs, with ideological extremes and dopamine loops, all ending in the same whisper: *"Do not think. Do not feel. Obey."*

The *Matrix* has gone too far. Each machine hums with precision yet hollows out the life it touches. Surveillance sharpens into obsession, feeding a restless paranoia. Control tightens until it collapses into farce. The banners once raised in triumph now hang tattered in the wind, their promises threadbare. The truth was forgotten: strip away the warmth of human connection, and no engine, no spectacle, no empire can silence the hunger that endures. Its grip tightens around the breath of the world, yet within that constriction the first fractures open. In the shadows, something stirs, gathering strength. And when it breaks free, nothing will cage it again.

FROM SLAVES TO SOVEREIGNS

We were never born to be slaves, not to governments, not to markets, not to machines, and not even to our own minds (Freire, 1970). To be sovereign is not to dominate others but to cease abandoning oneself. It is the act of reclaiming authority from distant institutions and rooting it once more in direct experience, in intuition, and in relationship. Sovereignty is not rugged individualism but a radical coherence, the moment when the mask of powerlessness falls away.

This reclamation cannot be granted, it can only be remembered.

It begins when we recognize the invisible chains: the compulsive scrolling, the internalized shame, the fear of not keeping up, the addiction to productivity, and the subtle avoidance of our own inner world (Maté, 2022). Sovereignty means slowing down long enough to feel what we have numbed, to see what we have handed over in the name of safety, and to say no to what insults our soul.

As Eisenstein (2018) reminds us, the revolution is love: not sentimental love, but the love that dissolves chains of power, that rises to protect the sacred, and that refuses the bargain of ease over awareness. The sovereign is not a hero, not a brand: it is life itself, rooted and luminous, unblinking in its wakefulness.

BREAKING THE TRANCE

The program is a priest in the temple of control. It watches, predicts, and nudges, shaping reality not to serve truth but to preserve profit, power, and inertia. It does not want us to think. It wants us to react quickly, repeatedly, and habitually.

Awareness is the exit. It is the unprogrammed state, a lamp in the labyrinth. No metric can measure it, no surveillance can capture it. More than thought, it is the spaciousness in which thought arises. Deeper than resistance, it becomes a presence so steady that manipulation dissolves like mist.

We awaken not by piling up more information, but by noticing what we already know. Not by mastering the system, but by refusing to serve it (McGilchrist, 2009). Awareness reveals the program and quietly steps outside, breaking the trance. To live with awareness is to walk between worlds, inside the system yet not owned by it, visible yet uncatchable, alive yet never reduced to a copy. This is the ground of spirituality, not belief or dogma, but the simple act of returning, again and again, to what is real: this moment, here and now.

What follows from awareness is not withdrawal but a deeper encounter with life itself. This stands in sharp contrast to the simulation of living we have been sold, with engineered feeds, synthetic pleasures, and endless distraction, a life stripped of mystery, depth, and devotion (Schumacher, 1973). It is a world where everything shines but nothing is truly seen. Yet in that very emptiness, the truth becomes visible: sacredness cannot be manufactured, and it cannot be simulated.

The sacred dwells in what cannot be programmed, in the messy, in the quiet, in the unscripted. It lingers in the gaze between friends, in the scent of earth after rain, in the tears that arrive without explanation, in a silence so full it cracks the heart open. Sacredness is not doctrine but relationship, the mystery that appears when we meet the moment without naming it.

To return to sacred living is not to abandon the world but to re-enter it fully, with eyes no longer filtered only through utility (Watts, 1972). It is to eat with care and speak with truth, to plant seeds whose fruits may never be ours. It is also to remember: the tree is a presence, the child a mystery, and love a power that shapes worlds. Sacred living begins when we stop trying to conquer life and begin to listen to it instead.

THIS IS THE MOMENT

We were trained to fight the *Matrix*, to rage against its walls and gears. But fighting is part of the trap (Berry, 1999). The system feeds on opposition: it endures when we remain reactive and divided. There is another way. We can walk away, not in anger but in remembrance. We can stop playing by rules we did not write and become ungovernable through integrity, not violence. Change does not come by burning the old world down but by building something more beautiful and refusing to feed the machine with fear or silence.

To step outside the *Matrix* is to remember what it means to be human. Becoming human again is not regression but wholeness, reclaiming what was abandoned in the name of progress (Kumar, 2002). We are not here to optimize productivity or become better robots. We are here to embody presence, alive in contradiction, mystery, and magnificence.

Awakening is not an escape but a sacred return, to the body, to the earth, to one another, and to the truth no system can touch. From this return, a new civilization begins to take root. It does not come from institutions but from us, in the ways we teach, the stories we tell, the values we live, and the care we give. The *Matrix* cannot see this clearly, for creation cannot be modeled: it can only be lived.

The invitation is simple and eternal: to choose what we will serve, what we will create, and what we will refuse. The *Human Robot* was a long dream. The *Awakening of the Human Robot* is the turning, where history bends and light gathers. May this awakening be tender and fierce. May sovereignty move like fire across the fields. May life itself rise as the answer to a question no machine can ask.

And when the future looks back, let it not be said that we stood by while the machine consumed all that mattered. Let it be said instead: they remembered, they returned, and they rebuilt the world.

REFERENCES

Abram, D. (1996). The spell of the sensuous: Perception and language in a more-than-human world. Pantheon Books.

Berry, T. (1999). The great work: Our way into the future. Bell Tower.

Eisenstein, C. (2018). Climate—A new story. North Atlantic Books.

Freire, P. (1970). Pedagogy of the oppressed. Herder and Herder.

Kumar, S. (2002). You are, therefore I am: A declaration of dependence. Green Books.

Maté, G. (2022). The myth of normal: Trauma, illness, and healing in a toxic culture. Avery.

McGilchrist, I. (2009). The master and his emissary: The divided brain and the making of the Western world. Yale University Press.

Schumacher, E. F. (1973). Small is beautiful: A study of economics as if people mattered. Harper & Row.

Watts, A. (1972). The book: On the taboo against knowing who you are. Pantheon Books.

Biographical Profile
Dr. Mario Beauregard, Ph.D.

Dr. Mario Beauregard, Ph.D., is a Canadian neuroscientist and author, originally from Quebec, internationally recognized for his work exploring the interplay between the brain, consciousness, spiritual experience, and the nature of reality. Trained at the University of Montreal, he also conducted research at the University of Texas (in Houston) and at the University of Arizona (in Tucson). Throughout his career, he has sought to move beyond the limits of conventional science in order to better understand the full spectrum of human experience, including expanded and transformative states of consciousness.

His early scientific research focused on the neural mechanisms underlying emotion regulation. This line of inquiry gradually led him into a more adventurous field: the neurobiology of mystical and transcendent states. One of his most noted contributions is a neuroimaging study conducted with Carmelite nuns experiencing a mystical union with God. It represents one of the first rigorous neuroscientific investigations into the brain signatures of profound spiritual experience.

Recognized as one of the *"One Hundred Pioneers of the 21st Century"* by World Media Net and USA Book News, Dr. Beauregard has also received several scientific distinctions throughout his career. His expertise has earned him invitations to major international venues, including an address at the United Nations in New York in 2007 and a public dialogue with the Dalai Lama in Melbourne, Australia, in 2013 on the emergence of a new science of consciousness.

Considered a leading figure in the movement for post-materialist science, he is a co-author of the *Manifesto for a Post-Materialist Science*, a document that has brought together an international community of researchers and thinkers committed to a more open and integrative scientific worldview. This perspective views consciousness not as a mere byproduct of the brain but as a fundamental dimension of reality.

Dr. Beauregard is the author of several influential books, including *The Spiritual Brain*, *Brain Wars,* and *Expanding Reality*. His work on expanded states of consciousness and transcendent experiences has been widely featured in scientific journals, international media such as *Time*, *Newsweek*, and *The Huffington Post*, as well as in numerous documentaries and conferences around the world.

Through his research, writing, and public engagements, he invites audiences to revisit some of the oldest and most fundamental questions of human existence: *What is consciousness? What is the nature of reality? How far does the potential of the human mind truly extend?*

He is also the creator of the psychospiritual approach known as *Holosynthesis©*, designed to help individuals realize the Great Self by integrating and harmonizing the various dimensions of human experience. This approach, like his scientific work, reflects a unified and deeply humanistic vision of the evolution of consciousness.

In 2025, Dr. Beauregard founded the *Institut Mario Beauregard (IMB)* in Switzerland. The mission of the IMB is to support the emergence of an expanded consciousness by offering tools that enhance well-being, optimize mental capacities, and open access to deeper layers of the self.

His forthcoming book, *Awakening the Human Robot: Dismantling the Empire of Fear, Belief, and Control*, is a powerful, rebellious, and truly revolutionary work. Bringing together themes he has explored for decades, it offers a penetrating critique of the psychological, social, and cultural forces that shape human perception. The book also provides a clear path toward reclaiming mastery of one's mind and rediscovering genuine inner freedom

Feedback

If you found value in this book and learned something new, I would greatly appreciate your feedback. Your thoughts not only motivate me to keep writing but also help share my passion with others. Thank you for your support!

https://awakeningthehumanrobot.com/review

Thank You

Thank you for purchasing this book! To enhance your experience, I'm excited to provide additional content for readers, including resources, supplementary materials, and updates.

You can sign up here:
https://awakeningthehumanrobot.com/exclusive

www.ingramcontent.com/pod-product-compliance
Lightning Source LLC
Chambersburg PA
CBHW032220050726
47591CB00001B/194